R/ 57897
B/99

CE

Loss and Bereavement:
Managing Change

Edited by

Ros Weston
Terry Martin
Yvonne Anderson

Blackwell
Science

© 1998 by
Blackwell Science Ltd
Editorial Offices:
Osney Mead, Oxford OX2 0EL
25 John Street, London WC1N 2BL
23 Ainslie Place, Edinburgh EH3 6AJ
350 Main Street, Malden
  MA 02148 5018, USA
54 University Street, Carlton
  Victoria 3053, Australia
10, rue Casimir Delavigne
  75006 Paris, France

Other Editorial Offices:

Blackwell Wissenschafts-Verlag GmbH
Kurfürstendamm 57
10707 Berlin, Germany

Blackwell Science KK
MG Kodenmacho Building
7–10 Kodenmacho Nihombashi
Chuo-ku, Tokyo 104, Japan

The right of the Author to be identified as the
Author of this work has been asserted in
accordance with the Copyright, Designs and
Patents Act 1988

All rights reserved. No part of this publication
may be reproduced, stored in a retrieval system,
or transmitted, in any form or by any means,
electronic, mechanical, photocopying, recording
or otherwise, except as permitted by the UK
Copyright, Designs and Patents Act 1988, without
the prior permission of the publisher.

First published 1998

Set in 10/12 Palatino
by DP Photosetting, Aylesbury, Bucks
Printed and bound in Great Britain by
MPG Books Ltd, Bodmin, Cornwall

The Blackwell Science logo is a
trade mark of Blackwell Science Ltd,
registered at the United Kingdom
Trade Marks Registry

DISTRIBUTORS

Marston Book Services Ltd
PO Box 269
Abingdon
Oxon OX14 4YN
(*Orders:* Tel: 01235 465500
        Fax: 01235 465555)

USA
Blackwell Science, Inc.
Commerce Place
350 Main Street
Malden, MA 02148 5018
(*Orders:* Tel: 800 759 6102
        781 388 8250
        Fax: 781 388 8255)

Canada
Login Brothers Book Company
324 Saulteaux Crescent
Winnipeg, Manitoba R3J 3T2
(*Orders:* Tel: 204 224 4068)

Australia
Blackwell Science Pty Ltd
54 University Street
Carlton, Victoria 3053
(*Orders:* Tel: 03 9347 0300
        Fax: 03 9347 5001)

A catalogue record for this title
is available from the British Library

ISBN 0-632-04787-9

Library of Congress
Cataloging-in-Publication Data
Loss and bereavement: managing change/edited
  by Ros Weston, Terry Martin, and Yvonne
  Anderson.
      p. cm.
   Includes bibliographical references and
indexes.
   ISBN 0-632-04787-9
   1. Bereavement – Psychological aspects.
2. Grief. 3. Loss (Psychology) 4. Life change
events. I. Weston, Ros. II. Martin, Terry.
III. Anderson, Yvonne.
BF575.G7L674 1998
155.9'3–dc21   98-20838
                                          CIP

For further information on
Blackwell Science, visit out website:
www.blackwell-science.com

To all those we have loved
and whose lives have informed this book

Contents

Preface

This book developed as a result of teaching a course on bereavement and loss at the University of Southampton and covers much of the content of that course. Many of the authors teach particular sessions.

Recent changes in mental health policy have been another influence. A topic which previously was taboo is now recognised and talked about more openly; this includes experiences of bereavement and losses arising from life transitions.

Acknowledgement of these processes of change, transition, loss and bereavement has meant that those who are sad may now ask for and receive help to move through these major life experiences. However, this is still not always the case for other shattering events such as violent death from crime, the loss of dignity from sexual crime or the loss of status from unemployment or redundancy.

The *Health of the Nation* is now a key driving force in enabling us to recognise situations which may cause individuals or groups (in the case of mass disaster) to feel intense pain and sadness and the need to offer support to those individuals through the change or grief process.

The increasing numbers of suicides in young men is a particular cause of concern. Strategies to help individuals become more emotionally competent are part of any teaching and training on loss and change. It is also with these issues in mind that this book has been written.

We hope by producing this book we will help more people to engage effectively with those who are undergoing change, loss or bereavement and also encourage such change processes to be opportunities for individuals to grow and develop. Even where this is not possible then we hope at least to help change the culture in which people grieve to one of care, support, empathy and understanding.

Notes to the reader

The text is organised in chapters, each of which is prefaced by an introductory paragraph which includes reference to the particular author perspective. These perspectives are discussed in the Introduction. Key concepts can be cross-referenced via the subject index and are defined in the Glossary.

Acknowledgements

Thank you to:

The authors for their contributions to this book; it has been a team effort and they have all responded to our many requests.

Anne Oestman who voluntarily carried out literature searches. Karen Regan and Peggy Herd for secretarial support. Brian Weston for help in proof reading. Griselda Campbell and Sarah-Kate Powell of Blackwell Science for their efficiency, clear instructions and on-going support.

List of Contributors

Yvonne Anderson MEd is a Senior Research Fellow in the Health Education Unit, Research and Graduate School of Education at the University of Southampton. She formerly worked as a teacher, lecturer, care worker and freelance trainer.

Sandie Arrell has been in the police force for 20 years and has extensive knowledge of working with both adults and children who have experienced abuse in both an investigative and training role.

Celia Di Massimo MA(Ed) is an independent trainer with the Health Education Authority's 'Look After Yourself' and 'Health at Work' projects and the 'Europe Against Cancer' programme. For the past 10 years she has specialised in Pre-retirement and Redundancy Education working with Cooke and Burns (Personnel Services) Ltd. She is a Member of the International Stress Management Association and the National Osteoporosis Society.

David Durston MA(Camb) undertook research with the Grubb Institute into the task of the Church in the community before becoming Vicar of St Paul's, West Bromwich. He has contributed to bereavement care and is the author of *Growing Through Grief*. He is now Chancellor of Salisbury Cathedral.

Pamela Elder was born in Bradford, West Yorkshire and trained at Neville's Cross, Durham. She married in 1966 and her first daughter, Kate, was born in November 1968, followed by triplet daughters in 1973. She has lived and worked in Portugal, Italy and Spain. She is presently a health consultant to the Health Education Authority and was awarded an MSc in Exercise and Health Behaviour in 1995.

Ann Eyre PhD completed a PhD in Sociology at Liverpool University. During this time she became a survivor of the Hillsborough football stadium disaster. She developed an interest in the sociology of disasters. She now lectures at the Centre for Disaster Management at Conventry University and is an active member of Disaster Action, an umbrella organisation made up of survivors and the bereaved from major disasters.

Anna-Michelle Hantler Dip.Psychotherapy is an independent consultant with 18 years of experience in educational teaching and advisory services, child protection and residential social work. She is also an Integrative Psychotherapist practising in Bath, predominantly with children. Her commitment lies in bringing emotional literacy to the school curriculum, through circle time, literature and the arts.

Terry Martin PhD is a lecturer in the Research and Graduate School of Education, University of Southampton; his research and teaching interests are in the areas of management, counselling and professional development.

Alastair McWhirter MA is Assistant Chief Constable of Wiltshire Constabulary. Formerly a teacher, he has been a police officer for 21 years in Hampshire and Wiltshire, policing in a wide range of communities and environments.

Jenny McWhirter PhD is a Senior Research Fellow at the University of Southampton. Her research interests are in young people's perceptions of health-related issues, curriculum development and evaluation of health education. She has been a youth worker, school governor and is a parent of two school-age children. Jenny is currently a member of a team researching and developing a health education curriculum for Hungarian schools.

Pat Usher MA(Ed) is Senior Registrar at the University of Southampton New College. She teaches Gender Differentiation and Feminist Approaches to Knowledge Creation in the Faculties of Education and Social Science at the University. She was an Open University Tutor from 1984–1996 in Post-Compulsory Education courses.

Graham E. Watkinson MA(Ed) trained as a nurse in the Royal Navy. He gained post-registration qualifications in both coronary care and intensive care nursing, and worked as a charge nurse and intensive care unit manager before becoming a lecturer in nursing. He is course leader for an inter-professional BSc (Hons) Health Promotion Degree and the Health Promotion Adviser to the University of Portsmouth. Current research interests centre around student health issues.

Ros Weston PhD has taught in comprehensive schools with responsibility for pastoral care and in special schools. She was a senior lecturer in health and teacher training in a further education college and lead officer for cancer at the Health Education Authority. She was UK co-ordinator for the Europe against Cancer Programme. She lectures in the University of Southampton and was Chairperson of Victim Support, Wiltshire.

Noreen Wetton MEd has been a teacher, head-teacher and teacher educator, before becoming a researcher in the field of health education. She is the originator of the 'draw and write' investigation technique which has enabled her to discover how children aged 4–11 perceive and explain health and health-related concepts. Noreen is currently a school governor and a member of a team researching and developing a health education curriculum for Hungarian schools.

Jackie Yardley MA(Ed) is a psychotherapist/counsellor specialising in neuro-linguistic programming (NLP) and hypnotherapy. She is a former nurse, health visitor, researcher and teacher. She was formerly director of counselling at Wessex Cancer Trust, and is currently campaign manager for the Colon Cancer Society.

Introduction

Ros Weston, Terry Martin and Yvonne Anderson

In the early hours of Sunday 31 August 1997 Diana, Princess of Wales, was killed in a car crash in a Paris subway, together with her companion Dodi Fayed, and their driver Henri Paul. Her death resulted in a great public expression of grief and mourning without parallel in this country in living memory. Several commentators, for example Young (1997), have suggested that this expression was in part due to personal unresolved losses which individuals had previously inhibited and that this is likely to have made a significant contribution to the strength of feeling expressed during the days that followed Diana's death. The lack of opportunity for previous release and expression is partly a reflection of the prevailing culture of excessive meanness and selfishness which has marginalised the caring dimension. The prevailing culture has also marginalised those who have come to be called 'the constituency of the rejected'. David Durston explores this theme further in the postscript to his chapter.

The cumulative impact, individually and socially, of such unresolved and unexpressed grief is a major contribution to the levels of mental illness in the community, documented in the Key Area Handbook on Mental Illness (Department of Health, 1993) and the primary targets for mental health set out there and in the *Health of the Nation* White Paper (Department of Health, 1992). Although we have some reservations about the discourse within which these are framed and we believe all texts (including the present one) should be subject to critical analysis and scrutiny, nevertheless we acknowledge the intentions behind them and hope that our work makes a constructive contribution to their realisation. Our over-riding concern for mental health focuses on two broad areas of mental health promotion:

- Long-term preventative strategies which develop a culture of caring
- Short-term interventions which support and help those who through misfortune and tragedy find their own resources depleted.

This book has developed from our experience of teaching a course, Bereavement and Loss Education, which is part of a higher degree programme. The rationale for both the course and now this book is to address precisely these issues of unresolved losses so forcibly and movingly brought to our attention through Diana's death.

Coming from this educational background highlights our commitment to the importance of experiential learning with its emphasis upon active engagement in the learning process and recognition of differences in learning style. There is also our commitment to the importance of concrete experience, both real-life experience and that created through activities on courses and also vicariously encountered in literature. The commitment is evidenced in the authors of the following chapters most of whom have contributed to the course programme and in the inclusion of a teaching and learning focus at the end of each chapter. We acknowledge in particular our indebtedness to the writings of Kolb (1984) on the experiential learning cycle, Heron (1989, 1990, 1992) on emotional competence and facilitation styles and Goleman (1995) on emotional intelligence, as sources of many of the ideas which underpin our own practice.

As authors and editors we are located in time in the condition that Giddens (1991) refers to as high modernity and others refer to as the postmodern. This context is characterised by a risk culture in which issues of ontological security and existential anxiety are foregrounded. It is also a context in which there is a widespread loss of plausibility in grand overarching structures of meaning within which former generations made sense of the ultimate existential issues of life and death. Nevertheless, it is still a context within which a spiritual dimension has a place even though this is not necessarily equated with traditional religious beliefs.

Perspectives

In this book the authors of the individual chapters approach the central issues of loss, transition, bereavement and change from a general background of constructivism, both psychological and sociological, and from a specific range of perspectives which give rise to associated concerns summarised in Table 1.

In the *phenomenological perspective* we place primacy on the *valuing of personal experience*, which is elaborated further in Chapter 1. There are also rich and moving accounts within other chapters of individuals' experience of loss and suffering. We need to attend to the immediacy and urgency of this experience, using theory to illuminate our understanding and frame our response. We resist, however, the temptation to neatly categorise such experiences into a normative mould. We respect and draw upon such experience, including that recounted in literature, acknowledging the rights and responsibilities of both clients and helpers.

The perspective of *professional practice* is a strong feature of the book through the wide range of *professional experience and expertise* represented. We are committed to improving the quality of care in the widest sense through sharing good practice and the understandings which inform it.

The *autobiographical perspective* highlights our commitment to *empowering and giving voice*. Those who grieve and those caring for them need to give voice to that experience of pain and anguish. In Chapters 2 and 5 and the

Table 1 Perspectives and associated concerns from which the authors of the individual chapters approach the central issues of loss, transition, bereavement and change.

Perspective	Concern	Chapters
Phenomenological	Valuing of personal experience and interpretation	1, 3, 6, 7, 10 and 11
Professional practice	Professional experience and expertise	1, 2, 5, 6, 7, 8, 10, 11, 12, 13 and 14
Autobiographical	Empowering and giving voice	2, 5 and 9
Empirical	Evidence and knowledge base	1, 2, 4, 7, 8, 10, 11 and 13
Theoretical	Understanding, explaining and clarifying concepts	1, 3 and 4

Afterword this perspective is explored with reference to the intersection of the public (professional) and private (personal), (Church, 1995), and the theoretical framework of discourse analysis.

From the *empirical perspective* we consider the *evidence and knowledge base* which supports our claims and our practice. This research perspective draws upon both the natural and social sciences in examining the epidemiological evidence and the methodological procedures on which it is based.

Kurt Lewin's famous dictum that there is nothing so practical as a good theory demonstrates for us the importance of a *theoretical perspective* to inform our *understanding* of the experience of loss and bereavement through theories and models. The related process of *explaining and clarifying concepts* are also important to the improvement of professional practice in a wide range of contexts.

These five perspectives and associated concerns give the book an essentially multi-perspectival and eclectic character. In addition, the different authors bring a diversity of personal and professional experience, although we realise that we are not, even in our diversity, a representative sample in terms of ethnicity and culture.

Aims and objectives

The immediate objectives of the book are to give you the opportunity to:

- Explore, evaluate and assess your own experience and knowledge about change, transition and loss and how these affect human beings
- Challenge common myths and misconceptions about change
- Assess, learn and practise your skills in caring for those who need help and support whilst experiencing change, as well as enhancing your own practice.

The longer term aims are to:

- Encourage positive mental health
- Raise awareness of bereavement care and support as a primary prevention health issue
- Reduce morbidity from unresolved grief and resulting health problems
- Improve the quality of life for those facing major changes in their lives
- Create a 'critical mass' of personnel with knowledge and skills to improve the quality of care and support for those who are undergoing transition or grieving.

We all experience at various times in our lives anticipated transitional events such as leaving school, marriage, death of a parent, etc. These, though occasionally traumatic, can be prepared for but are less problematic than the unforeseen stresses that confront us all. Redundancy, a sudden death or serious illness are obvious illustrations. The fundamental difference between the anticipated and the unexpected is the lack of opportunity that we have to plan and this can give rise to a sense of being out of control.

Some change can be positive; examples are personal change which enables growth and development and organisational change which can enhance personal and collective achievement, motivation and reward. Some change is negative and damaging and almost always is related to the loss of personal power, self-esteem or able-bodiedness; examples are crime, accident or violence. Other change may hold mixed blessings and therefore means there is a struggle for growth pitted against the need for change; examples are the loss of a partner or loved one through death or divorce, moving house or country, or changing job. The struggle may result in very positive development but it can also be painful and is almost always one of uncertainty.

One of our aspirations for the book is to highlight the challenge that change can bring and the resulting pleasure and achievement through dealing with adversity in a way that can be both positive and ultimately rewarding. This is not to deny that change can be unpredictable, dangerous, frightening and risky and frequently not a question of choice. Theoretical models can easily give the impression that there is some kind of answer. There is sometimes no answer and no comfort but only an awful void.

We hope that the theory and strategies documented in this text will help you to play your part in reducing the devastating effects of mental illness, encourage prevention strategies and help to engender positive approaches to the support of those in transition. This will allow their lives to become meaningful again, realistically related to their lifestyle, culture, age and physical condition. Change is rarely easy but if the positive elements can be emphasised then strength can be gained from such experiences. For many loss brings an enhanced child-like sense of the value and wonder of life.

It has been a costly and difficult book to produced both in terms of the intrinsic painfulness of the issues we address and also in the consequent challenging and disturbance of our own assumptive world, Parkes (1993,

1996a). We hope you will enjoy reading and using it and that by such use you too will be equipped to contribute to the *Health of the Nation* targets for the promotion of positive mental health. More importantly it gives us all an opportunity to contribute to the health promoting community whatever the setting in which we work, to optimise the opportunity for every individual to reach their full potential.

Teaching and learning focus

Chapters 3 to 14 end with a teaching and learning focus. A teaching and learning focus is an activity or set of activities through which course facilitators and participants have the opportunity to engage with a topic or issue and learn about it in an active and experiential way. Although essentially group activities, they can be used for personal reflection.

The topics in loss and bereavement are sensitive and potentially threatening and there are therefore important ethical considerations in the design and delivery of a teaching and learning focus. A group needs to establish some clear ground rules in order to create a safe learning environment and these should include clear understandings of:

- Confidentiality – the content of what is shared must be kept within the group
- The right to opt out of any activity without the need to offer any reason or excuse
- Time boundaries – prompt beginnings and endings of sessions.

The facilitator has a number of responsibilities to fulfil during a teaching and learning focus:

- Clarify the ground rules
- Explain the purpose of the activity
- Set up and run the activity
- Debrief the activity giving opportunities for feedback, reflection and conceptual clarification.

A teaching and learning focus will be set within a wider context in which the issue or topic is being considered. It will often be complemented by some other form of teaching input and discussion. We have identified intended learning outcomes for each activity; however, experiential activities are inherently open ended and risky and often participants construct unintended or unforeseen learning outcomes, which may nevertheless be very valuable.

Through experiential activities we generate or create experience, the elements of which are thoughts, feelings, decisions and actions. Through the use of observers both the verbal and non-verbal behaviour of participants can be analysed. This forms data for feedback during debriefing. The state of mind of participants can only be inferred by observation. Each participant has the choice of which elements of experience to disclose during debriefing. As participants both contribute to and attend to the processes of feedback and disclosure so they are enabled to create new meanings through reflection and analysis.

Chapter 1
A Theoretical Framework for Understanding Loss and the Helping Process

Terry Martin and Ros Weston

This chapter explores the relationship between our personal experience of loss and bereavement and our theorising about that experience. Specific theories and models are considered together with the caring strategies they imply. The authors emphasise the importance and value of theory whilst also stressing the need to see these as provisional and tentative ways of framing our understanding and action. Central to this process is the role of language, the medium in which our understandings are embedded and through which our concerns and caring for each other are expressed.

The perspectives from which this chapter is written are: phenomenol,gical, professional, empirical and theoretical.

Introduction

Loss is an inevitable part of life in some shape or form, and those of us in the caring and training professions are just as vulnerable as anyone else. The playing field of life in this regard is level and we are not in any privileged position. What we may have to offer to ourselves and those for whom we care and teach is greater insight and understanding of some of the complex issues involved.

Most of us experience loss as painful; the bigger the loss the bigger the pain. We would consider someone who denies such feelings as abnormal and their reactions unnatural. A moving and eloquent expression of this experience of loss comes from the pen of C.S. Lewis who, after the death of his wife Joy, kept a private diary into which he poured his feelings and reactions of fear and restlessness. The story of his love for Joy Davidman has been vividly and movingly portrayed in a book, TV programme, play and film all sharing the same title, *Shadowlands*, which poignantly capture the kind of world that bereaved people often feel they inhabit. The popularity of these portrayals and the now published diary (Lewis, 1961), suggests that many have found his candid expression of pain and his struggles to understand it both helpful and encouraging.

Because loss is painful we often go to great lengths to minimise and avoid it. Whether such tactics are, in the long term, helpful or unhelpful, healthy or unhealthy, is an issue to which we shall return later.

Why is loss painful?

The question almost seems superfluous because we so intimately associate loss with feelings of pain. We might just as well ask: why is picking up something very hot painful? The obvious answer to *this* question is that this is just the way the world is; hot things burn and being burned causes painful sensations. However, the experience of pain associated with loss and the experience of pain associated with being burned are fundamentally different. The difference is grounded both in the situations giving rise to the experience and also in terms of causation. In the latter situation there are clearly identifiable physical and physiological processes at work, whilst the former is essentially a complex set of psychological processes, although other associated processes may also be at work depending on the type of loss. The psychological processes are both emotional and also cognitive. The cognitive processes are in terms of making sense of the experience.

'Above all, if we deny grief, we deny the importance of the meaning each of us has struggled to make of life. Loss is painful because we are committed to the significance of our personal experience.'

(Marris, 1986: 103)

What does it mean to be *committed to the significance of our personal experience*? Before proceeding further with answering this question we must first clarify what we mean by personal experience. As human beings we are experiencing subjects, aware of both the external world around us and an inner world within. In the present moment we experience the external world as it is mediated through our senses. It is a world rich in sights, sounds, tastes and smells.

The sights and sounds of immediate sensory experience are also accompanied by thoughts, feelings, memories, anticipations and intuitions arising within us. Staying close to, and capturing the immediacy of, human experience is a preoccupation and concern of phenomenology (Heron, 1992). These phenomenological categories of thoughts, feelings, intuitions, etc., constitute the basic dimensions of all experience. We share with other animals, presumably, visual and auditory experiences of some kind, but what makes human beings unique is their capacities for language, conceptualisation, the recollection of past experience and the anticipation of future experience. We live in time but can also step outside time through imagination and memory.

Each person is unique, in a sense different from, for example, the way in which a chair is unique. Our uniqueness springs from both what we came equipped with when born into this world and what we have experienced whilst in the world. The particular social and cultural configuration within which we have each lived our lives has resulted in our own unique standpoint or perspective from which we view or experience the world. For each of us it is a world like no-one else's and brought into being, in part at least, in and through language. Language is central to communicating and sharing our own personal experiences. Even if my experience of a sunset is different from yours we can nevertheless share our experiences, albeit imperfectly, and assume they refer to something real in the world outside us both.

In ways we still scarcely understand, through interactions at the sensory boundary of ourselves and the world, we build up inside ourselves a model of the world around us that is unique and personal to ourselves. Our experience of the world enables (most of) us to build up a picture that provides a measure of security through the predictability of events. This assumptive world (Parkes, 1993, 1996a) is both a social (Berger & Luckmann, 1967; Burr, 1995) and a psychological construction (Kelly, 1955, 1963). It is crucial for our sanity and survival. We come to take for granted certain features and processes and they become an unquestioned backdrop for our purposeful actions within the world.

We inhabit both a natural world and a social (or cultural) world and a systematic exploration and understanding of both has led to the creation of the natural and social sciences. The natural sciences, for example physics and chemistry, have been conspicuously successful at creating explanations, understandings and knowledge of the natural world through the scientific method. The precise epistemological status of these scientific explanations, understandings and knowledge is the focus of much discussion and dispute amongst philosophers, although rarely amongst scientists who tend to regard the philosophical basis of their endeavours as unproblematic.

These scientific explanations, understandings and knowledge have in turn led to enormous technological changes that have radically altered the kind of social world we now inhabit compared to our forebears. It is a world that many would regard as a mixed blessing as we are increasingly forced to recognise the environmental impact of technological change and the prospect of nuclear annihilation. These and other concerns have raised serious doubts for many about the supremacy of natural sciences in providing a single true account of the world and our place within it. These doubts are expressed in the ambivalence within the caring professions towards an exclusively scientific approach to the solving of human problems. This approach is usually referred to as the medical model.

Social scientists have for a long time been divided in their attitudes towards the natural sciences. At one extreme are those who wish to model their disciplines upon the natural sciences, the positivist paradigm, whilst at the opposite extreme are those who adopt a more humanistic and interpretative stance. In the latter approaches we take seriously the meaning-making nature of human beings and value the primacy of experience.

As human beings we have, it seems, a deep need to give meaning to and make sense of our experience. Even at the most basic perceptual level we are unconsciously seeing meaningful patterns, even if, as visual psychologists have demonstrated with illusions of various kinds, our perceptions are sometimes 'wrong'. This capacity for making sense has been formalised and developed through the methodologies of the natural and social sciences. We are also the inheritors of this accumulated knowledge, can contribute to its dissemination through educational processes and can subject the knowledge claims to critical scrutiny.

There is now a substantial body of systematically gathered evidence about the experience of loss and a number of theories and models purporting to explain and understand this evidence. This epidemiological evidence concerns the prevalence of mental disorders, the efficacy of different intervention strategies and the accounts of personal experience of those affected by loss. The theories and models are many and varied and are human constructions which seek to make deeper and more comprehensive sense of human experience.

Part of the commitment to the *significance of our personal experience* is the acknowledgement that theories of loss, like all theories, are human constructs, tentative, provisional and subservient to the primacy and immediacy of individual human experience. Much as we might wish for clear cut answers to the complex questions of life we have to be able to tolerate ambiguity and uncertainty both in ourselves and those we seek to help.

The experience of loss

To lose something or somebody is to be deprived of and separated from a presence, often taken for granted, around which or whom we have organised our lives. It represents a challenge to our assumptive world (Parkes, 1993, 1996a). We have become attached to and have come to assume the reliability and dependability of this presence, and have invested emotionally in the relationship something of ourselves. If 'it' is a person, then the reciprocity of the relationship implies mutuality of attachment and dependability. If 'it' is a physical object then alongside its functional utility will be an emotional attachment that derives its importance from the human associations and relationships with which it is enshrined. It was not just a bicycle, in the sense of a two-wheeled mode of transport that I recently had stolen, but my son's bicycle, which he had customised in his own way, expressive of himself and his interest in, and enjoyment of, cycling.

As was shown so convincingly by Bowlby, and usefully summarised in Holmes (1993), the patterns of such attachment behaviour are prototypically laid down in the early months of life when we were most vulnerable to the vicissitudes of the care we received from our parents or other primary care givers. Normally, although not exclusively our mothers, these people played a pivotal role in establishing, or not establishing, our fundamental ability to create and maintain significant attachment relationships throughout our subsequent lives. Herein lies a paradox, for the intensity of pain experienced through loss would seem to relate to the depth of attachment formed to the lost object or person in the first place. So one strategy for avoiding the pain of loss is not to get attached in the first place. Yet as Bowlby and others demonstrated, those who are insecure in their attachments, uncommitted in their relationships to others, condemn themselves instead to the pain of loneliness and isolation. What for most of us gives life its deepest meaning, purpose and fulfilment is mediated through just those attachments whose severance and loss causes us most grief.

The pain of grief comes from the readjustments we have to make as we are forced to detach and separate ourselves from these lost 'objects' and find new relationships to invest in emotionally. The related concepts of investment of psychic energy in lost objects, or cathexis in the mourning process, were first formulated by Freud (1917a) and developed by Klein (1959) in terms of the inner organisation of our experience. Organising our experience and creating meanings takes time, and experiences like bereavement happen so fast and are so disruptive of our basic sense of self that we often cannot process them and they remain frozen inside us. This is the hallmark of a traumatic experience; it is unfinished business that we have failed to work through and remains inside at an unconscious level but still influencing current behaviour and emotional response. These ideas are also fundamental to a theoretical understanding of our experience of loss and change.

Loss and change

Marris (1986) demonstrates how any experience of change can evoke similar reactions and feelings to those evoked by loss, so that for all practical purposes we can equate the two processes. Change is loss, and loss is change. The former assertion reminds us that when the expected routines of life are rudely interrupted we experience grief-like reactions as we seek to readjust to the loss of the familiar patterns around which we have organised our lives; the latter assertion reminds us that any loss inevitably will bring in its wake changes both internal and external to all those affected by it.

Although as human beings we may all share in attachment-like behaviour and depend upon the secure emotional base from which it comes, we will vary enormously in our grief reactions depending upon the intensity of particular attachments and the significance and meaning they hold for us. We can anticipate certain patterns as they are widespread and common, whilst others will be unpredictable and surprising, often as much to those who experience them as to those close by who observe them. Most people, for example, would experience the death of a parent as painful and maybe traumatic, depending upon the precise circumstances, yet some people can be apparently unmoved and unaffected such as Camus:

> 'Mother died today. Or maybe yesterday. I don't know. I had a telegram from the home: "Mother passed away. Funeral tomorrow. Yours sincerely." That doesn't mean anything. It may have been yesterday.'
>
> (Camus, 1983: 9)

Other people can be deeply upset and thrown by a change in their life's routine which from the outside looks trivial and inconsequential. However, if the change disrupts and severs an attachment of importance to the individual then the loss will be painful to them.

How do we cope with and process these painful experiences of separation and the inevitable levels of anxiety which come with them? Again there would seem to be enormous variation between the ability of different individuals to cope with loss depending upon their emotional resourcefulness and the external support that is available. Ultimately how we react or respond is influenced by, and in turn influences, our basic sense of the trustworthiness of life. Studies of life events that precede the onset of mental illness, such as Caplan (1961), Brown & Harris (1978) and Rahe (1979), suggest the most dangerous life-change events are:

- Those that require people to undertake a major revision of their assumptions about the world
- Those that are lasting in their implications rather than transient
- Those that take place over a relatively short period of time so there is little opportunity for preparation.

The risk factors are:

- Intense loneliness, being without a close relative or friend or some form of social support
- Death of a child
- Sudden death, one that happens without warning and for which you cannot prepare
- Lack of perceived support, that is isolation
- Reduced material resource, income and financial problems
- Concurrent crisis, one change or grief after another, compounded.

In his well-known conceptualisation of the human life cycle, Erikson (1980) locates the origins of trust and the emergence of hope at the very earliest stage of our development. A satisfactory foundation to our personality and life, equivalent to forming secure attachments in the language of Bowlby, would seem to provide the origins of this basic sense of the trustworthiness of life.

The construction of reality

Although writing from the perspective of a qualitative case study researcher, Stake (1995) usefully and concisely gets to the heart of the issues surrounding the nature of reality and its relation to our experience:

> 'Most contemporary qualitative researchers nourish the belief that knowledge is constructed rather than discovered. The world we know is a particularly human construction.'

> 'We may conceive of three realities. One is an external reality capable of stimulating us in simple ways but of which we know nothing other than our interpretations of those stimuli. The second is a reality formed of those interpretations of simple stimulation, an experiential reality representing external reality so persuasively that we seldom realize our inability to verify it. The third is a universe of integrated interpretations, our rational reality.'

> 'Denial of an independent reality is unsupportable by evidence – but more important, it is socially disconcerting.'

> 'The aim of research is not to discover reality one, for that is impossible, but to construct a clearer reality two, and a more sophisticated reality three, particularly ones that can withstand disciplined skepticism. Science strives to build a universal understanding.'

> (Stake, 1995: 99–102)

He also, drawing upon the work of von Wright, draws a helpful distinction between understanding and explanation, which derive from two broad traditions in the history of ideas. These notions are important in evaluating specific models and theories about the experience of loss and the epistemological and ontological status we wish to give them.

The notion that reality is a construction has both a psychological and sociological aspect which we consider separately below.

Personal construct theory

This is an idiographic approach stressing the uniqueness of each individual and it is also a phenomenological approach in that it attempts to understand the person in terms of his or her experience and perception of the world; a view of the world through the person's own eyes and not an observer's imposed interpretation or analysis. We are all considered as scientists putting our own interpretation (or theories) on the world of events and from these developing hypotheses and predictions about future events. Every time we act we test our theory by conducting an experiment, with behaviour as the independent variable. Depending on the outcome our hypothesis is either validated or not, and this determines the nature of our next behaviour. Although a real world of objects and events exists no one organism has the privilege of knowing it. All we can do is place our 'constructs' upon it and see whether they fit the world; the better they fit the better will be our control over our own personal world. All we have is our own interpretations. We are constantly engaged in checking, modifying and revising these unique sets of constructs. The individual actively constructs reality by interacting with it. This is also the basis of cognitive-experiential self-theory described by Epstein (1993). He emphasises:

> '... the importance of distinguishing between consciously held rational beliefs and preconsciously held experiential beliefs. Of primary importance with respect to adjustment is the meaning of an event in the experiential system. A person in his or her conscious, rational system may believe that he or she should be deeply distressed following the death of a sibling. In the experiential system, however, the death may be perceived as the defeat of a rival, and evoke feelings of victory along with those of regret.'

> (Epstein, 1993: 115)

Feelings of ambivalence over those most close to us have long been recognised within the psychodynamic traditions; Epstein gives fresh understandings. His theory is based on:

> '... four basic needs that are sources of motivation in a personal theory of reality and four related beliefs. The basic needs are to maximise pleasure and minimise pain, to assimilate the data of reality ..., to maintain relatedness to others, and to maximise self esteem.'

> (Epstein 1993: 116)

The related beliefs concern the degree to which the world is viewed as benevolent-meaningful, predictable and controllable; other people are viewed as a source of affection and support; the self is viewed as worthy, competent, lovable and good. Each of these dimensions will significantly affect the experience of grief.

Social constructionism

Burr (1995: 2–3) outlines the following key assumptions of the social constructionist position:

(1) *A critical stance towards taken-for-granted knowledge* – our observations and categories do not unproblematically reveal the nature of reality. This includes those observations used in enquiries into the processes of dying and grieving to construct models and theories.
(2) *Historical and cultural specificity* – which includes knowledge generated by the social sciences. The implications at one level are compatible with

the liberal/humanist dimension of equal opportunities. However, some knowledge comes to be privileged over others and becomes normative. Issues of power and powerlessness affect individuals in so far as they are expected to conform to these normative structures.

(3) *Knowledge is sustained by social processes* – the personal meanings we come to create are negotiated through social interaction and this emphasises the importance of language and discourse in constituting, as well as communicating, understanding. Agreement as to what constitutes valid knowledge is arrived at by consensual validation.

(4) *Knowledge and social action go together* – different constructions invite different responses in terms of social action and policy. Constructing grief as a disease requires a different response from constructing it as a normal reaction to an event inherent in the human condition.

Even if we consider all human beings as equal, whatever their culture, sexuality, able-bodiedness or gender, we also know that because of the way society and meanings are structured all are not treated so. Sometimes positive discrimination in bereavement care may be necessary with certain groups; for example the catastrophic effects of AIDS/HIV have drawn attention to the bereavement needs of gay and lesbian individuals.

Theories of loss and the helping process

In understanding any phenomenon or experience in life, models and theories can play an important part. There is a danger in detaching and distancing ourselves from the immediacy and primacy of experience in abstractions and generalisations. Nevertheless without some way of organising experience we will learn little from it and face new experiences without resources to guide and inform our response. The importance of models and theories of grief is not to interpret events in a rigid and inflexible way, but to provide generalisable clues and patterns to the unfolding of what would otherwise be a bewildering variety of human experience.

Our understanding of likely patterns of response to loss is now greatly enhanced by the pioneering works of Kubler-Ross (1969) and Parkes (1996a) and subsequent developments, refinements and challenges to them. Their theories are based upon qualitative research through interviews carried out with terminally ill patients and widows respectively. They conducted these with great sensitivity and care as they sought to find out how these people were thinking and feeling about their predicament. They independently developed stage models identifying different psychological processes that were dominant in an individual as they responded either to the realisation that they were shortly going to die, or to the death of their husband. The stages in the model of Kubler-Ross are:

- Denial
- Anger

- Bargaining
- Depression
- Acceptance.

The stages in the model of Parkes, closely linked with ideas of Bowlby, are (as cited in Archer & Rhodes, 1987):

- Shock or numbness, involving a feeling of disbelief and an urge to deny the truth of the news
- Pining and 'yearning and protest' that includes pangs of grief and anxiety interspersed with feelings of anger, which may be accompanied by bitterness, irritability and self-reproach
- Disorganisation and despair, characterised by feelings of depression and a tendency to withdraw socially
- Readjustment, including redefinition of oneself and one's circumstances.

The models have been influential in deepening our understanding of how people experience the imminence of both their own death and also all kinds of losses and bereavement. The danger with these, and indeed any model, is that they become normative, telling us how people ought to experience loss. Not everyone, however, necessarily goes through (or needs to go through) all the stages or in the order outlined. The elements of the experience nevertheless seem to be widely experienced and for reasons that we can make some sense of in the light of earlier ideas. Denial and associated defensiveness are often seen negatively within psychodynamic perspectives; however, the processes have an essentially protective function as we react and respond to the initial experience of shock. We thereby create space for ourselves in which to come to terms with what has happened. Anger is a natural and appropriate response to situations where we experience loss of control. The experience and expression of anger are considered in more detail in Chapter 12.

An alternative, complementary approach to the experience of loss is provided by Worden (1991) who describes a series of tasks which have to be worked through in resolving grief.

- Task One: to accept the reality of the loss
- Task Two: to experience the pain of grief
- Task Three: to adjust to an environment in which the deceased is missing
- Task Four: to withdraw emotional energy from the lost one and reinvest in another relationship.

The focus on tasks links with the idea of grief work and the effort and energy required. It is not surprising therefore that at such times we are particularly vulnerable and in need of appropriate help.

Adams *et al.* (1976) proposed a model charting the changes in self-esteem that occur during transitions:

(1) *Immobilisation* – shock, being overwhelmed by the situation and incapable of making plans. The amount of shock experienced is proportional to the level of crisis experienced.
(2) *Minimisation or denial* – can even be accompanied by feelings of euphoria or mood swings from elation to despair. There can be an attempt to trivialise the situation or even deny that a change exists.
(3) *Depression or self-doubt* – a time of uncertainty accompanied by feelings of powerlessness and of not being in control. Mood swings between anger and helplessness can occur.
(4) *Acceptance of reality* (letting go) – a gradual awareness of the new reality which is one of the most important phases because it marks the point at which a person is detaching from the emotions of the past and is moving forward to the future.
(5) *Testing* – time to experiment and try out new options. It can be a time of activity when new behaviours and lifestyles can be tested, and coping skills brought into play.
(6) *Search for meaning* – making sense of what has happened and learning from the experience. Knowing what the changes mean and how they affect our lives help us to move on to the next stage.
(7) *Internalisation or integration* – the transition has been accepted and the changes have been incorporated into the new lifestyle. Self-esteem is restored and confidence returns.

The dual process model of grieving (Stroebe *et al.*, 1994) is based on the way in which:

'Bereaved people oscillate back and forth between grieving and the other demands of life – eating, sleeping, caring for surviving children and so on.'

(Parkes, 1996a: 53)

More recently Walter (1996a) has challenged the dominant normative model which:

'... sees grief as primarily a working through of emotion, the eventual goal being to move on and live without the deceased.'

(Walter, 1996a: 7)

Bereaved people do not necessarily want to so lightly dispose of the dead, but need to find a place for them. This place is partly a psychological construction but the process needs a viable social context in which to take place.

'The purpose of grief is therefore the construction of a durable biography that enables the living to integrate the memory of the dead into their ongoing lives; the process by which this is achieved is principally conversation with others who knew the deceased.

(Walter, 1996a: 7)

The epidemiological evidence and the need for interventions

It is important before we look further at theories and models for transition, change and grief that we are clear about the epidemiological evidence which suggests that interventions based on such understandings are necessary in the first instance.

Mental illness is a leading cause of illness and disability. It accounts for about 14% of certificated sickness absence, 14% of NHS inpatient costs and 23% of NHS pharmaceutical costs. The cost in human misery and suffering to individuals and their families is incalculable. Table 1.1 illustrates estimates of the prevalence of mental disorders in the population. Most common are illnesses such as depression and anxiety. Less common, but more severe, are the psychotic illnesses such as schizophrenia and affective psychosis.

Table 1.1   Estimated frequency of mental disorders in the adult population over age 16 based on *Key Area Handbook: Mental Illness* (Department of Health, 1993).

Mental disorder	Point prevalence (percentage [%] of the population over age 16)	Lifetime risk (percentage [%] of the population over age 16)
Schizophrenia	0.2–0.5	0.7–0.9
Affective psychosis	0.1–0.5	1
Depressive disorder	3–6	>20
Anxiety states	2–7	
Dementia (over age 65)	5	
Dementia (over age 80)	20	

The figures on depression are worrying and in some instances may well be the result of unresolved or ongoing loss. Mental illness also leads to death caused by physical illness and from suicide. There were 5567 deaths from suicide (and undetermined injury) in 1991 in England. Trends in suicides differ by age and sex. There is a particularly worrying rise in suicides among younger men. In relation to behaviour change the *Health of the Nation* sets out the targets for reduction of chronic disease and life-years lost through these:

(1)   To improve significantly the health and social functioning of mentally ill people.
(2)   To reduce the overall suicide rate by at least 15% by the year 2000 (from 11.1 per 100 000 of the population in 1990 to no more than 9.4).
(3)   To reduce the suicide rate of severely mentally ill people by at least 33% by the year 2000 (from the estimate of 15% in 1990 to no more than 10%).

Two million people can be expected to die in a single year in the USA alone. Of these more than 16 000 are children between the ages of 1 and 14 and as many as 38 000 are young people between the ages of 15 and 24 (US

Dept Health and Human Services cited in Department of Health, 1992). These show an alarming infant mortality rate of 40 000 babies dying before they reach 1 year. For each of these deaths there are many people left behind, all of whom are at risk of detrimental affects on their mental and physical health. However, most of these people given supportive environments and care will move through their own grief journey at their own pace. Only approximately one-third will experience difficulty and need psychological help. This not only shows the strength of the human psyche but that the development over the years of a more supportive culture and training may be helping to reduce risk. There is no room for complacency as we cannot tell easily how many individuals try and cope, appear to cope but perhaps are very distressed and yet afraid to seek help and support. We do know there are some people who face life events which could result in mental illness, particularly depression and increased anxiety.

The helping process

There are now numerous practical books on bereavement counselling, Lendrum & Syme (1992), Humphrey & Zimpfer (1996), Parkes (1996b) and Tschudin (1997) for example; it is not our intention to replicate the material in detail here. Such theories and research are well documented in Dickenson & Johnson (1993), Stroebe *et al.* (1993) and Raphael (1996). Dickenson & Johnson also include ethnic and cultural issues along with gay and lesbian death and grieving. It is useful nevertheless to look at the theoretical basis of the therapeutic strategies recommended in such texts and research evidence for their effectiveness.

There are three broad approaches to counselling and psychotherapy based on different assumptions about the nature of human beings and the way they function (Macleod, 1993):

- *Person-centred* – a focus on the 'here-and-now' relationship with counsellor or therapist
- *Psychodynamic* – a focus on the influence of past events on present experience and behaviour
- *Cognitive-behavioural* – a focus on learning new ways of thinking and behaving in the future.

Most counsellors, in both the voluntary and professional sectors, acknowledge their indebtedness to the pioneering work of Carl Rogers in the development of person-centred approaches. He formulated the core conditions or qualities for effective counselling and listening and we consider each of these in turn in the light of the ideas above:

- *Empathy* – understanding – sensitivity – communication
- *Unconditional positive regard* – acceptance – warmth – respect
- *Congruence* – genuineness – authenticity – transparency.

Firstly, the quality of *empathy*, which is essential for effective listening, can be usefully defined as:

'... the ability to perceive accurately the feelings of another person and the ability to communicate this understanding to him/her...'

(Kalisch, 1971, quoted in Tschudin, 1989: vii)

Rogers & Stevens (1967:92–3) describe empathy as:

'To sense the client's inner world of private meanings as if it were your own, but without ever losing the "as if" quality...'

The aim, according to Rogers & Stevens, is to sense the client's uncertainty, anger, or rage, without experiencing your own at the same time. This level of understanding is probably rare, certainly in our close relationships. Often a painful disclosure to a friend is met with 'I know just how you feel, something very similar happened to me ...'. Goleman (1996) suggests that the roots of empathy are in self-awareness; if we cannot tune in to the pains and pleasures of our own lives, how can we begin to put them to one side in order to put ourselves in the place of another?

If from a constructivist perspective we all inhabit separate worlds then we can only by an effort of imagination project ourselves into someone else's world. It is as much a cognitive as an affective achievement. This, however, is only the first half of the expression of empathy because if we fail to convey this achievement to the other person then they will never know of our efforts to see the world through their eyes. Hence the importance of communicating this understanding to them. This is the fundamental bridge between individuals which enables us to know that in some measure others understand our predicament and the way we are experiencing it. Such understanding may be offered freely (by voluntary counsellors) but it is very costly in terms of the emotional demands required.

Every person perceives and experiences loss in their own cultural, personal and individual way, so what might seem an unimportant loss to us may be devastating to them. We cannot use our own mind map and perceptions to judge the effects of loss for other people. There is a need to emphatically view it through their own perceptual world or frame of reference.

Secondly, there must be *unconditional positive regard* or respect for the individual and this includes adults recognising that children are individuals in their own right and not mini-adults. Adults need to review the use of paternalistic and maternalistic approaches to helping children; children are able to be active on their own behalf, they do know what they are feeling even though they may have difficulty in articulating it (see Chapter 13). Through respect we validate and affirm each other and the integrity of our experience.

The value of respect, based on Egan (1994), is manifested in both our attitudes towards and the ways in which we work with each other. Our attitude towards each other is respectful if we:

- Care about the welfare of ourselves and others
- Consider each child or adult to be a unique human being
- View them as capable of determining their own fates
- Assume the good will of children/adults until this assumption is demonstrated to be wrong.

Our attitude when working with others is respectful when we:

- Develop competence in helping, and use it
- Attend and listen actively
- Suspend critical judgement
- Communicate empathic understanding
- Express reasonable warmth or friendliness
- Help them identify and cultivate their own resources
- Provide encouragement, support, and appropriate challenge
- Help them get the work of each relevant step of the helping process done.

Thirdly, the quality of *congruence* or genuineness which presents particular challenges when we are in our professional roles. We are genuine in our relationship with each other when we:

- Do not overemphasise our professional role and avoid stereotyped role behaviour
- Are spontaneous but not uncontrolled or haphazard in our relationships
- Remain open and non-defensive even when we feel threatened
- Are consistent and avoid discrepancies between our values and our behaviour, and between our thoughts and our words in interactions with others while remaining respectful and reasonably tactful
- Are willing to share ourselves and our experience with others if it seems helpful.

In addition to individual counselling and therapy the use of group therapy in relation to issues of loss can be powerful and effective. Individuals in a group can be unrelated and working on their own agenda, related (family therapy) or brought together as a result of having shared some common disaster and trauma (see Chapter 11).

The three core conditions are conducive to healing and growth in all counselling contexts and particularly for those in trauma and crisis. They are also the basis of long-term preventative interventions and the basis for the creation of a culture of care.

A culture of care

In a health-promoting climate and environment the culture is one which supports and cares for all of its members, developing their self-esteem and confidence as well as their academic potential. This care also extends to respect for the environment. The result is a culture which helps all of us to have the confidence to know ourselves and to grow and develop. If we live and work in such a culture (and many do not as it is in constant tension with accountability theory and practice), then we already have the bedrock of all we need to support those who are in a process of change, feel sad, lonely, hurt or who are grieving. We also have these skills to use with one another. These qualities imply a relationship of interdependence, thus avoiding the unhelpful extremes of dependency and independency. They express solidarity particularly in times of loss when our personal resources may be temporarily depleted and our capacity for the hard work of constructing new meanings temporarily disabled. An important part of the task is to enable people in telling their story to use the language of feelings. There are many ways we can encourage the use of feeling words in our everyday work which helps us all, including children, to express our feelings and the emotions behind the words.

Practising these skills enables us to become more effective carers and supporters. As well as integrating work about feelings with our everyday activities, there may be times when we and colleagues or children need very special understanding and love. The experience of loss and bereavement can be inexpressible and unexplainable; we just feel it as a deep inner pain.

The process of reconstruction

Unfortunately, quite often as professionals, we are unable to help and support either clients or colleagues because we fear being overwhelmed by our own sadness, grief, anger and powerlessness. The will is there but fear gets in the way. Training in change theory, counselling, loss and bereavement can encourage us to explore such fears, sensitising us to more reflective practice which enables us to help others to cope and to grow.

Much theory of the promotion of positive mental health requires that we acknowledge and work with change and grief to encourage learning and development. Out of such experiences we are then able to invest anew in our future: to reconstruct our lives. This work is the promotion of positive mental health and to achieve it training is aimed at encouraging a critical mass of individuals who can prevent ill health from unacknowledged or unresolved grieving. This is not to make grief a pathological issue, most people are quite capable of achieving this themselves especially if they have sound social supports, it is only a minority that cannot. Using the concept of reconstruction, even those who can help themselves need a culture in which they feel supported to do so.

The message is simple yet profound, nowhere will you find someone who has not grieved or experienced loss. It is a universal experience for all of us and we all therefore have the possibility of showing empathy. We may not, however, have felt bereavement. Susan Hill (1974) uses the concept and distinguishes between the sadness of loss and the process of grief we experience when we know we have been bereaved. The core self, deep inside, is shattered, painful, hurts and feels it will never be whole again.

Many of us face situations of loss or bereavement, through divorce, separation, illness, unemployment, redundancy, changes to systems and practices in work, death, abuse, burglary, or violence to property or self, this includes bullying. There is no way of grading which of these experiences has the highest collateral in terms of loss and bereavement.

Normative values and professional training, however, often mean we believe professionals know best. This is not always the case. Many lay volunteers are involved in support and counselling. All of us every day may help and support in the course of our everyday lives. The key aspect of helping, as Kubler-Ross demonstrated, is understanding what is happening for the grieving person, their needs and perspectives.

Starting where the person is enables us to work with them and at their pace, with everything in their control – we reinvest them with power which is an antidote to powerlessness. Grief, or experiences for which we have to grieve, leaves us powerless in the present and immediate future. This concept of starting where the individual is at is grounded in the concept of becoming from the philosophical work of Tillich (1967).

In order to enable us to support and help others to cope, other techniques, in addition to talking and listening, can be used. People can draw or paint or explain through music; sometimes they just want to be quiet and someone to hold them, metaphorically and physically, until they can explain. There is no time limit for these things, individuals can take days, weeks, months, years. There should only be holding and no pressure. Being able to hold someone in their intense pain, just being there, is sometimes enough and it is a privilege as well as a skill to be able to do it. Many times it will require more than this.

Some people may not want or be able to share their feelings. Some may find their feelings too strong to reflect on, to try to put into words, especially when these relate to fear, aggression, hatred, uncertainty, being bullied, anticipation, joy, love and delight. Those who help and support need to explore ways which may encourage them to do this when they are ready.

Conclusion

We can gain useful understanding, and insight into the experience of loss from the theoretical ideas of constructivism, both social and psychological, and from the psychodynamic traditions. They illuminate the emotional cost of reorganising our inner world in response to uninvited changes in the external world as we attempt to provide the much needed continuity of coherence and meaning around which we organise our lives. Taking this perspective has significant implications for how we manage the educational process for both children and adults.

Chapter 2
Identity and Power

Pat Usher

This chapter provides a theoretical framework for understanding the contributions in this book which deal with the use and abuse of power. Using her experience as a union representative and feminist, the author deconstructs the nature of power in the context of patriarchal society. Adopting a Foucauldian approach to discourse analysis she develops critiques of the nature of power and suggests that intimidation, bullying and violence are socially constructed and culturally reproduced.

The perspectives from which this chapter is written are: professional, autobiographical and empirical.

Introduction

I take as my focus the themes of power and gender as an aspect of loss and bereavement. The intention is to explore the nature and abuse of power in a society which has its origins in patriarchy. Although my main theme is gender, the argument applies to other dimensions such as race, culture and social class. Using discourse analysis I highlight issues about being powerless and argue that as some abuses are institutionalised they continue without challenge. The accompanying loss of self-esteem leaves victims with the same sense of anguish that is found in bereavement.

Power has a multiplicity of expressions and is exercised by everyone. The view that power resides only with and in particular individuals or groups needs to be challenged. The hierarchical nature of society is reproduced in all its aspects, even within the caring professions where bereavement care takes place. To understand this requires the very notion of power to be deconstructed.

Subsequent chapters will describe and discuss issues of violence and crime; it is noteworthy that longitudinal and cross-cultural studies indicate that women continue to play relatively minor roles in violent crime (Simon & Baxter, 1989; Weiner & Wolfgang, 1989).

'It seems to be one of those facts that escape notice by virtue of its very conspicuousness. It is surely, to say the least, very odd that half of the population should be so significantly immune to the criminogenic factors which lead to the downfall of so significant a proportion of the other half. Equally it is odd, too, that although the criminological experience of different countries varies considerably, nevertheless the sex differential remains.'

(Weiner & Wolfgang, 1989: 171)

These studies give a clear indication that violent crime is linked to gender and may be linked to the way power is used in society.

Experiences of power

There are three ways I use my experience of power to illuminate this debate. These are as a feminist, a trades unionist and an educator. I confront the central, but disguised operation, of power along gendered divisions and the interdependency of power and justice in institutional decision making. I therefore value experience as crucial in the formulating of knowledge. Any explanations about grief, loss and conflict which do not take account of analyses about how identity is formed, how power is exercised and how gender difference is implicated, are unconvincing. I have increasingly come to realise that the structures in Western thought, through which we create meanings about how to grieve or confront conflict in personal relationships, limit our vision and capacity to create 'new maps of the terrain' of the whole panorama of human activity (Rorty, 1979).

My focus is on gendered relations but I am well aware that, in drawing on critical theoretical analyses, I am offering insights that apply equally to other social divisions such as class, race, and age. Using gender as an example I perceive power as relational, productive as well as oppressive, contradictory and unitary. New ways of understanding all the facets of conflict (including those in the caring professions) may mean that much of our previous thinking proves unsatisfactory.

The hidden agenda of power

It is the underlying structures of power within society that makes possible and organises individual actions within a context where sexual inequalities are taken for granted. Sexist behaviours are the visible symptoms of a patriarchy which assumes it is acceptable to treat women in ways unequal to men. It is certainly true that as individuals women can intimidate men junior to them and other women, but in the context of our patriarchal structures, where women lack social, political or workplace power, women as a group cannot harass men as a group. It is through the meanings which society assigns to masculine and feminine behaviours that men can rely on customs, conventions, attitudes and norms which support or render invisible their discriminatory acts against women.

The visibility of sexual harassment and bullying is a relatively recent development. In 1991 the Equal Opportunities Commission in the UK received 403 claims alleging sexual harassment and in 1992 there were 502 claims. Virtually all their surveys have shown that sexual harassment is perpetrated predominantly by men against women. A survey carried out by the Industrial Society (in 1993) found that 54% of working women had suffered sexual harassment (IRS (1996) *Employment Trends* 615). Making a complaint is often as stressful as the original experience of harassment and in most cases (in my experience), the complainant is the least likely to gain anything. Losing a job or having to move are the most likely outcomes (IRS (1996) *Employment Trends* 615; 618; 621).

Tension between the sexes at the workplace and in other social and political situations has long existed. Feminist writers (Alexander, 1984; Hall, 1992) have revealed how men historically have used their social power to exclude women from paid work by claiming the greater entitlement to work, maintaining power of definition over the skills needed to do certain jobs and exclusion from training. Trades unions have been dominated by men concerned to protect their jobs and wages and historically women were prevented or discouraged from joining. It has only been in recent decades that the unions have shown a systematic concern about women's interests (Beechey, 1983) whereas hitherto the objective has been to protect male workers from female competition.

The critical interpretation of experience

In reviewing personal experience of these issues and how I interpret the incidence of sexual harassment and bullying within the historical and conceptual context of gendered power relationships in the workplace, two autobiographical details are relevant. In parallel with my full-time job of administrator, I have been a part-time educator working in post-compulsory education and my experience has led me to become a feminist. In constructing a text such as this it is important to make explicit the paradigms through which my thoughts and assumptions are constructed.

In common with many adult educators (Dewey, 1925; Boud & Griffin, 1987), my ideas and practice about education have developed through a discourse of experiential learning. In coming to appreciate that significant learning arises from experience, closely linked to social interaction in relationships, I acknowledge that my emotional subjectivity is deeply implicated in the intellectual part of me. Each of us creates a meaning out of specific experiences and in so doing we draw upon our memory of the past. We bring a unique interpretation to experience even when the same experiences have been shared. In holding such views, it is evident that this is outside of the mainstream perspectives on learning which relate to the transmission of externally defined bodies of knowledge to be communicated through curricula, syllabi and assessments (Church, 1995).

However, as Boud *et al.* (1993) state, while experience is the precursor of learning it does not necessarily lead to it. The added ingredient must be an active engagement leading to some form of analysis. Writers like Boud *et al.* (1993) and Usher (1993) have drawn attention to the special role that reflection plays in creating meanings from experience. Drawing on the work of Kolb (1984), they argue that we are involved in two processes, one of grasping the nature of experience and the other of transforming it. The value of Kolb's work is that he draws attention to the extent to which Western societies favour external knowledge and abstract, analytical thinking and those who excel; but goes on to argue that reflection on direct experience, giving rise to personal definitions, should be equally emphasised within formal education.

Why is it that out of the myriad of experiences and created meanings about my workplace roles, certain aspects have been focused on rather than others? Usher is helpful:

'Once we start analysing something, we make something the object of our investigation, we do so within and through a discourse. It gives us a vocabulary, a set of concepts and pre-understandings, a motivating focus and direction for our investigations – above all a disciplined and systematic way of talking.'

(Usher, 1993:169)

In using the concept of discourse, Usher is drawing on a Foucauldian concept. Foucault's (1969) objective is to analyse the contexts from which discourses emerge and hence make claims for truths, that is, knowledge and understanding of a particular phenomenon. In *Madness and Civilization* (1967) his study of the history of madness starts from the institutions which enclosed the insane. He looked at the institutional practices within the asylum and asked questions about the sets of rules, norms and conventions which gave rise to modes of speaking and interacting. Through the systematic organisation of representations and definitions certain individuals were accorded status giving them the power to make medical decisions. In Western culture Foucault argues that the human sciences have increasingly constituted discourses which provide reasons, criteria and justifications for creating particular identities or subjectivities through which people have been classified, examined, trained, excluded from others and disciplined. This analysis can provide new ways of viewing the epistemological question, what is it we do in change and bereavement work and the ontological question – what is this world in which we do it?

The significance of Foucault's work for me as a feminist will become clear later in the chapter. It is appropriate to state at this juncture my perspective that experiential learning is a discourse. It has developed its own rules and conventions that present experience as a form of knowledge.

Usher's work (1993: 170) provides an insight into understanding experience as akin to the process of reading a text. He develops reading as a metaphor to show the similarities between reading a text and reading experience. Both must be interpreted since neither has an intrinsic meaning;

this is relational since each meaning owes its significance to a contrast with other meanings; furthermore as it is contextual it is interpreted from experience founded within a particular position in time and culture. The process of reading experience is never entirely personal because, as he points out:

'. . . any reading whether it be the reading of written texts or of the text of experience, depends on an interpretive culture, a discursive tradition within which our pre-understandings are located.'

(Usher, 1993: 173)

Within a discursive framework of an interpretive culture, women in patriarchal structures are afforded an opportunity to offer a critical interpretation of their everyday experience.

It is clear that many of the contributors to this book are working within interpretive discourses. In different ways we argue the importance of personal narrative in creating intelligible meanings about vitally important areas of human experience. Various stages in feminist theory have been equally committed to giving voice to women's experience because politically and personally it provides a direct link to their consciousness and identity. Within such humanistic discourses, the assumption is that people's experience can be represented in an account and that it will be authentic. However, Usher is unhappy with such idealistic notions because what is omitted is the insight that numerous other interpretations could have been selected in representing experience.

Examples exist within this book of contributors drawing on post-modern critiques of both positivist and humanist perspectives and arguing that people's subjectivities are produced through discourses and the meanings they give their experience. How they create themselves is derived through the rules and conventions of one or more discourses. In the following, I draw on both experiential and radical feminist discourses to give an account of the gendered nature of power relationships in the workplace. However, in using the rules of such discourses it is accepted that personal accounts do not constitute the whole 'truth'.

The discourses which exclude women from equality

Women are positioned in society in relation to men. Their significance as voices is also afforded a lower status in relation to those cultural values embedded in masculine discourses which render invisible the power men exercise over the lives of women.

Given the patriarchal nature of structures it would be tempting to believe that the status quo should remain unchallenged. The ideology of masculinity and men is that it is part of a natural order which provides for stability and a rational acceptance that hierarchies are inevitable; founded on fundamental values from which all benefit most of the time.

The aspects of personal experience on which I choose to focus are the injustices which arise when power is exercised within a discourse that excludes women from their entitlement to equality. Barriers to women's needs and progress, whether conscious or unconscious, go largely unnoticed because they are intrinsic to the status quo. This has always been the case. The difference is that women now have the benefit of critical analyses which allow the reflexivity to reinterpret experience, create new meanings and argue for new behaviours which will expose abuses of power.

For most of us who have been active in the politics of social change over recent decades the dominant paradigm within which we constituted our meanings and activities has been that of equal opportunities. Its concerns are to remove barriers to women's participation in all aspects of public affairs and to argue for a greater share for women in the rights, duties, privileges and responsibilities of society.

This particular approach to feminism derives from liberal theory which in turn owes its tradition to Enlightenment thought, the assumptions of which are a belief in an essential human equality, a scepticism towards prejudice and tradition and a commitment to the power of rational thought as the guarantor of truth and knowledge. Location within this discourse has led to campaigns resulting in legislation for abortion (1967), equal pay (1970) and sex discrimination (1975). The assumption constituting the discourse is that female subordination is the result of the operation of sexism and if the unwarranted differential treatment of women can be identified in empirical terms, it can be removed. If women and men are treated as equals both in politics and the paid work environment there is the rational possibility that women's views and activities can be afforded the same degree of significance.

However, as time has passed, many women have become disenchanted with the contradictions embedded in liberal feminism which they believe account for the failure of the politics emanating from this position. Although there has been much change, progress is slow and institutional forms of patriarchy are still evident. The real challenge has, perhaps, not begun in earnest.

What are the implications of this analysis on individual and organisational change? I have attempted to bring together the insights gained from experiential learning and radical feminism. The incidence of intimidatory behaviours leading in particular to bullying and sexual harassment is ever present. The organisation of work has been examined through a feminist lens and its patriarchal structures and normative values presented as positioning women in subordinated roles and status. Gender and occupational status interact to shape women's experience at work in ways that men do not experience because definitions of masculinity privilege their exercise of power and position them in status roles.

The processes of discrimination are widespread and operate at the level of overt structural barriers such as lack of child-care facilities, role models or mentors; as covert barriers through prejudiced attitudes, beliefs and exclusionary behaviours defined by men; or as unconscious effects on women's self-esteem. Given these factors it might be tempting to rationalise that this reflects a naturalised order and that we should remain with the modest efforts offered by equal opportunities approaches as a means of attempting change.

However, feminist studies which ally themselves with post-modern arguments have developed a more sophisticated account of gendered power relations and from this we can construct different approaches to the use of power in the workplace which do not treat men and women as unified groups in opposition. What is needed are theories about patriarchy which do not neglect the differences or similarities within the category of men and women. Theory is required that permits thinking in terms of pluralities and diversities of experience rather than accepting the traditional norms and unities out of which so many fixed stereotypes emerge. We need a critical discourse that allows us to break out of the conceptual hold of long traditions of Western philosophy that have constructed our thinking through rigid hierarchies and universal categories. The association of masculinity with rational, autonomous, objective behaviours sets up a complex set of meanings and cultural processes which is the starting point for the way that institutions are organised and identities created. If change is sought then it is necessary to ask, how do meanings change, emerge as normative or become submerged?; how is power constituted and operated? (Walter, 1996a).

Difference and diversity

Foucault's work on discourse mentioned above offers insights for feminists into a critical discourse about the operation of power which can subvert the hold which masculinity has over the power of definition.

Foucault's use of discourse permits the insight that truth is not outside of human construction but is the product of meanings that are historically, socially and institutionally derived. It can be argued that discourses overlap, influence and compete with one another in making appeals to know what is valid knowledge about experience. Biological and essentialist theories which argue that sexual differences determine that men and women are naturally disposed to behave differently and so legitimate the association of power and masculinity are but two discourses among many and have no greater claim to validity than any other.

Foucault's work provides a different way of thinking about the politics of creating meanings. If that is combined with the concept of critical reflexivity derived from experiential learning, we have at our disposal the intellectual tools to create new meanings. These meanings allow women to subvert the dualities of thought which have traditionally positioned them as inferior, being other, excluded, the specific, by comparison with the masculine claims to neutrality and universality.

To illustrate how this approach may be applied, Scott's (1988) discussion of the 'equality-versus-difference' debate is at the heart of competing discourses in feminist theory. Liberal feminists put their emphasis on seeking equality because they argue that women have the same capacity to act as rational beings as men and therefore should have the same access to rights and responsibilities in the public exercise of power. However, in living such an approach, women must often disavow what it is about their identities and experience that makes them different. This is, in effect, a binary opposition between equality and difference – the former must minimise or exclude the latter.

Scott argues that the two terms should be seen as interdependent, and that the opposition between them should be broken. Definitions may be developed which see equality not as the elimination of difference, but as a respect for diversity of differences and difference as a concept which eliminates a hierarchy of status. In contrast to liberal discourse on equality-difference, Scott argues within a post-modern discourse for the following approach: it is not sameness or identity between women and men that we want to claim but a more complicated, historically variable diversity than is permitted by men vis-à-vis women (Scott, 1988: 33).

Until now concepts suppressed our capacity to take differences into account and so conformity to unified categories dominates our assumptions. This means that all men and women are expected to conform to rigid notions about who has power, how it is exercised and how definitions of worth are constructed.

The implications of such a stance are far reaching. To escape the stereotype that femininity predisposes women to certain jobs or styles of management, women will have to surrender any privileged position they might try to defend based on essentialist categories. In other words, men are as capable of caring and relational behaviours as women if the stereotypic categories are to be broken down in favour of the contingent nature of categories. None of this denies the existence of gender difference but it does mean both sexes have to surrender the normative rules in favour of new meanings.

Instead of positioning rationality and emotion in binary opposition, we need to reconstitute their meanings so that we define each not by excluding the other, but by acknowledging the interconnected relation between them and how each can only be defined by relation to particular constructions in specified contexts. Unless we argue for this contingent approach, we are always pressured into accepting normative rules which take no account of personal or group diversity or need. There are situations in which it is both rational and emotional for women to claim that their role as mothers should be recognised and integrated into workplace organisation and other situations in which the rational approach should be to ignore motherhood as a relevant consideration.

Similarly, the patriarchal approach which regards men as workers without emotional lives that affect their judgement is neither rational nor good management. Men are as much constrained by current definitions of masculinity as women. Critical studies on both men and masculinities are beginning to argue that they are not homogeneous, unified or fixed categories (that is, white, heterosexual, middle-class) but different and shifting categories related to age, class, ethnicity, religion, sexuality, parental/ marital status, occupation, size and propensity for violence. Once one dispenses with taken-for-granted ways of thinking, one can deconstruct existing 'meanings' and reorder them to create more accurate representations of men's lives, or in the case of bereavement care or health issues, constantly question why we have come to theorise and practice in certain ways, why professional training is constructed as it is. Men live gendered lives and how they operate in the workplace and how, in particular, they manage has until recently been presented as if it were all gender neutral activity.

This points to an important challenge which both sexes must face if we are to learn new behaviours of the distribution and operation of power in the workplace. As I have argued earlier, dominant discourses about workplace organisation fail to address two aspects of organisational power; the first related to hierarchy and the second related to gender and men. If we are to address the abuse of power in the workplace which produces intimidatory behaviours and the resulting stress and trauma, we need critical discourses which problematise power and control, ideology and men's control through an association of masculinity and control.

In their attempts to work with power, men and women are attempting to control employees, colleagues and themselves, and depending on the discourse within which they speak, they may either reflect and reinforce oppressive environments, attempt to subvert them or encourage change, growth and development.

Foucault has developed an analysis about the relationship between power and knowledge which underpins our understandings of truth and rationality. He asks us to see the links between power and subjectivity and shows us how power grips us in the process of constructing our own identities and giving expression to our own desires (this can be the desire to 'care' or do 'good' just as it can be an unwitting acceptance of normative value; see also Murdoch (1970)). Walter (1996a) speaks about this in his work, our acceptance of the need to 'let go' rather than 'hang on' to the dead. This is cultural as well as a way of establishing an outcome of grief which has medical connotations, that is, get back to normal as soon as possible, once you have proved you have, you are perceived as having recovered. He challenges other concepts of bereavement work in the same way, see also Chapters 1 and 9. Foucault's theory of power differs from the model offered by liberal and Marxist approaches in these three ways:

(1)   Power is exercised rather than possessed; it is not held by the state. Therefore in the caring professions there is no ownership of the 'power and knowledge' but many that contribute to theory and practice.

(2)   Power is not primarily repressive, but productive; it does not flow from a centralised source from top to bottom (see theories on growth, development and change).

(3)   Power is analysed as coming from the bottom up; it is not based simply on repression backed up by coercion (see theories on hermeneutics, interaction between individual and the social and Fox (1993) on arche-health, that is, the constant resistance through desire to change power or repression that human beings are capable of exerting).

While he does not deny that power operates in repressive and imposed ways, he has developed approaches which show that power is exercised through relationships and that the most effective power systems are ones that work through certain institutional and cultural practices that in effect discipline individuals by creating them in certain identities. The rise of the human sciences during the nineteenth century helped create practices of disciplinary power which both increased the power of individuals at the same time as controlling them. In modern society, disciplinary power has spread throughout all the social sciences through the emergence of disciplinary techniques that allow professionals the right to survey, examine and create definitions about other people's lives (see Walter (1996a) on grieving and healing). In his view, ways of knowing equate with ways of exercising power over individuals (see warnings about therapy, counselling, therapists and counsellors as well as professional and lay carers). For the educator and the social scientist power over definitions such as healthy/ill, mad/sane, legal/lawbreaking confer a great deal of personal power over others' lives but also are the means through which they create their own identity and betray their own desire to control.

Such ideas are deeply uncomfortable because they remove the liberal notion that individuals can exercise power in an innocent and disinterested way. Foucault firmly points to the interrelatedness of power and desire and the propensity we all have to control others. However, while he argues that power is everywhere he also argues 'we're never trapped by power; it's always possible to modify its hold in any determined condition by following a precise strategy' (Foucault, 1980: 13). Power relations are thus not inevitable, unchanging or unalterable. By offering us a theory of resistant subjectivity, Foucault opens up the possibility of developing critical discourses which can resist hegemonic ideas about the relationship between power and masculinity. Alternative approaches can be adopted which resist the splitting of concepts into binary opposites such as rational/irrational, autonomous/dependent, objective/biased. We can argue that such attempts are in fact the means by which individuals have power over others and in so doing act defensively against their own anxieties about losing control in both their personal and professional lives (see also Chapters 1 and 3).

We need to practise the critical reflexivity which generates personal and political empowerment by naming the abuses of power we witness in our everyday working lives. Analysis, naming and refusal to collaborate with intimidation and bullying whether it be between the sexes, or by the same sex, can only become a reality if it is done within an understanding that power relations are capable of change. The feminist project which I would advocate is not to overturn one system of domination and replace it with another, but rather to deconstruct power relations and reconstruct them in a different value structure. We need to expose hierarchies that are built on divisions and argue for the similarities and interconnectedness of concepts. Too many people, most usually men, but now the few women who access powerful positions, exercise power within the terms of an oppressive discourse which requires them to live up to a masculine ideal. In doing so, too much emphasis is placed on achieving conformity, and the masculine cultures of toughness, competition and aggression. Not only are people's individual characteristics distorted in the process, women are most often the victim of these projections and their own specific characteristics are marginalised or rendered invisible.

Unless we continually practise self-reflexivity, the exercise of power is a potentially dangerous activity. We create the illusion of control by seeking the power of definition in the name of wanting to get things done or make things better. We cannot disassociate ourselves from the outcomes of our desires and yet we still hanker after transcendence. All we can achieve is the appearance of transcendence: like control it is an illusion. We need to situate ourselves in a discourse that says power is a fragile dynamic interaction, we are not in control and do not need to be. We must subvert our traditional association with power and gender, reintegrate our experience, redefine new ways of understanding masculinity and femininity within resistant cultures.

Conclusions

If we are to minimise the conflicts and stresses endemic to work environments (or change the culture in which bullying, violence, rape, abuse, discrimination, extermination and war can take place and be justified) we need analyses which discredit and challenge patriarchal systems of power. We need to acknowledge that seeking control and exercising power over others is central to the human condition. How we exercise that power is related to the types of discourse which make claims to function as the 'truth'. We need to move on from the liberal discourses which are themselves sexist and work with the new intellectual tools offered to us by discourses privileging the validity of experience and link them to resistant discourses which challenge the structures of Western thought. We need to explore the hierarchies in conceptual thinking which have divided, privileged and dis-privileged ideas and people. We need to deconstruct and subvert the narratives which disguise their domination and transform the hierarchies and relations of power they create.

Gender roles can change but only do so grudgingly and very slowly. Unless we grapple with these ideas, power will continue to be abused not just by men but by women too: those who gain access to status roles too often feel they have to prove themselves by acting out the values of masculinity. Existential uncertainty, our human inability to know or control our lives, affects us all. The sooner we acknowledge that the more likely we are to confront the illusions of control offered to us by patriarchal power relationships.

Chapter 3
Personal Mortality

Terry Martin

In this chapter the concepts and exercises are all designed to generate 'thinking' and 'feeling' about personal mortality and raise awareness about our preferred ways of negotiating our 'lived world and experience'. There would be many ways to think about these difficult issues; this is only one. Reflection and opportunity to think about these issues is most important if individuals are to think seriously about the existential questions in more depth.

The perspectives from which this chapter is written are: phenomenological and theoretical.

Introduction

Those who presume to work in the area of bereavement and loss, or even write books about it, need to be as clear as possible about their own motives for helping. We tend to situate ourselves in life with tasks and responsibilities which to some extent meet our own needs. Those of us in the helping and caring professions must therefore be particularly aware that our own unmet needs can sometimes lead us into compulsive helping. However caring our conscious intentions may be, these can still be undermined by unconscious processes. We can so easily rationalise our own behaviour and motives and hide behind professional roles which can become convenient masks to our true selves.

In seeking to help those who are bereaved, terminally ill or victims of tragedies, we will be placing ourselves in ultimate boundary situations. We will be testing our capacity to face the inevitability of our own death and vulnerability to tragedy. In line with current understandings of grief these involve ongoing processes rather than finished tasks, and the issue is whether we can continue to strengthen our personal resources rather than our defences and thereby better equip ourselves to help. In this chapter I consider some of these demands and challenges within the particular context of high modernity.

Modernity and self identity

As we draw to the close of the twentieth century it is proving for many to be an appropriate time for reflection and taking stock. With respect to the issue of death, we have witnessed this century extraordinary and para-doxical events and changes. As a result of two major world wars and countless other 'minor' wars and conflicts more people have been forcibly and violently put to death than at any other time in human history. The developments in technology throughout the same period have increased the sophistication of:

- The instrumentation of death and its institutionalisation in Western societies, the military-industrial complex
- The means of communication and the media, and thereby the capacity to project the details of each horror into our living (sic) rooms
- The services of medicine and nutrition and the supplies of fuel and water, so that a large proportion of the populations of Western societies have been given a longer life expectancy and more comfortable lifestyle than any other generation ever before.

However, we are now realising that many of the technological develop-ments, which have given some of us these great improvements in our standards of living, too easily equated with quality of life, have been bought at a cost of deep and possibly irreversible damage to the life-support system of our shared planetary home. The gains have been largely for a privileged minority of all of the fellow travellers on space-ship earth. As a consequence we now contemplate, think and worry about death in new and hitherto unknown ways. The combination of a Cold War, in which our deepest security needs were met through a bizarre arrangement of mutually assured destruction (MAD), and an environmental/ecological crisis of potentially catastrophic proportions, confronts us with the threat not just to our own personal mortality, but to the possible annihilation of the whole of human and biological life. We are all prone to planetary anxiety (Heron, 1990).

Anxiety plays a central role in contemporary understandings of both psychoanalysis and existentialism. In the face of death we are confronted with the threat of non-being, the annihilation of our self. Despite the increase to our life expectancy we are all vulnerable and we can never defend our-selves totally against the inherent insecurities of the human condition. An illusion of immortality seems to be a precondition of engagement with our project of life. Some see this as intrinsic to the ultimate tragedy of life and the human condition, others as a positive virtue, essential for sanity and sur-vival. Firestone (1994) discusses the various psychological defences against anxiety and the differing attitudes, healthy and morbid, towards death. Defending ourselves, individually and collectively, against anxiety is always at a cost, and we are therefore confronted with the need to assess the value of the benefits against these costs. In order to make this assessment some reference to personal values is inescapable and the clash of values between individuals and groups can become the source of much deep-seated conflict. 'Healthy' and 'morbid' are not neutral but value-laden terms.

The particular conditions of what he refers to as high modernity and the implications for both our sense of self and attitudes towards death are described most eloquently by Giddens (1991). Compared with traditional societies where to some extent identity is pre-formed through position in the existing social matrix and death is a real and immediate experience, in high modernity identity is a reflexive project and in day-to-day life we are separated:

'...from contact with experiences which raise potentially disturbing existential questions – particularly experiences to do with sickness, madness, criminality, sexuality and death.'

(Giddens, 1991: 244)

This 'sequestration of experience' is explored in further detail in relation to death in Mellor & Shilling (1993). They draw upon the work of Elias (1985) in which he considers the tendency in modern times for death and dying to be out of the public view leading to what he calls 'the loneliness of the dying'; Elias takes as unquestioned fact that there is no afterlife, which for him adds poignancy to the loneliness he describes.

Others have contested this view that death and dying are taboo, drawing attention to the intense media coverage of death in catastrophes and a growing literature in the area. Death is no longer the last taboo (Walter, 1991; Gerrard, 1997).

There are a variety of cultural approaches or responses to death (Walter, 1994); Walter identifies traditional, modern and neo-modern (or post-modern) which constitute ideal types for the purpose of sociological analysis. Neo-modernity is what Giddens refers to as high modernity and Gergen (1991), like many others, refers to as post-modernity. As explicated in the title of Gergen's book, in contemporary life we experience dilemmas of identity and a 'saturated self'.

The medicalisation of death is described by Walter (1996b) – the majority of the population now die in hospital, and in the UK their bodies are disposed of by cremation. Peoples' concerns now focus on the process of dying and the grieving of the bereaved, rather than the fate of the deceased in the afterlife.

The dysfunctional effects of anxiety in the organisational setting of a hospital are described in a classic study by Menzies Lyth (1960, 1988). The nurses who were the focus of her study were professionally committed to care but in an occupational context they were in constant and close proximity to disease and death.

It is impossible to guarantee total security against the uncertainties of life, although insurance companies would have us believe otherwise. In the wake of Dunblane and other recent tragedies in schools, there have been understandable pressures to increase security in access to premises and also to outlaw the possession and use of handguns. Worthy, reasonable and necessary as these measures are they could never ensure that similar tragic events never occurred again. The demand for complete control over uncertainty is illusory, and the challenge therefore both individually and collectively is to manage the attendant anxieties in constructive ways.

Self and personal identity

We cannot explore the notion of personal mortality without some sense of what it means to be a person. There are several interrelated concepts involved here: person, self, identity, awareness, consciousness, individuality, I, me, subjectivity, reflexivity, etc. A way of experientially engaging with the deep issues involved is through the twenty statement test (TST) originated by Kuhn & McPartland (1954) and described in more detail in the teaching and learning focus at the end of this chapter.

In his best-seller *Sophie's World* the author Jostein Gaarder (1995) commences with Sophie, a Norwegian schoolgirl, finding a mysterious note in her mailbox with the single question 'Who are you?' written on it. Her response is not unlike that of many of the individuals to whom I have set the TST in learning groups. She experiences a combination of puzzlement, confusion, frustration and intrigue. As pursued in the book the question is an opening into the entire history of Western philosophy from the pre-Socratics to modern existentialism. The enduring sense of self, our personal identity, is both fundamental and central to our being human and yet conceptually elusive.

In the TST exercise the responses given to the question can be roughly divided into two main groups:

- Those concerned with personal qualities, traits or evaluations
- Those concerned with roles, particularly those associated with home and work.

The former responses tend to be couched in the form 'I am...', whilst the latter in the form 'I am *a*...'. It is important in setting up the exercise not to influence the outcome by stressing one type of response at the expense of another as it can be significant to explore the balance of responses in the two categories for different individuals. On average the responses divide roughly equally into the two groups but there are wide variations for individuals with some at the extremes of giving only one kind of response. It is also interesting and significant to note how easy or difficult individuals find the exercise. Some people produce a list with no difficulty at all whilst others struggle to come up with anything.

There are significant variations across cultures; for example some people's sense of personal identity is closely tied up with their national and religious identities. 'I am Welsh' (or Irish, or Scots) is often on the list for those with such backgrounds, but rarely has anyone in my experience (in England) put 'I am English' on their list. No doubt context plays a part; if the exercise were being done abroad then the sense of being English would probably come more to the fore. The sense of who we are appears to depend, to some extent, upon where we are and whom we are with. In a context, for example, where everyone is Muslim (or Christian, or Hindu) then there is nothing remarkable or unusual about being Muslim (or Christian, or Hindu) and it is part of our assumptive world (Parkes, 1993, 1996a). However, in a context where we see ourselves as different in some significant way from those around us, cultural, religious, personal, or whatever, then the difference is foregrounded and we become more self-conscious of this aspect of ourselves.

Issues of gender are usually apparent with women often including an explicit reference to gender on their list; 'I am a woman' or 'I am female'. Men rarely do so; it is as if their default assumption is that a person is assumed to be male unless there is explicit evidence to the contrary.

The list of statements will also reflect levels of self-awareness and self-censorship; some individuals are in touch with themselves having been validated and affirmed through significant relationships. Other individuals struggle with deep-seated issues arising from the past, never having achieved permission to be or to grow in important ways. The exercise can be further developed by inviting individuals to reflect upon any pattern or organisation inherent in the list of statements. This can be partly in terms of a hierarchy of importance or significance attached to the items, and also the extent to which they interrelate and are interdependent. By displaying the roles and qualities on paper with the self at the centre, then those items of most importance are placed nearer the centre and those of lesser importance further away with links between items explicitly made. A map or representation of ourself is thus created and can be checked out with how others see us. A different conceptualisation is that of the heuristic device of the Johari Window (Luft, 1970); the different areas of ourselves and the processes of self-disclosure and feedback.

Individuals can be invited to engage in a thought-experiment and imagine what it would be like if, through some eventuality they were deprived of one of the items on the list For example, through the eventuality of divorce or death I could cease to be a husband and then the statement 'I am a husband' would cease to be true. That particular role would no longer feature on my map and my sense of who I am would be altered. Some statements can be lost in this imaginary way relatively painlessly, or even with delight, 'I am a taxpayer', whilst others would require a radical reorganisation of my sense of self. In some cases our sense of identity is so inextricably bound up with the item in the statement that the loss or negation of the item is literally inconceivable.

The inductive exploration of self through the TST exercise can be complemented with various psychological models of self and related concepts of self-concept and self-esteem. Hamachek (1978), for example, distinguishes the following components of personality:

- *The self:* That part of us of which we are consciously aware – what we know about ourselves.

- *Self-concept:*   Cluster of ideas and attitudes we have about our awareness at any given moment in time. An organised cognitive structure derived from experiences of our own self.
- *Self-esteem:*   Feelings about our self; the affective portion of self. The extent to which we admire or value the self.

We construct our sense of self and personal identity and forming a secure sense of self is seen as a major developmental task and achievement, which even if never fully completed, is essential for our sanity. The term identity crisis, Erikson (1980), is now common parlance, drawing attention to the problematic nature of the task in the context of high modernity as discussed above with reference to the work of Giddens (1991).

The constructivist perspective in psychology derives from the work of Kelly (1955, 1963); using techniques developed by him and others, for example the repertory grid technique, we can identify the personal constructs we use in relation to other people. This gives insight into our own personal unique perspective on the world, but it can also be used reflexively upon ourselves to characterise our self-concept. Constructions have both a cognitive aspect – the way we think about ourselves – and an affective aspect – the way we feel about and value ourselves – now commonly referred to as self-esteem.

Two features of a person's construct system are of particular interest:

- The specific constructs used to make sense of some area of experience
- The way that the constructs are organised with respect to each other.

A useful technique for eliciting the organisation of constructs is laddering; the term suggests that constructs may have an hierarchical organisation like the rungs of a ladder. Depending upon your metaphorical preference either higher or lower rungs of the ladder will represent constructs of greater generality or significance. Using depth to indicate a probing into areas of greater significance (as in depth psychology) then the technique takes us deeper into an individual's frame of reference. The technique applied to how we each give meaning to our personal existence is discussed in Rowe (1993), and is described in more detail in the teaching and learning focus at the end of this chapter. Based partly upon the ideas of Jung and personality types, Rowe claims (1993: 24) that each of us experiences our existence in one of two ways:

- As being a member of a group, as the relationship, the connection, between our self and others, focused on external reality (extrovert)
- As the progressive development of our individuality in terms of clarity, achievement and authenticity, focused on internal reality (introvert).

The greatest danger we can ever know is the threat of not-self, the annihilation of the self which is feared far more than bodily death, and each of us sees the threat of the annihilation of the self in one of two ways, depending upon whether we are extroverts or introverts (Rowe, 1993: 25):

- As complete isolation, being left totally, utterly and forever alone, thus withering, fading away, disappearing into nothingness
- As losing control of yourself and your life and falling apart, falling into chaos, fragmenting, crumbling to dust.

The ultimate fear of deprivation revealed in the laddering exercise often relates closely to one or other of these threats depending upon whether we are extroverts or introverts.

'We spend our lives maintaining and elaborating how we experience our self and in avoiding and defending our self against the threat, as we perceive it, to our self.'

(Rowe, 1993: 26)

This can lead to many dysfunctional, addictive and self-destructive behaviours, including suicide, which is explored further in Chapter 7. The needs for a sense of attachment to others and control of ourselves and circumstances are basic to all human beings and are precisely those needs most threatened by situations of change, loss and bereavement. More recent developments in psychology draw attention to the importance of discourse and narrative, see for example Edwards & Potter (1992) and Harre & Gillett (1994). The importance and relevance of these developments to issues of self and identity is expressed by Giddens:

'A person's identity is not to be found in behaviour, nor – important though this is – in the reactions of others, but in the capacity to keep a particular narrative going.'

(Giddens, 1991: 54)

It is precisely at times of loss and bereavement that our personal resources and hence capacity is most diminished and the disruption to our own particular narrative most severe.

The concept of role can be considered in both a psychological and sociological sense (Reed, 1985), where managing roles is seen to be a positive strategy to reducing stress and improving effectiveness in organisations. Roles are defined in terms of wider systems, like the organisational contexts in which we work, and through them we identify with aims and purposes which can give meaning to our individual lives.

In an interesting case study of primary teachers, Nias (1993) shows how as a result of major redefinition of their role through the considerable changes in education and the curriculum in recent times, many are in an identity crisis, grieving for their lost selves.

Managing the boundary or intersection between role and person, the public and private, can be a challenging task. In particular, as professionals we can readily hide behind roles thereby withholding ourselves in the encounter with clients. In helping relationships there is a fine line between protecting ourselves through such defensive hiding on the one hand, and excessive and overwhelming levels of self-disclosure on the other. However, if as Johnson & Johnson suggest self-disclosure means:

> '...to share with another person how you feel about events that have just occurred. Self-disclosure does not mean revealing intimate details of your past life.'
>
> (Johnson & Johnson, 1987: 31)

then it is perhaps not so difficult to maintain a degree of openness. Validating the emotional component of each others' experiences is fundamental to the approaches we are advocating in this book, and the importance therefore of hearing the voices of those who are expressing pain and hurt (Williams, 1997). It means expressing acceptance to those feeling rejection (Pritchard, 1995).

Other perspectives on the self and death

There are a variety of other perspectives from which to view these concepts of the self and death in addition to the psychological and sociological perspectives considered above. For example, biological/neurological, philosophical and spiritual perspectives, which are interdependent and not exhaustive and will be considered below.

We are embodied selves and dependent upon the continued existence and health of our physical bodies and, most crucially, our brains for our continuing sense of identity. There is currently much scientific and philosophical interest in exploring the relation between conscious awareness and brain function (Dennett, 1991, 1996; Greenfield, 1995). Much of this debate is conducted within a reductionist discourse which is essentially a continuation of the Enlightenment project to explain and control the world. Some human beings are nothing more than highly complex chemical computing devices.

The dependence upon our brain for our existence as conscious aware beings has enormous ethical implications (Singer, 1994). The dramatic impact of a brain tumour on her personality and life is described vividly by Martin (1997), and in a series of publications Sacks (1984, 1985, 1990) has shown how vulnerable our sense of self is to neurological damage and malfunction, and how bizarre the behavioural and experiential consequences can be. On a lighter note most of us are familiar with the effect of drugs on our mood and behaviour through the deliberate use of alcohol.

With, for example, brain stem death (Chapter 10), a body can be kept alive artificially and despite appearances, in the absence of consciousness, no-one is at home in it anymore. There is a similar situation for those suffering from senile dementia, Alzheimer's disease. These can be profoundly distressing and disconcerting experiences to close friends and relatives.

The complex issue of personal identity is discussed in detail by Noonan (1989) from a philosophical perspective, and from both philosophical and psychological perspectives by Glover (1988). A crucial element to a secure and enduring sense of self and personal identity is memory. The kind of doubts about personal identity expressed by philosophers when intensely experienced and enacted are usually considered evidence of deep psychological disturbance.

In considering our own personal mortality we confront our own finitude and personal death. Our own personal views about whether or not there is any continued existence beyond, and what nature this might take, will influence our attitude towards our own death. As well as this ultimate boundary and the profound threat it poses, there will be lesser personal deaths through tragedies and catastrophes which impinge directly upon us. We each have so much we can bear; some are overwhelmed in the face of what they construe to be the ultimately tragic and meaninglessness of the human condition and take their own lives.

Many poets, philosophers, artists and writers have sensed that confronting our own mortality can be both enabling and fundamental to the project of making sense of life. Psychotherapist and writer M. Scott Peck (1993) has written extensively on these themes in his popular writings:

'...as you struggle with the mystery of your death, you will discover the meaning of your life.'

'In my practice of psychotherapy, I found that I had to push at least half of my patients to face the reality of their death.'

'We cannot live with courage and confidence until we can have a relationship with our own death. Indeed, we cannot live fully unless there is something we are willing to die for.'

(Peck, 1993: 49–50)

'In the final analysis, if we can find meaning in life, then it is not unreasonable to assume there must be meaning in death.'

(Parkes & Sills, 1994: 514)

It is significant that it is so difficult to find words to give expression to our thoughts and feelings in this whole area, but that art and music can evoke and carry the burden so much more effectively. Bertman (1991) draws upon a rich selection of such material in her handbook for educators, healthcare professionals, and counsellors.

Conclusion

Those of us in the helping and caring professions (the intended readership of this book) are characterised by:

- A need to act – both through the professional demands of where we are situated and by personal predisposition
- Not normally having the luxury of disinterested speculation and philosophising about issues of life and death.

However, we do need to be reflective and thoughtful about our practice. Unless we have come to terms with, or are actively coming to terms with, our own personal mortality our professional practice in the areas of bereavement and loss are likely to be contaminated with our own agenda. The perennial challenge to all helpers and carers is to honestly face the question:

Who am I really trying to help – the client or myself?

The answer invariably is both, but if we are aware of this we can draw upon our personal experience and needs in a creative way. If we are not aware then our need to help will probably get in the way.

Skynner (1989), in a challenging address to social workers, draws upon his own experience of going into the mental health profession. He had to face the truth that his choice of career was motivated by personal need. However, having faced this truth he was able to become a most effective and successful practitioner. If he had denied the truth he would have manipulated clients unconsciously to his own ends. A contrasting view is expressed by Parkes & Sills:

'It is sometimes said that psychotherapists who work with the dying have got to come to terms with their own death. This is a tall order since none of us can know until we get there whether or not we have "come to terms" with anything of the kind.'

(Parkes & Sills, 1994: 514)

However, coming to terms with death is not exactly the same as coming to terms with our own personal mortality. It is also different from acquiring self-awareness about our own motivation to help in these areas of loss and bereavement and being clear about our own expectations, life goals, and how and why we set these.

The challenge for those in the caring professions is to turn the human condition, which for many is still full of sadness and pain, into a humane condition, where we reach out in genuine compassion and thereby contribute to the healing and survival process.

Teaching and Learning Focus

Rationale

The rationale is to enable course participants to reflect about their sense of self and personal identity and to confront the threat of not-self, the annihilation of the self.

Activity 1: Twenty statement test (TST)

A way of experientially engaging with the deep issues involved with self and personal identity is through the twenty statement test (TST) originated by Kuhn & McPartland (1954). As facilitator you ask the group participants to repeatedly answer the question:

Who am I?

and write down their answers in the form of statements:

I am ...   or   I am a ...

Ideally they produce twenty different answers, but using the activity in a learning group ten or more answers are quite sufficient to work with. The response can be shared by the participants working in pairs. You can then work with the whole group exploring the issues and explaining models of the self as outlined above.

Activity 2: Laddering

Laddering is a powerful and effective technique for surfacing an individual's core values. Like any powerful technique it has to be used with great care and sensitivity. The procedure is best demonstrated with a volunteer in front of the group; they can then work in pairs taking turns to take their partner through the following steps:

(1) Think of three examples of any type of object, concrete or abstract. For example three different colours, flowers, cars, people, schools, etc.
(2) Describe one way (quality or property) in which two are the same and the third is different.
(3) Decide which you prefer – the two the same or the one that is different.
(4) Why is this quality or property important to you?
(5) What would happen to you if you were unable to realise this; that is you were deprived of this quality?

Step 4 can be repeated until some fundamental ultimate quality or purpose is identified.

The rationale is explained in detail in the main text of the chapter; the exercise puts us in touch with the greatest danger we can ever know which is the threat of not-self, the annihilation of the self. Depending upon whether we are extroverts or introverts each of us sees the threat of the annihilation of the self in one of two ways, and the ultimate fear of deprivation revealed in the laddering exercise often relates closely to these threats.

Learning outcomes

The learning outcomes stimulated by the activities are for the course participants to acquire:

- Greater self-knowledge and self-awareness
- An awareness of the ways in which:

  'We spend our lives maintaining and elaborating how we experience our self and in avoiding and defending our self against the threat, as we perceive it, to our self.'

  (Rowe, 1993: 26)

- An understanding of the relevance of the concepts of self-concept and annihilation when working with clients.

Chapter 4
Bullying: Coercion and Control

Yvonne Anderson

Bullying is widespread in settings from school to workplace. The psychological origins of the phenomenon are explored through a classic experiment and also the political implications when regimes institutionalise extreme forms of bullying which are focused on internal minority groups or external enemies.

The perspectives from which this chapter is written are: empirical and theoretical.

Introduction

> *Sed quis custodiet ipsos Custodes?*
> But who is to guard the guards themselves? (Juvenal)

Everyone knows about bullying. We have either done it, seen it, read about it or been a victim. We know that it happens in schools, we also know that it has always existed and probably will continue to do so. But do we understand why it happens and why some people, including children, are driven to suicide because of it? Do we comprehend the misery of volunteers who resign from the military, or workers who give up careers, because of bullying? If it is not epidemic, then the potential for it is endemic.

The following discussion emphasises the importance of the settings in which coercion and force can most easily take place. The intention is not, however, to imply that we are solely the products of our environments in some passive way. Such deterministic notions belie the power of free will. The environments in which humans act and interact are created by all of us and are imbued with meanings by us. Hitler, with a handful of gangsters, was able to construct an environment of persuasion, coercion and fear across an entire nation. In order to achieve the aim of annihilating the Jews, that hostile environment had to be maintained with the help and compliance of the rest of the German population. Conversely, Nelson Mandela's government has chosen to create a climate of tolerance and amnesty in the new South Africa, dealing with the atrocities committed under apartheid through the Truth Commission, with the purpose of reconciliation. Mandela could not achieve the environment he desires without the contribution of the rest of the black South Africans. Despite their outrage at the past they are creating an environment of peace for the future. In both cases it is self-evident that environments have been created in the first instance by a small, but influential group and have been developed and maintained by the cooperation of a mass of people. The environment which was Nazi Germany was one in which bullying could, and did, thrive – to such an extent that six million innocent people were wiped out. The new South Africa is yet to be judged by history, but is set to become an environment in which intimidation and coercion will not be able to thrive on a wide scale.

Are there similarities to be found in smaller settings in which bullying occurs? If so, there is much scope for planned prevention.

A simulated prison study

In the early 1970s a psychological experiment was carried out at Stanford University, USA, to study captivity behaviour (Zimbardo, 1973). The findings have far reaching implications and in order to consider them a brief description of the experiment is given below.

Seventy five people replied to an advertisement to take part in an experiment into prison life. Of these, 24 men were selected, after screening out those displaying any tendency to particularly aggressive or anti-social behaviour. The resulting group was felt by the researchers to be emotionally stable. The volunteers were assigned arbitrarily to two groups, the 'guards' and the 'prisoners'. The guards were briefed about the running of the prison (a realistic mock-up), though the researchers deliberately gave only minimal instruction, in order that the guards would make their own rules. The prisoners were arrested on invented charges, without forewarning, by the local police. On their arrival at the prison they were stripped, deloused and issued with short smocks, caps to cover their hair, but no underwear. The guards, in contrast, wore khaki uniform with police whistles and reflective sunglasses, so eye contact could not be established. From that point, the volunteers were left to conduct themselves as a prison population. Their actions were covertly observed by the researchers.

What occurred over the next few days was shocking, both to the volunteers and to the research team. The behaviour of the guards was punitive and hostile in the extreme and, despite being prohibited from the use of physical violence, they found many ways to belittle and degrade their charges. In contrast, the prisoners became passive, withdrawn and anxious. Some prisoners had to be released early on in the experiment because of their obvious acute distress. The entire experiment so disturbed the researchers that it was brought to an end before its intended finish. Both the prisoners and the guards were generally confused and shocked by what had occurred and debriefing continued for months and sometimes years afterwards.

There are very many aspects of Zimbardo's prison experiment which continue to provoke discussion and debate. From a methodological standpoint, what would have been the outcome if the experiment had been conducted using women, or a group of men and women? Does the fact that only men were used invalidate the results? The essential question it raises for many people is that of the dubious ethics of carrying out such research (Savin, 1973). Can the end be said to justify the means? For some that can never be the case. Others, more pragmatically, might argue that provided the findings have made a highly significant contribution to a field of knowledge which will benefit humanity, then the temporary damage to a small group of paid volunteers was justified. This important debate begs the question of what we can learn from Zimbardo's work. Ostensibly the research was conducted to investigate captive behaviour. It was part of the work of the US Office of Naval Research and had been stimulated by studies into wartime captivity which suggested that certain types of personality seem to fare better than others (Watson, 1980). Valuable lessons were learned from the prison experiment into the understanding of both captives and captors, which could be used to develop new ways of training military personnel and prison officers. More fundamentally, however, the results provoke serious questions about the human propensity for aggression and hostility, but furthermore, about the situational and contextual factors which perhaps promote these tendencies.

The 'guards' in this instance were, of course, only role playing. They were not in any real sense paid to do the job; they invented the rules for themselves and what is more, they invented some highly punitive rules in a very short space of time. The guards knew that it was only chance that had assigned them to their role and that equally they could have found themselves in the prisoner group. They therefore also knew that the 'prisoners' were, unlike normal prisoners, not deserving of incarceration. The rationale for hostility, which could conceivably be offered by a guard in a conventional prison, that the inmates themselves are hostile and anti-social, could not be offered in this situation. What motives could the guards have had? That we are all capable of aggression and violence is perhaps such a truism as to be hardly worth stating, but many of us would imagine that the circumstances under which we would resort to such actions would need to be extreme. Not so in this case. The important factors would appear to be:

- *The investment of power* – this was granted by the researchers when they assigned the volunteers to the two groups and confirmed in the first briefing.
- *The cultural emblems of power* – these were the familiar accessories, with military association, which were granted to the guards; uniforms, whistles, sunglasses, etc.
- *An institutional setting* – a totalitarian regime existed for that short time, within the prison confines.

Before going on to consider these factors in a wider context, it is worth considering the role of the 'prisoners'. They knew they were not tried and convicted criminals, yet they allowed themselves to be humiliated and degraded – why? If it is true that in all human beings exists the potential for aggression, then is it also the case that in all lies the ability to be victimised and rendered passive? These are important questions. It cannot be forgotten that the volunteers were assigned to the groups by arbitrary means, so we have to agree that the likelihood is that their actions were influenced more by the setting and their expectations of the role they should play within it, than by any individual characteristics or personality variables. Being captive cannot, in itself, be seen as the most crucial factor in explaining the prisoners' actions, since, as stated already, they knew they were in a role play and presumably could demand to be let out and thus forfeit the fee. Certainly their position was not comparable to that of real prisoners, prisoners of war, or hostages. For the prisoners passively to accept what was meted out, the important factors would seem to be:

- *Feelings of powerlessness* – initiated by the shock of being arrested for 'crimes' unknown and maintained by institutional routines and processes.
- *The absence of familiar affirmations of dignity and standing* – all possessions and personal clothing were removed, replaced by a mode of dress which caused embarrassment and feelings of vulnerability

Settings

When considering bullying as a wider concept, the same questions are raised. Some individuals will always have a greater tendency towards hostile acts; these are a minority group consisting of persistent offenders and others with psychopathic personalities. Leaving those individuals to one side, there are countless examples in society in which bullying, the wilful intimidation of one individual or group towards another, occurs. Might it be that these cases arise out of settings which, by their nature, promote such behaviour? If so, then it is to institutions and organisations that we must look if we wish to prevent and control bullying, rather than focusing on the supposed common characteristics and inherent tendencies of either bully or victim. We must also question whether it is ever helpful to talk of a typical bully, or a classic victim. Perhaps given the right circumstances any one of us could become the bully or the victim.

Some institutions actively promote bullying, though they may not describe it as such. Many autobiographers have recounted their unhappy experiences as children in English public schools, recalling the ritual humiliations of fagging and flogging. References to bullying in literature are arguably amongst the most well known. *Tom Brown's Schooldays* does not give rise to an impression of a pale youth, but rather the sneering cad that is Flashman. Dickens regularly returned to the subject; the Beadle in *Oliver Twist*, Whackford Squeers in *Nicholas Nickelby* and so on. Even Henry Fielding's rollicking yarn *Tom Jones*, could not resist the punning of Jones' tutor, Mr Thwackum. All of these characters shared one thing in common; they were in charge of minors and this permitted humiliation and corporal punishment to be dispensed frequently under the guise of discipline. The late Roald Dahl wrote bitterly of the callous way in which physical punishment was administered at his prep school:

'There is nothing wrong with a few sharp tickles on the rump. They probably do a naughty boy a lot of good. But this Headmaster wasn't just tickling when he took out his cane to deliver a flogging.'

(Dahl, 1984: 131)

He goes on to describe in painful detail the account given to him by his friend of such a flogging. The head had slowly and deliberately paused between each stroke of the cane on the boy's bare flesh, to fill and light his pipe, whilst delivering a ponderous lecture about sin and wrongdoing. Dahl states:

'At the end of it all a basin, a sponge and a small clean towel were produced by the Headmaster, and the victim was told to wash away the blood before pulling up his trousers.'

(Dahl, 1984: 132)

A closed institution, such as Dahl's preparatory school, is like a totalitarian state. The power of the head teacher and his staff was absolute, even letters home were censored. The cultural emblems which served to remind small boys of the power held over them would have included the staff rooms and offices, the differentiation in clothing between boys and masters and that powerful totem, the cane. Meanwhile boys would have worn regulation clothing and would live and sleep communally, with a minimum of personalised possessions. During term time and, for some, even in the vacation, the boys were captive. The regime was one in which they did not have control. Just like similar total institutions, such as prisons, psychiatric hospitals and military camps, the distribution of power between staff and inmates ensured that the former retained control, rendering the latter passive (Goffman, 1968). Little wonder that such settings are well known as places in which coercion and systematic abuse are known, tolerated and sometimes sanctioned by the institution itself. Kesey's novel, later a successful film, *One Flew Over the Cuckoo's Nest* captures brilliantly the dehumanising tendency of institutionalisation, the coercion of the vulnerable group by those invested with power (Kesey 1973). Recent investigations across the UK have revealed that abuses of all kinds have routinely occurred in children's homes over many years. Similar cases occur periodically in homes for elderly people. In all cases, the common features are a group made vulnerable by circumstances – frailty through old age, lack of support through parental and familial absence, lack of advocacy because of a disability – living in closed institutions in which another group holds almost total power and control.

Other settings in which recent cases of bullying have come to light include schools and workplaces. The notion of playground bullying is hardly new –

the very word 'bully' for many evokes a childhood memory of a playground demon. However, bullying in the workplace has more recently been recognised as a problem. Once again the setting cannot be ignored. Places of work are institutions in themselves, in which there are clear divisions of power and control. The workplace is not quite analogous with total institutions, such as prisons, since, in theory, there is a means of escape – as a rule we are not captive as employees in quite the same way as we are when imprisoned, for example. However, the experience of employment is that we often feel entrapped; by our strong motives in wanting to succeed and perform well and our need to be rewarded for those efforts in gaining a regular income. Therefore, the group of workers with the least power are by definition vulnerable to coercion and control. Bullying happens in workplaces because those with power and control can intimidate those lacking in power without fear of being found out. This theme is explored in more depth in Chapter 2.

In schools widespread concern about bullying is now being followed up by programmes designed to prevent and deal with the problem. Extensive research in Scandinavia (Olweus, 1987) revealed a number of noteworthy findings, including a gender bias: boys being more frequently involved in bullying than girls and an age difference; younger and weaker children being more often the victims and older stronger children the bullies. The most interesting finding though, was that there was no support for the popular notion that children who are different are more likely to be targets, for example, those who are fat, wear spectacles, speak with a regional accent are no more likely to become victims. Over 160 000 children were used in the studies, which employed a variety of techniques. Research into bullying in British schools has been more modest and has relied mostly upon self-reports from children. A difficulty has been the suspicion that in many instances bullying has not been viewed as a serious problem, rather as part of normal school life (Stephenson & Smith, 1989). Tattum & Lane (1989) have gone further, suggesting that in addition to viewing bullying as inevitable in school life, some teachers are themselves bullies, whilst others only regard the academic side of school life as their concern. Furthermore, Roland (cited in Tattum & Lane, 1989) asserts that bullying is by nature a covert activity, surrounded by secrecy.

Prevention in schools

Despite the paucity of large-scale studies, the indications from a range of small-scale projects are that bullying in schools – particularly in the playground – is a real problem (MacFarlane, 1995). Many schools have developed interventions designed to prevent and discourage bullying. A recent innovation, in line with the more general principles and practice of health promotion, is the 'whole school approach'. Roland (1989) has stated that schools which embraced a whole school approach were more likely to succeed in their anti-bullying programmes. A framework for this perspective has been suggested by MacFarlane (1995), who is opposed to 'crisis management' and favours a more proactive approach.

The point of the whole school approach is that every aspect of the school environment can be assessed and improved. As well as the more obvious environmental aspects, such as the dark corners of the playground or bicycle sheds, factors such as staff attitudes and procedures for dealing with pupils come to be considered. The curriculum is itself examined and opportunities for raising self-esteem and promoting openness are identified. As Herbert (1989) put it: 'The caring ethos must be made explicit through the curriculum and the daily dealings with individuals.'

Furthermore, in recognition of the contribution that everyone makes to their environment, everyone in the school is involved in the process in some way. The governing body will be consulted, informed and perhaps will take part in awareness raising exercises. Children will be asked for their experiences and ideas, perhaps conducting a school survey. Staff, including non-teaching staff, may take part in awareness raising training and be asked to review policy (MacFarlane, 1995). The benefits of raising children's self-esteem are outlined in Chapter 13. If a feature of bullying is that the victim is vulnerable and weak, then equipping children with increased self-confidence and skill in assertiveness must help them to avoid being victims at all. What of those who bully? Children who bully are themselves often experiencing some emotional difficulty and some are being bullied by others, creating a hierarchy of bullying (Stephenson & Smith, 1989). Perhaps instead of judging we should consider the benefits to these children of enhanced self-esteem and personal effectiveness. Expressions of unprovoked anger and hostility are often the result of inarticulacy; an inability to express negative feelings appropriately (see Chapter 12).

Other school-based interventions have included assertiveness training, group discussion, including peer counselling and school tribunals, or 'bully courts'. One initiative has been called the 'no blame approach'. Here the focus is on stopping the bullying without exacting retribution, in recognition of the fact that bullies are often being bullied, or are victims of some other abuse, or have other problems of self-esteem. The idea that there is no sense of blame involved in deliberate acts of intimidation is problematic: it may be more helpful to think of it instead as a no revenge approach. The wider issue of no blame is taken up later.

Loss

In many cases victims of intimidation lose all confidence in themselves, particularly in their ability to fight back. It is as if their self-worth becomes quite destroyed, or at least held in suspension. There are notable exceptions. Nelson Mandela, for example, has stated that nothing in his 27 years of imprisonment could ever have stripped him of his dignity. Brian Keenan (1992), among his many extraordinary recollections of his time spent as a hostage, tells of one particular occasion on which one of the guards, angered by Keenan's non-compliance with an instruction, chained his ankles to his wrists and flogged him for 15 minutes. Keenan, despite appalling injuries, was able to retain his sense of humanity, writing:

'Abed was on the very edge of emotional collapse and exhaustion, just as I was. I felt his tears in the hot sting welling up in my own eyes, but I would not cry. I knew that in that moment he was very close to me in everything he felt and thought.'

(Keenan, 1992: 244)

Keenan was aware of the strains and pressures under which his guards were placed, although he could not excuse them. Bettelheim (1960), too, wrote with considerable empathy:

'To the persecutor too, the victim appears to be much more dangerous than he really is.'

(Bettelheim, 1960: 225)

These words seem to convey the paradox of coercion. However tempting and righteous it may be to judge harshly the bully in every instance, we have to consider that he too suffers, albeit less knowingly. Bettelheim, as a psychoanalyst, expresses strong views on the inner workings of the persecutor. He goes on:

'The SS, by externalising their own undesirable tendencies and projecting them into the stereotyped picture of, for example, the Jew, tried to shake off their own inner conflicts.'

(Bettelheim, 1960: 226)

Again an interesting parallel can be drawn with the writing of Keenan, here referring to the same incident in which the guard, Abed, was beating him:

'His excitement was beyond control. At times I thought he was almost singing. His rage was spitting out of him like fireworks ... Nothing in him could control himself. He was not even beating me, he was beating something bigger than me. Maybe he was beating himself.'

(Keenan, 1992: 242)

Another facet of those doing the bullying is that often they have been bullied themselves, as mentioned earlier regarding schoolchildren. There are many eye-witness accounts from prisons, camps and chain gangs, describing the behaviour of 'trusties' and 'turnkeys', those favoured by the regime and lifted a notch above their fellow incarcerates, only to change from victim to bully. In the concentration camps, or *Lagers* of Nazi Germany, the prisoners chosen from the ranks to conspire with the SS, were called *kapos*, here described by Levi (1989):

'[Becoming a kapo] was sought by the frustrated, and this too is a feature which in the microcosm of the Lager reproduces the macrocosm of totalitarian society: in both, without regard and merit, power is generously granted to those willing to pay homage to hierarchic authority, thus attaining an otherwise unattainable social elevation.'

(Levi, 1989: 32)

Mandela (1994) reveals another insight into the bully. He writes of a particular commanding officer on Robben Island, who was well known for his sadistic tendencies and for his physical abuse of many prisoners. On the day that the officer was to leave the island for another post, he shocked Mandela by wishing him and the other political prisoners good luck.

'Badenhorst had perhaps been the most callous and barbaric commanding officer we had had on Robben Island. But that day he had revealed there was another side to his nature, a side that had been obscured but that still existed. It was a useful reminder that all men, even the most seemingly cold-blooded, have a core of decency, and that, if their hearts are touched, they are capable of changing. Ultimately, Badenhorst was not evil; his inhumanity had been foisted upon him by an inhuman system. He behaved like a brute because he was rewarded for brutish behaviour.'

(Mandela, 1994: 448)

In such grievously unjust and inhumane conditions, Mandela was able to empathise with the bully. This does not necessarily imply a doctrine of turning the other cheek. In cases of bullying, whatever the magnitude, there can never really be a no blame approach. The blame for bullying lies with the bully, albeit viewed in the context of the environment. Bailey, in the introduction to Levi (1988), quotes Levi as having said that he could never forgive the Germans for what they had done, but that he refused to take part in 'the bestial vice of hatred'. Logically, no blame approaches imply some degree of responsibility to the victim, but this is a dangerous road to follow. At the end of that road are undeserving blacks, dirty niggers, sneaky Jews. The easy way out is always to blame the victim. In the past women who continued to live with men who violently abused them were seen as deriving some perverse satisfaction from their situation. Children who dared not complain about sexual advances from adults were seen as sexually precocious. Rapists were able to plead, 'She asked for it'. Those responsible for wilful intimidation and cruelty must shoulder the blame and accept responsibility. But their losses are also great. The bully risks the loss of human warmth and dignity and may spend years suffering guilt and shame. Added to the experiences of victims, this seems to create a huge amount of suffering and grief.

Whole communities and groups suffer loss when bullying reaches epidemic proportions. The shame and guilt of the German people is testament to that, indeed, even denial tells of guilt, if in a more cowardly way. Levi corresponded with a number of Germans following the publication of his first book. These are quoted in his last book (Levi, 1989), published shortly before his death. The following are typical:

'I can come to terms with this terrible levity of mine, cowardice and selfishness only by relying on Christian forgiveness.'

(Levi, 1989: 150)

'There remains the great mass of those who, to save their own lives, keep silent and abandon their brother in danger. This is what we recognise to be guilt before God and mankind.'

(Levi, 1989: 146)

'I spoke of "shame". I meant to express this feeling – that what was perpetrated by German hands at that time should never have happened, nor should it have been approved of by other Germans.'

(Levi, 1989: 154)

Conclusions

The examples used in this brief discussion of bullying environments have ranged from nation-wide settings for intimidation, such as Nazi Germany or South Africa under apartheid, down to small-scale institutions such as schools. Firstly, this has been an attempt to draw parallels between environments of very different magnitude; to say that the detail and complexity may be different, but the essence is the same. Secondly, there is, of course, an important link between schools and all other social institutions. Schools are the first organisations to which we belong and as such are agents of tremendous influence upon us. Ways of behaving in our formative years may be difficult for us to question or change later. Levi (1989) stated:

'The term torturers alludes to our ex-guardians, the SS, and is in my opinion inappropriate: it brings to mind twisted individuals, ill-born, sadists, afflicted by an original flaw. Instead they were made of our same cloth, they were average human beings, averagely intelligent, averagely wicked: save for exceptions, they were not monsters, they had our faces, but they had been reared badly. They were, for the greater part, diligent followers and functionaries: some fanatically convinced of the Nazi doctrine, many indifferent, or fearful of punishment, or desirous of a good career, or too obedient. All of them had been subjected to the terrifying miseducation provided for and imposed by our schools created by the wishes of Hitler and his collaborators, and then completed by the SS drill.'

(Levi, 1989: 170–71)

There is hope. In all regimes of terror there are resistance workers and refuseniks, who risk their lives by standing up for right. On a much smaller scale, we can return to Dahl and his account of small boys. After a caning from the head teacher, Dahl returned to his classroom, where he was welcomed with sympathy and outrage at the injustice of his beating. One boy in particular was incensed and decided to write to his father in complaint, convinced that his father would immediately return from Athens in order to 'do something about it'. Dahl concludes:

'There and then little Highton sat down and wrote to the father he admired so much, but of course nothing came of it. It was nevertheless a touching and generous gesture from one small boy to another and I have never forgotten it.'

(Dahl, 1984: 111).

Surely the lesson is to change the environments in which unjust and unwarranted acts of intimidation and hostility occur. Schools, public and state, should be places in which individuals are valued and respected and where bullying of any kind is not tolerated. Let us have all institutions – prisons, hospitals, homes for children and vulnerable adults – held accountable. They must be run with the full involvement of the clients, or residents, using systems which are transparent and do not allow for secrecy and collusion. In all our social institutions there must be external, impartial involvement which gives power to the powerless and grants them a voice.

The lessons we can learn from history are shown in essence in the awful implications of the simulated prison study. The conditions in which bullying may flourish are so easily fulfilled. In the words of Bettelheim:

'If having to live under certain conditions which I called 'extreme' could modify personality to such an extent, then I felt we must understand better why and how this can be so; not only to know what extreme situations can do to man and why, but because other environments, too, shape personality, though in different directions and ways.'

(Bettelheim, 1960: 108)

I am indebted to Kay McFarlane for her comprehensive literature review on bullying in schools, which was very helpful in the preparation of this chapter.

Teaching and learning focus on bullying: coercion and control

Rationale

The rationale is to encourage course participants to explore and relate the text of this chapter to a real-life situation they have encountered and to think about strategies for intervention.

Activity

Think about an incident of bullying which you have experienced – you may have been the bully, the victim, or a witness.

- What was the nature of the incident? Describe it briefly.
- In what setting did it take place? Identify the features of the environment which made the bullying possible.
- In order to minimise the opportunity for further intimidation, what changes would you make to that environment?

Discuss your ideas with a colleague.

Learning outcomes

The learning outcomes stimulated by the activities are for the course participants to:

- Compare their own experiences with the concepts discussed in the chapter
- Gain insights into their experience by considering it from a new perspective.

Chapter 5

A Search For Understanding Murder and Violence

Ros Weston

This chapter explores the personal experience of violence, both state-sanctioned violence and individual, non-sanctioned violence. Many issues are raised such as the social context of violence and state justification, the concepts of good and evil, punishment and forgiveness. The author explores the benefits and the problems of autobiographical research as a legitimate way of writing social science.

It also illustrates the author's attempt to develop an ongoing narrative about herself. The chapter concludes with recommendations for supporting those who have been bereaved through murder and is based on her experience with Wiltshire Victim Support where she was responsible for training, a management committee member, Vice-Chairman and then Chairman of the Management Committee.

The perspectives from which this chapter is written are: autobiographical and professional.

Introduction

There are five sections to this chapter each comprising a separate narrative:

- An autobiographical narrative which describes two particular events which shaped my views about non-violence
- A reflective narrative which illustrates how I made sense of these events as a child, teenager and adult
- A methodological narrative which explains the 'meanings' inherent in any autobiographical account and the challenges such methodology poses for researchers
- A reflexive narrative which engages with the ongoing reflexive project that is 'myself' (Giddens, 1991)
- A concluding narrative 'supporting victims of murder and other violent crimes'.

Autobiographical narrative

There have been two major influences in my life which have engendered a deep and abiding belief in non-violence. As Partridge (1996) suggests this does not mean that it is easy to be a pacifist. The first major influence was the experience, as a child between the ages of 4 and 10 years of visiting my ailing and subsequently dying father in Dunston Hill Military Hospital. The second was the murder of my cousin, to whom I was very close, in her own home, a military camp in Germany by person or persons unknown. Let me explain the influence these events had on an impressionable child and teenager.

Dunston Hill Hospital: an example of sanctioned violence and its aftermath

For more than five years my mother, younger brother and I travelled most weekends, and sometimes in school holidays on Wednesdays, to see my dad in hospital. We had to take two buses, one into Newcastle and another over the Tyne Bridge to Dunston, usually $1\frac{1}{2}$ hours in all. Sometimes my dad was well enough to walk in the grounds, play snooker or sit in the restaurant. Most times he was not. We played snooker (or tried to) and he watched. We were very lucky that we could visit as most hospitals in the 1950s did not allow children to visit. My dad was a gentle and sensitive man who had been conscripted into the army even though his medical records stated that his fitness was certainly in doubt at that time. He continued under the care of the military hospital until his death from cancer in 1959. At this point my mother was told she was no longer entitled to a military pension as he had not died of causes related to his military service. The British Legion fought this decision for us but was not successful.

These experiences following a death were disturbing in themselves and they have continued to happen to many war veterans, their widows and families following military service throughout the world. Neither have these practices only been employed by the UK. The long months of litigation and the final disappointment were a crushing blow to my mother. However, this was not the most disturbing aspect of the relationship we had with Dunston Hill and the Ministry of Defence. What was most distressing about Dunston Hill, for me, was the men in the blue serge suits.

Time and again I asked why they were all wearing the same pyjamas or suits. I never did get an answer. Usually I was told not to ask so many questions. Jumbled up with this Dunston Hill memory is my memory of the fear my dad generated over Kennedy's handling (or mishandling) of the Cuban Crisis. My dad was an inveterate newspaper reader and when he came home, which he did during periods when there was an improvement in his health (sometimes he went back to work for short periods) he loved to argue and discuss. He was at home during the Cuban scare and he involved anyone and everyone who came to the house (except my mother who had an abiding fear of discussion and argument) in listening to his fears about the possibility of a third world war and total destruction. This too had its effect on me, after all he took things very seriously, was a thinker, so if he felt frightened, as I trusted his feelings, I felt it too.

I knew my father had been in the war and that the badge he wore meant he had no longer been able to fight and that he had been brought home in a hospital ship. I cannot say when I came to any realisation that the men in the blue serge suits were casualties of war.

I have often wondered whether the hospital (Ministry of Defence) insisted on these suits as a way of ensuring that men who became sick, weak, ill, traumatised or frightened were some kind of coward and thus stigmatised by this mode of dress, or, that it was valedictory; they were heroes. Or, was it a gesture, albeit rather a clumsy one at that, of recognising their suffering and their contribution?

I wonder still what happened to all the women at Dunston Hill; there must have been some!

An experience of murder: non-sanctioned violence

I was introduced to individual violence as opposed to state or political violence when I read in the local paper, the *Newcastle Evening Chronicle*, of the murder of my cousin Monica. Her mother and sister found out in a traumatic way too. Monica's husband had sent two telegrams, one to his brother and one to Monica's sister, Pam. The first arrived but not the second. When the brother and his wife arrived to see Pam she answered the door laughing and joking. The wife of the brother turned to her husband and said 'my God she does not know!' They told my aunt who was at work and that night it was on the local news. The telegram had just said, 'Monica passed away'. How she had 'passed away' was on the news. Monica lived with her husband and 5-year-old daughter on an army camp in Germany and the army had released the story before the relatives had been fully informed. I have not remembered the date, the day or the year and if I am told I cannot retain such information. I can remember my reactions to what I read and having to tell my mother. I remember too reading that Monica's husband had been taken for questioning by the Military Police. I knew then and now that he was not guilty. I know I was 17 years old and in the sixth form .

Communication, or rather the lack of it was not the only problem the family faced. It was only the beginning. Lack of information became the norm. The military defences were starkly erected to protect themselves with no thought for those of us who needed to know more. From beginning to end (23 years) we knew nothing and to add insult to injury the army refused to fly her body home for burial. We had no funeral to go to (see Chapter 14). My aunt and her younger daughter Pam flew to Germany for the funeral. They returned with Monica's 5-year-old daughter. Her husband, having been released with no further charges, returned later following his resignation from the army.

All we knew then, and later, and until very recently, was that whoever the perpetrator was, he/she had replied to an advertisement Monica had placed in the NAAFI about selling her electric mixer. This pointed to how he/she had gained entry and that Monica knew him/her and therefore felt it safe to let him/her in. The mixer, usually stored in a box was out on the kitchen table. The perpetrator had stolen a radio and a few pounds and then beaten her to death; she had put up an incredible fight and had traces of skin and clothing from the perpetrator on her clothes and under her finger nails. The killer would have been badly scratched.

Reflective narrative: how I made sense of these events

Dunston Hill

Almost ten years ago my daughter and I were on holiday in Cornwall and suddenly I felt an urge to write. For four days and nights with little sleep words poured forth from me in an never-ending stream. I called this collection *Living Under a Concrete Pyramid*, it was a form of consciousness writing (see Church, 1995) and the men in the blue serge suits, were there. I cannot remember consciously thinking about them, the words seemed to form themselves. I entitled it:

Military Hospital for Invalided Soldiers

Children don't understand:
Travesty of adult thought!
No need for peace studies
Or understanding pacifism
Explanations and justifications
When you see, the men
In their blue serge suits.

Paraplegics, quadraplegics,
Tremblers and limbless.
Chronic sick and nervous diseases,
Comfortably cared for
A long way from home.

Children quick to see,
Medals and victory are vain prizes
For those, who are maimed
Left to suffer alone,
For what are mostly
Political ends.

For those who remember the sight
Can never be bought
By calls of patriotism, freedom
And just wars.
For it is many who pay the price for the freedom of a few.
Blue serge suits was the price paid.

With military pensions.
Suffering and death

Of the many
For values which profited the few.

All cultures, left, right or centre,
Blue, green, red or black,
Convincingly lure the many
To comfortably benefit the few.
Pawns in a game,
Encouraged to dream
It is for you, too!

I have always been safe in the knowledge that my father loved me (and us) and I loved him. I also knew that the above events were not personal (unlike my mother who believed that they were). I can only assume that my then love of theology and the Church allowed me to judge and explain things differently to my mother. There have been numerous examples of this throughout our lives. I can always see some rational explanation for events, she on the other hand could only ever see that the world was against her. The events were sad and I suffered immense grief but events were explainable. As I got a bit older I worked out for myself that it must have had something to do with the war. We all make sense of the world in our own way and I probably made sense of this experience through Church and school and of course ceremonies such as Armistice Day and parades with the Girl Guides. Come to understand it I did, but able to dismiss it or deny it never.

How can anyone define such a moment or process? It is so gradual. There are so many experiences which contribute to such understandings and the dawning of knowledge (Kelly, 1955; Bannister & Fransella, 1986). Sometime late in my teens I knew why they were there, why they were all dressed the same and only partly men. The rest is hazy. Was I drawn to reading Wilfred Owen, Robert Frost, Vera Brittain, Solzhenitsyn and others because I had a morbid fascination with war or death? Was it chance because I read widely anyway or was it to do with the changing ideology of the time, socially and culturally, and much questioning about the Vietnam War or a subliminal search for meaning? Who knows, but my personal journey led this way and gradually I understood about war. My jigsaw (or developing narrative) regarding war, Dunston Hill and the men in the blue serge suits, was gradually pieced together, the last pieces being put in place in the last few years. My pacifism was further confirmed by wars around the world, the bitterness and misery of Vietnam, the Falklands and the Gulf War. I knew then and I know now why there should not have been, and should not be, men in blue serge suits. There is a tension here in also knowing that civil war is just as destructive as defensive war and yet knowing that freedom fighters may well have a *cause célèbre*. Yet still I cannot condone any form of sanctioned/non-sanctioned violence for whatever outcome. This has been brought home to me very forcibly in my recent reading of Nelson Mandela's autobiography. I cannot yet come to terms with the fact that he was the main protagonist of an armed struggle and also the negotiator to end it. These are the tensions which are part of the intertextuality of any autobiographical account, the personal narrative cannot be separated from that in which it is inextricably embedded, the ideological stance at historical points in time, the social, political and economic. Man's continuing inhumanity to man. This tension was made manifest for me during the Gulf War and the possibility of dreadful casualties. I had the dilemma of acknowledging that if I was a pacifist I should do nothing at all, even by helping the casualties I could be seen to be sanctioning the war itself. However, my human feeling self felt that the casualties would need some help and support (following the Quaker approach). After much thought I did sign up to sit at the bedside of any casualties brought to the army or air force bases in Wiltshire. This was a personal, human and moral decision (see McGinn, 1997). The human decision feeling the right one at the time. Francis Partridge (1996) discusses this aspect of pacifism in her diaries, her husband would do nothing at all as doing anything, in his view, would contribute to the war effort whereas she felt very depressed at not being able to do anything. She did not really resolve this dilemma for herself but rather went along with his view.

It is all too easy to become cynical as we have much recent evidence of the callous way war veterans can be treated. My opening scenario is in this vein and the recent agreements by the last and this government to refund some war widows pensions is a case in point as is the recent agreement for a proper investigation into Gulf War Syndrome.

The murder

When I started writing in Cornwall my feelings, emotions and questions relating to this tragedy were once more voiced poetically in:

Summer Wedding Turns To Winter Chill

Disease and death
Can be understood
As natural.
Violence from a stranger's hand, defies intellect and emotion.

Trusting Wife and Mother
Cruelly beaten to death
At Home
By person unknown, or known
Who called to buy an electric mixer,
Secondhand.

A husband's discovery
At lunch time
Brought interrogation
And recrimination.
Family set against family

Loved against loved
Innocence to be proved.

Sympathy and empathy
Love and support
Gone. Flown like a feather in the wind.
What strange ways of trusting

Shocked and hurt people
Display.

To one who needed
Every shred of love
In that dark night of the soul.
All were found wanting.
Too suspicious, frightened
To respond. Driven by the need
For revenge.

It did not help to be told that if Monica had been found earlier she may
have lived. All the 'if onlys' in the world are useless in the face of man's
violence to woman, man to man, woman to man or woman to woman or
indeed relating to any tragedy (see Chapters 6 and 11). This also encourages
victim blaming and associated guilt (Walklate, 1989; Weiner & Wolfgang,
1989; Karmen, 1990). One of the most hurtful things we faced when we tried
to talk about it with anyone was the suggestion that she may have been
having an affair; she was not that kind of woman. This is a common sup-
position on the part of relatives which may on closer scrutiny not be true. On
the other hand it may well be a myth that is scotched in court if there is a
trial. We were not in the position to do this then or now whatever her marital
relationship may have been, and we had no evidence whatsoever that there
were any problems or that such an affair or passion may have been the case.

I cannot tell what any of our family felt or thought because we have never
talked about it. I know that my mother was driven mad by grief through
these multiple losses. I know it contributed to my aunt's premature ageing
and ill health. I know that my mother and stepfather wanted only revenge
and they saw this as the only recompense for such violence. They themselves
would happily, driven by intense anger, have killed the person responsible.
They would be happy only if they got there first or if the state sanctioned
capital punishment and did the dirty deed for them. Only death, for death,
would be enough to help them in their anguish. Sadness never left us from
that day. There was always a terrible, terrible sadness. There is anger that
remains and even now disbelief at the senselessness of it all. Only recently
did I discover that Monica's sister has felt that everyone had forgotten it all.
What a terrible burden of senseless and lonely pain she has had to bear.

I could not feel the same sense of revenge, for me that was not the
answer and is still not. I have never quite understood, then or now, why if

human beings are not entitled to take life, they feel they have the right to do so in revenge. I cannot condone this whether it be by oneself or through the state apparatus of capital punishment. To me this suggests that we sanction someone else to do our violence for us thus distancing ourselves intellectually and practically from this last act. Giddens (1991) discusses execution as the acknowledgement of the criminal being beyond state control, in other words the state cannot succeed in restitution. This would seem to suggest the failure of the state to be able to deal with such violent acts. I believe that the punishments we inflict must reflect the values we seek to promote. Here we see the tensions between individual thought and reasoning and the Church, religion, and the justice system. For me solutions must be just and fair and in relation to the crime committed. As Christ said 'inasmuch as you do it to the least of these my brothers you do it unto me'.

I would have liked the perpetrator to be found, charged, and tried justly and fairly if only to bring a conclusion to the case and to sweep away once and for all suspicion and innuendo. This line of thought was in keeping with my relationship with religion and the Church. I was able to see that forgiveness is necessary whatever the magnitude of the wrong doing as I also knew intuitively that if I could not forgive and try to understand the pain would kill me.

This is not a retrospective justification. I argued fiercely at the time, with my parents and relatives, the importance of doing this and that I believed further violence would bring no comfort and no answers. At that time I attended church regularly and found great solace in prayer and I suppose God. That was then, and over the intervening years I have had to explore my beliefs and practices and have left this rather cosy relationship with religion behind. I left a belief in a personal God and an afterlife behind too. However, I have not left spirituality behind and still draw much strength and comfort from my spiritual values and beliefs. My aunt did not go to church again, it destroyed her belief in a caring God.

And what of acceptance? It happened, it was senseless, that is accepted, but the crass way in which this tragedy was handled, the lack of understanding and support, the misinformation, these can never be understood or accepted. I still reel at the thought of so many people telling me it would be best if I forgot all about it and did not talk about it. This was mostly friends and relatives but also teachers (see Chapter 13). It was not until I was in my thirties that I really understood that as a child and teenager I had already had experiences that were outside the norm of experience for most people around us at that time; they could not have understood, they had not the experience of such an event and particularly rapid multiple loss. One thing I used to try to tell my mother, but was unsuccessful in getting her to understand, was that of course there were people who had had similar experiences and some that had had much worse. Some, having lost four sons in war, etc., (see Wilkinson, 1996). I understand now, I did not then. This is expressed in more of the consciousness writing in a piece:

For Whom Will It Call Next

Grandad, Grandma, Dad, Nana, Granda, Uncle, Uncle, Friend, Cousin,
Aunty, Friend, Cousin,
All gone in ten years;
Is it neurotic
To wonder
When death will call again
For me?

The fear,
Expressed
In palpitations, panic attacks
And sleepless nights,
Feelings of unreality as though I were
Already dead and observing.

No-one asked for the story
or listened to the fear,
All consuming anger,
Grief and defeat.
Brave child, such courage
Shown in conquering.

Sham face of conformity
And achievement!
Camouflage for the lost Self.

The most profound effect on me was Fear! Fear of being left alone, fear of
being left in the house, fear of unlocked doors, terror at unrecognised foot-
steps, suspicion of men, fear of men, fear of the knock at the door, terror at
turning a dark corner, terror in the dark, fear of the dark, fear of dark on the
landing, a need for open doors, fear of going out at night, fear of travelling on
a bus, fear of talking to strangers, feeling I was not safe even in my own
house. This led to some near incapacitating behaviours such as panic attacks,
anxiety states, risk taking, overspontaneity and overtrusting.

Once I recognised that I needed to learn to come to terms with my fears if I
was ever to live I overreacted and forced myself to take risks travelling alone,
here and abroad, and doing spontaneous things which arose from feeling I
might not have a long life. I had to pack as much into the one I had as
possible and have few if any regrets. Achieving a balance in this way of
living is still a learning experience.

Another phenomenon was that of being good. Oh yes, I too had absorbed
the message that such things only happen to those who are not good. I
became a very good girl in the sense of trying to be good at everything.
Achieving, marriage, motherhood, professionalism, listening to others, so
good that I was a pain to myself and probably others too. I do not under-

stand this but can shed some light on in it in the sense I believe I then viewed it as a protection related to a belief in an afterlife and God, a kind of insurance policy. If I was really good perhaps these terrible things would stop happening to me/us and on the other hand only if I was good would I get into heaven thereby being united with all whom I had loved (see also Jung, 1964). I remember thinking when I was about 18 years old that I only went to church in case I died during the week and so I could be assured of getting in through the pearly gates. This raises issues of social conditioning and culture. In another culture I may have used different perspectives. None of this was conscious and it has taken a long time to come to this awareness and for me to be able to articulate it. All I know is that being so good is wearing physically and mentally and is very guilt generating. It was not until 20 years later that I knew I was also very, very angry. When that anger surfaced it was so overwhelming and violent that I did not know how to cope. My family found it difficult too. A different person had emerged, a demon. How I had displaced it, controlled it, denied it previously is still a mystery to me. The anger took almost two years to work out and it ruined the harmony I had so carefully engendered in my home, with my daughter and my husband. How we resolved this is a story in itself but I can say that the brunt of my anger was the loss, not only of a major part of myself, but of my childhood (as I became the mother and took up all the emotional responsibilities that engendered) and of my teenage years too.

Autobiographical narrative as a research method

Swindells (1995) discusses the problems social scientists sometimes find with autobiographical accounts:

> 'In the very process of making room for the necessary connection between autobiography and the social world, for an interpretation of auto-biography as something more than a simple presentation of individual existence, this way of analysing autobiography fails to accommodate any sense of the tension, struggle, contestation, or outright conflict between consciousness and environment, between people and their surrounding ideological world, rather, whatever the distinctive characteristics of the different authors included in the tradition, there is a drive towards the inscription of the autobiographical norm. The critical treatment of roland barthes gives an example . . .'

(Swindells, 1995: 2)

She goes on, using Barthes as an example to challenge the way his writings have been played with by the critics. These games (of the critics) she suggests act as further challenges to the value of autobiography which itself challenges the norms of society. Norms such as the importance of reticence, coping and the dismissal of painful or unpleasant events as well as possible private and public guilt. The counter challenge being that individual memory and remembering may be distorted and is therefore not scientific. In other words logical positivists and some social scientists (phenomenologists) challenge the notion that autobiography can be representative of one's experience or have any value in understanding the social world. The authority of selfhood is thus derided using discourses of derision (Usher & Edwards, 1994).

However, as Usher also argues this (my story) is not a privileged account and neither does it try to make a truth claim (Usher & Edwards, 1994). It can only be seen as one interpretation of my story. I could equally have chosen many other ways of presenting these experiences, that is, other discourses could have been used to interpret and explain as well as other research paradigms used for analysing these personal experiences. Readers may interpret this account using their own preferences in many different ways. As Swindells (1995) argues, however, this story is part of my identity. It is a developing and ongoing narrative and an important aspect in my search for selfhood, (Giddens, 1991). Giddens cogently describes the importance of an ongoing reflexive narrative throughout the life span as an important tool in negotiating a complex and changing world as well as a sense of self.

I am very aware as I construct this particular narrative of the possibility of many challenges, particularly from social scientists and academics, to my interpretation of my story. Schenck (1988) issues a warning to those of us who challenge the traditional genre of social science writing (see also Church, 1995). Schenck speaks of those who exert a powerful control in social science writing, deciding what is acceptable and what is not and explains this using the term *homo taxonomicus* that is, the way the borders of the genre are policed. As Church (1995) would argue, writing an auto-biographical piece is going to be difficult in more ways than one, not the least of which is that it challenges the status quo and is not comfortable either for the author, the reader/academic or the researcher, so often defined by ideas of masculinity and rationality (see Chapter 2). I know that I still have not come to terms with the tensions, particularly those of an ideological nature, such as the need to defend the state while retaining a belief in non-violence and in particular the support of both state and church for war and defence (see Partridge, 1996).

This complicated issue is dialectally explored by Wilkinson (1996) in his text *The Church of England and The First World War*. Not all clergy were supportive of the war or the state view. Many were against the war and spoke out against it, others supported the concept of a just war and some saw it as destruction of the anti-Christ. These issues now are no less easily untangled as McGinn (1997) discusses in his text on ethics. Individual and collective positions are dependent on what he calls meta-ethics and normative ethics. I know I still have a problem when it comes to contributing to the British Legion in the sense of purchasing a poppy. Every year I find myself explaining that I wish to contribute to the British Legion but that I do not want a poppy and why. I explain that the red poppy, to me, is a symbol of war. I will wear a white poppy but these are usually few and far between. I contribute and they accept my explanation. Neither do I know how I worked these things out but I do know I had no adult help or support to do so. I just tried as any developing human being does to make sense of what I observed, was part of, therefore I made sense of it in my own way by using the resources at my disposal which included the conventional/traditional valorisation of war and heroism so prevalent in the 1950s and 1960s.

On attending a Myers Briggs (1987) workshop I confirmed my own understanding of my coping strategies in terms of my personality type which is introverted, intuitive, thinking, judging (abbreviated to INTJ) and whilst I do not wish to label myself quite so categorically, it suggests that my intellect and introversion helped me to understand and explain these events and others throughout my life. It is interesting too that this type is rare in the population, less than 1% of the population and even more rare in the female population. However, I have no wish to deny the fact that I had a mask (Jung, 1964; Church, 1995). This took the form of being able to cope and for which I had positive feedback. The consequence of this was my lost self (see poem *For Whom Will it Call Next*). Whether this account makes sense to anyone else is not at issue, they have a right to both question and interpret it but they cannot cancel it out, my account remains. However, as Church says there are alternative ways of writing academic social science (see Afterword). I draw your attention to the autobiography of Nien Cheng (1995), *Life and Death in Shanghai*, and suggest that it is possible to be consciously aware of what is happening to you and be able to explain it and work with such explanations to survive; see Chapters 1 and 13 on how children make sense of their world and events, it may be no sense but it is not nonsense. It is also important to note that it is possible to be both conscious and unconscious of the tensions too, in that you can survive at the expense of other parts of the self being denied or suppressed (Jung, 1963, 1964; S. Freud, 1917a; A. Freud, 1936). I have certainly been both unconscious and conscious of the tensions which existed in me of coping and not coping at one and the same time.

One of the things I found hardest to work out and understand was people's attempt to be helpful. In terms of autobiography as a research method this is hard to categorise. Obviously much of the current explanations are also contaminated by my professional experience and training, reflected in the fact that I have become involved in the teaching of these subjects in the first place. I draw here on the work of Church (1995) to help me understand that this is not anti-scientific. Church argues that one of the most difficult things to do is write about personal shattering events hence the title of her book, *Forbidden Narratives*. She explores ways of writing about these events and suggests that unless one has a confrontation with self it is impossible to become involved in professional or lay activities to help others who may be suffering or struggling to survive. I have some sympathy for her point of view and agree with confronting the self. However, I can also see that this is a developmental process which may indeed cause some kind of dislocation of self, a crisis. I do not believe that this is either necessary or that it is inevitable. For some people the process may be painful, slow and deliberate. In this sense it resembles Piaget's developmental growth. For others it may be triggered by more external pressures interplaying with the internal which remain beyond the conscious mind and more resemble Freudian processes. Jungian explanations come somewhere between these two and it his work which has offered some help to me, especially as an adult.

Whichever discourse, or combinations of these, one prefers, autobiography is a powerful tool in not only understanding ourselves but in changing the social world around us. We are constantly in such an interactive relationship (Giddens, 1991; Fox, 1993; Usher & Edwards, 1994). Victims and survivors, whatever the stage of healing and development, are not passive but active in their struggle to make sense of the world. This can only be encouraged and helped if the world is sympathetic and empathetic to their concerns, Usher suggests, 'has a purchase with those concerns'. This is best illustrated by an example from my own experience. Many people, when I took the risk consciously or unconsciously to talk of these things (determined I suggest by the level of my internal pain and confusion), always told me to forget about these terrible things, and also in the case of the murder tried to explain the event away by suggesting that Monica may have been having an affair. This was not helpful and was also misguided. It was an attempt to understand on their part too. Yet this somehow suggested that such reasons justified murder. However, the suggestion itself is predicated on an erroneous premise which is that any man (woman or child) would be justified in killing out of passion or jealousy. Love, jealousy or passion somehow justifies violence. This is a simplistic argument just as it is in rape, abuse and assault (see Chapter 6) and is much more to do with institutional structures which support power relationships that may result in bullying, dominance and violence. For those who are in shock and grief it is also a very cruel accusation even though it may be intended to offer an explanation and comfort.

Many writers have tried to explain the defences we all put up when faced with embarrassment, fear or an event which seeks to overwhelm us. All have suggested that such defences are ways of distancing the pain of such an event and based on a misguided need to sympathise and help the victims to cope and explain the unexplainable. It also has the effect of dividing the good from the evil, or in terms of religious explanations, it could be seen as a protection of those who are not the victims. Many people still believe that bad or evil things only happen to those who somehow or other have not been good. Therefore by this paradoxical belief and process they can convince themselves they have been saved from such tragedy because they have been good but at the same time distance themselves from the fear that it could possibly happen to them. By doing this they need not confront how they might cope or survive such overwhelming events; see Chapter 3 on annihilation and the Introduction of *Sophie's Choice* by Styron (1992).

The media are very fond of this type of categorisation (see reports of murder cases especially the James Bulger case) which somehow can give the impression that the potential for violence resides only in some people, but not me, and that others are evil and born that way (see next section for explanation). This resolution is ongoing and has taken most of my adult life to work through. Giddens (1991) refers to this as the reflexive project of the self. These remain sound reasons why autobiography is not just a personal story but can also change the nature of the social and help and support others. Although much progress has been made over the years in sensitising the social and professional world to cataclysmic events, much still remains to be done and autobiography has an important role to play in this as well as offering further knowledge and experience to social science in general, especially about human development. Much progress has been made already, otherwise I could not as a professional write this story, thereby mediating other discourses. My professional credibility may well have been called into question had I done so some years ago. Intertextually this shows the progress that has been made socially and politically especially in equal opportunities policies, health care, the caring services and bereavement care and the changing nature of what counts as acceptable knowledge.

Reflexive narrative

There are three issues I wish to engage with in this section. These are:

- The ongoing reflexive project which is myself
- The link with the professional development of myself and others and the relationship with teaching and training in bereavement and loss
- The concepts of good and evil and possible explanations.

As Giddens (1991) suggests for some individuals and groups the reflexive project is a lifetime work. This has certainly been true in my case. It has not been a deliberate search, by that I mean I have not sought out therapy or specific forms of help and not always been conscious of such a process. What I have been conscious of is my learning from all forms of education in which I have been involved as well as literature and other texts such as film and theatre. I have also had the support of my family and some very good friends. In the Piagian sense I have actively used my intellect and the process of reconstruction. However, I have had some minimum help from counselling and it is interesting that I also chose cognitive counselling (6 weeks) seeing it as the most useful medium for my needs (see Chapter 1).

Jung suggests that the process of individuation is one that is ongoing and of which we are not always consciously aware. It is part of the developmental nature of human growth. Others such as Rogers (1961), Erikson (1980), Rowe (1988, 1991) and Egan (1994), would empathise with this view. Therapy or counselling can act as a catalyst, help or support. Sometimes it is necessary because of a personal crisis, the confrontation with self of which Church (1995) speaks. I am conscious of having numerous confrontations with self throughout my lifetime and of having to step back from the daily round of routine and work and allow myself time to reflect and, at times, heal. It is interesting that others have often used the term neurotic to describe my mood and behaviour at such times. Giddens (1991) explains and challenges this way of viewing behaviour and the reflexive project as does Rowe (1988). It is a process which is necessary to the development of self, the clarifying of the personal and ongoing narrative so essential to our understanding of ourselves, our relationship with others and the social world, and for negotiating the complex world in the context of high modernity. It is interesting that it is often viewed as a negative process rather than a positive one.

Goleman (1996) is encouraging professionals (such as teachers) to teach such exploratory and emotional skills as part of the curriculum and illustrates the benefits of this for some American schools, pupils and teachers. Wetton & McWhirter (1997) also make a plea for such work based on their research with children here and in Hungary (see Chapter 14).

As Usher & Edwards (1994) explain, the reflexive project is not just an autobiographical one but rather a complex part of the more global nature of the social context in which we have our being. We are intertextually linked and are inextricably part of the cultural, economic, political, religious and environmental world (see Giddens (1991) on embeddedness). Their impact on us, rather than the internal process of individuation or personal motivation may be the catalyst which encourages growth and development. Similarly the stresses of high modernity (and the reflexive project) may be too much and encourage what Lasch (1980) describes as unhelpful narcissistic tendencies. There is an inevitable and perhaps unresolvable tension in all of these. Further challenges to therapy and counselling are issued by Deleuze & Guttari (1984) and other post-modernist thinkers. They see there could be a danger of power relationships being redefined through these processes. In Foucauldian terms, the nature of the gaze of the professional counsellor/therapist and hence their power may change and may well be seen as controlling (Foucault, 1986). That is, the aim of the game is to re-establish the societal norm rather than engender growth based on the need of the client and an equitable relationship.

However, as I have come to be involved in teaching and learning about transition, bereavement and loss it has been essential for me to both be clear why I am involved, how much of myself I reveal and use in such teaching and what it is I do. This is important when as a teacher I am involved in asking others to study not only the theory but existential questions too (Giddens, 1991). This can be dangerous work but also handled sensitively can be developmental and constructive. These issues cannot be ignored and relate to those raised about bereavement theory and practice in Chapter 1. All I can say is that I am/we are very careful to acknowledge these important questions throughout our experience of working in this field and they remain an important part of planning and teaching. We have learned much from Heron (1990, 1992) and especially his facilitation techniques. We are aware of archaic agendas in ourselves as facilitators and for students. I suggest that mechanistic/medical/biological models of behaviour change, bereavement care and development, whilst useful with certain personalities and situations, fail to acknowledge these issues just as some of the humanist approaches overemphasise them. It is a balance between them all which is important, succinctly explained in philosophical terms by Derrida and his concept of 'differance'. It is the space between the polarities which require our attention or in his words, the slippage.

I wish now to return to the discussion of good and evil as this I believe is important in our understanding of violent crime. Jung describes one particular way of understanding this process (and there are many other discourses which would be equally valid) in his work on symbols (Jung, 1964) and the shadow self. Shadow does not only refer to individuals but also to families, biological ties, and communities. There are many manifestations of such processes such as making scapegoats, racism, chauvinism, enemy making, homosexuality, unemployment and so on. This is supported by the work of Miller (1984). War, abuse, rape, murder and ethnic cleansing are sinister manifestations of individual and collective shadow selves. If we cannot recognise and integrate the shadow in ourselves, the dark side, how can we hope to recognise it in the community or in the collective sense.

These issues are discussed in Wilkinson (1996) and McGinn (1997). McGinn discusses the importance of learning from literature and the portrayal of the shadow in such; the good evil divide. Murdoch (1970) also discusses this in her seminal work on *The Sovereignty of Good*. Individual nation states sanction all sorts of violence from war to capital punishment with a tolerance of other forms of violence masquerading as discipline (Chapter 4; Miller, 1984). Structures and functions within societies continue to support such beliefs and values. However, as Norris (1987) in explaining the work of Derrida suggests such polarisation may not be useful as by privileging one or the other we immediately create a power (value) relationship. Perhaps the Derridian concept of 'differànce' (sic) can help us understand that truth cannot necessarily be established in this way. I suggest, (using Derrida's work) that by privileging good and subjugating evil we immediately establish the fact that good is preferable, better, something to aim for and evil is bad and negative. By this association power relationships are established, supported by traditional truth claims, grounded in philosophy and ethics, and so allows us to separate ourselves from the evil. We are good therefore we cannot be evil. Jung (1964) immediately challenges this with his work on the shadow. We all have, he suggests, a dark side. We are all therefore capable of being influenced by this, especially if it has been subjugated and not integrated within our personalities (see fairy stories and literature such as Faust, Dorian Gray, for examples of the shadow and its effects).

There are numerous recent and current examples; the extermination of the Jews, the troubles in Northern Ireland and recently the ethnic cleansing in Bosnia, Slovakia and Rwanda. In any newspaper account it is possible to read of individuals and groups who apparently undergo some kind of metamorphosis during the night and then carry out the most appalling acts of violence from then on. Others who know them being amazed that it was possible because they are and have been such nice persons. It is this grey area which is so difficult to understand and explain in a culture which has privileged the good. There are many other psychological and sociological explanations, see Gross (1993), of these concepts but I prefer the Jungian explanations.

Fortunately we have learned a great deal and those who suffer the murder of a relative whatever the circumstances, are better cared for than we were. Rightly so, as such caring can help recovery and survival. We do need to acknowledge, in my view, the fact that different people have different needs and want different helping or supportive approaches. Even within one family our approach to support needs to be defined and led by individual need. Survivor needs need to be defined by them, not by professional or lay people (Walter, 1996a). It is at this point I refer back to my challenge on the dominance of models of grief in bereavement training and counselling and their inappropriateness as any more than a guide to the helper. They are not the only representations and interpretations of grief or helping. Neither are all victims/survivors helpless and powerless or incapable of solving problems and overcoming intense grief. Even multiple and complex grief are not necessarily pathological, but they could for some persons become so. The need to know when to refer to other professionals is of paramount importance. Neither is denial necessarily a negative thing as Stroebe *et al.* (1993) document, it can be a survival technique in itself, see Giddens (1991).

Concluding narrative: supporting victims of murder and other violent crimes

A few years ago I was approached by Victim Support, Wiltshire to become a trainer for their volunteer training. I was approached for my reputation in training and especially in sensitive issues not my experience of murder, indeed they knew nothing of my experience. I neither see myself as a victim nor as a survivor, just someone who has struggled. I was unsure and said so and explained about my experience. I felt I had to be very sure that I had come to terms with events. I took time to consider and then agreed. I was to use, as Church (1995) suggests, such experience to translate between worlds. I am very glad that I did. The sensitising effects of my experience meant I was able to sensitise others to the possible needs of those who suffer and ask for help to survive. However, in no way does my experience privilege me neither does it mean that I know more about this topic than others or work better than anyone who has not had such experience or indeed similar experiences.

I believe one of the most important aspects of the training we did together was the acknowledgement that there may be violence in all of us. We do not know under what circumstances or conditions we might be driven to such extremes. It is not a question of good or evil, these two exist in us all (although I like neither value-loaded term), but rather a question of the complex factors that come together in any one human being at any one time shaped by their experience, personality, life chances, context and history (Gross, 1993). National Victim Support (NVS, 1996) carried out research into the needs of victims which has encouraged enlightened training in the police force, other helping services and in victim support. However, in any murder there will always be some harrowing experiences which may complicate grief. These are as follows:

The temporary or long-term *closure of the house* to protect the scene of the crime. Individuals may not be able to return to the house for personal belongings. Children are particularly vulnerable as they may leave without the comfort of their toys and personal things. Victim Support do offer loans to help such families and individuals. The police attempt to be as sensitive as possible and forensic services try to do the work as quickly as possible. However, until such forensic work is complete there can be no return to the house or scene of the crime. The building of a case and evidence can be difficult and we have high expectations of the police and the justice system. There can be many cul-de-sacs and blind alleys. This can be very frustrating and needs to be carefully explained to relatives. However, relatives under such stress and shock may not be able to take in or understand what is being said. In the medical profession the use of tape recorders or videos has helped in explaining traumatic news. People can replay when they feel ready. Much recent training in the police force has increased the sensitive explanations to those who find themselves in this situation.

- The *interviewing of witnesses* can be harrowing although the police have been trained in sensitive techniques, especially for the interviewing of children. However, some personalities may not be able to benefit from such training and its application is not always as general as we might like to think.
- Near relatives or friends may be *questioned* and have *samples* taken in order to rule them out of the enquiry. This is not always made clear and often misunderstood by distraught relatives. In some circumstances they may be a suspect and this can be hard for any family or friends to accept. Many murders are indeed carried out by near relatives or friends.
- The law relating to the *ownership of the body*. The body does not belong to the family but to the state via the coroner. He may only release the body for burial when there is sufficient forensic evidence to proceed with a case, or when the police are satisfied that they cannot do more. Where there is a suspect who has been charged with the murder it is part of our legal system that his/her solicitors/barristers have access to the forensic evidence and this may include the body. This is immensely upsetting for the relatives and is not a reciprocal arrangement, as the victim's family do not have the same right over the perpetrator. Anger may be expressed at this point.
- The body may be released for *burial* only, in case it has to be exhumed, and therefore the family have no choice between burial or cremation. This can be particularly difficult if the 'culture' of the victim or family requires cremation, as in the Hindu religion.
- Coroners are improving their services in the sense that they are allowing relatives to *view the body*. Previously it was thought, especially where the injuries were dreadful, that it was less upsetting for relatives to not see the

body than to see it. This is not necessarily the case. Relatives need to be able to make a choice. To do this they require a careful explanation of the injuries which will enable them to make such a choice. If they are denied such a choice this may compound grief and result in nightmares, imaginative replay and trauma.

- The delicate balance between explaining the need for *evidence* and the protection of their loved one's *privacy and dignity* is a delicate one and needs some careful management. This process needs to be led by the families and individuals. There is no one way to help this process.
- If there is a court case Victim Support now operate *support services* in court. This has helped as there is no right for the family to have a seat in the court, often they only know the date the previous day. The police, the coroner and courts, along with Victim Support, are continually improving this service. However, after a court case the family may be very upset by the verdict. This relates to the sentencing on the grounds of manslaughter or murder. The first is defined as killing with no pre-meditated intent and the second planned and pre-meditated. Both have to be proved through the process of evidence and the families often cannot understand these judicial definitions and feel duped and upset that the sentence does not give them the revenge or the comfort they need. Doubt may remain but the sentence has to be respected.
- The *media* can be a problem, invading privacy and re-telling the story in different ways and not always accurately. This can be a major pressure on families, the police and the justice system. This too needs careful management both to protect the relatives but also to help in appeals for witnesses or evidence. Sometimes a press appearance is necessary to give facts and to lessen the demands from the press in general. It may also be arranged to keep the case in the 'public eye'. This could bring valuable witnesses and evidence for the police. However, another aspect of this is that the family can rewrite the history and biography of the person killed in any way they wish. This may not match with the facts known and can cause immense distortions and fantasy which ultimately may mean that verdicts and evidence do not match the relatives' view or image of the person who has been killed.
- *Forgiveness* in relation to the perpetrator; this is a difficult issue and one which has undergone an ideological change in recent years with a call for stiffer sentencing and harsher punishment. Every person who completes a sentence of imprisonment is entitled to be forgiven and to be helped and encouraged to live within society once again, rehabilitated. This is an issue about civil rights and human rights. They are entitled to a second chance. This is a basic premise of our justice system. However, victims have rights too and unfortunately these have tended to be overlooked. Victim families need to be kept informed about the perpetrator and especially the arrangements for release. This can be a trying situation for all concerned. Once again the police, Victim Support and the probation service are trying to improve services to victims and acting as advocates on their behalf.
- *Compensation*; the rules for compensation for victims were changed

recently. Compensation is available and Victim Support does help people to file claims. This process can be particularly stressful with long waits and enquiries followed sometimes by despair and anger at the final sum awarded. Physical, mental, psychological and emotional trauma cannot be separated as though the body is a machine operating with separate parts, but under the recent change to the system this is the way compensation is awarded. We should remember that it is totally inappropriate to award compensation on this basis as the body operates as an integrated system, hence the move to holistic medicine. Psychological injuries should be given equal weight to physical and each are inextricably bound to each other. Whilst I endorse the need to control financial resources I believe the previous system was less traumatic for relatives.

- *Trauma* (see Chapter 10). Sudden death poses some issues for grief counsellors and others. It can be more difficult and there could, for some people, be the risk of post-traumatic stress syndrome or compounded grief (see Stroebe *et al.*, 1993). Counsellors do need to know the signs for post-traumatic stress syndrome and know when there is a need to refer; see Chapter 11.

Conclusion

Grief has many manifestations and each individual will behave differently, there is no one way to cope with devastating circumstances and grief counsellors and supporters need to understand that no amount of training and theory (grief models and processes) can give them a direct or perfect map for dealing with these situations. It is important that they too are supported and come to terms with what they can do; if they do their best it is good enough (see Bettelheim, 1960) and often better than in the past.

Teaching and learning focus on a search for understanding

Rationale

The rationale is to enable course participants to explore the needs of the different family members bereaved through murder.

Activity

Having read the chapter consider:

- The practical, emotional and personal needs of immediate family members when their property is sequestrated by the police for forensic purposes

- The help and support these family members will need through the process of coming to terms with the crime but also the building of evidence for the police
- The skills and knowledge a detective who is investigating the crime will need to interview the husband, parents and a child in a murder case
- The emotional and practical help a Victim Support volunteer can give to a bereaved family in the period between the crime and the court case.

Learning outcomes

The learning outcomes stimulated by the activities are for the course participants to:

- Clarify the needs of the different members of the family
- Explore the skills of the police to enable them to gather evidence whilst being caring towards the family
- Explore the role of carers in supporting families throughout the period before the court case.

Chapter 6
The Effects of Sexual Violence on Individuals and Families

Sandie Arrell and Alastair McWhirter

In this chapter the authors take the reader through:

- *How rape may leave a victim feeling*
- *The law relating to rape/sexual assault*
- *The journey of recovery for the victim.*

The perspectives from which this chapter is written are: phenomenological and professional.

Introduction

The purpose of this chapter is to discuss the effects of sexual violence on individuals and families. It aims to help the reader explore his or her own attitude to sexual crimes and the needs and feelings of victims. To do this we will discuss the concept of violent sexual crime and its definition in law. We will address the way that the police investigate sexual crimes; how they work with victims to provide support in helping them cope with the grief and loss that sexual violence often brings with it. We will discuss the joint working with other agencies to help provide a network of support for victims through the investigative and judicial process and beyond. We intend to help the reader dispel many of the myths which surround rape and other sexually violent crimes.

'Rape is totally and utterly destructive, striking right at the roots of a person's sense of self and worth.'

'It has nothing to do with the fulfilment of a committed relationship, special and complete. It is sordid, dirty and violent.'

'All I can do is pray, "God let me come out of this alive".'

This is how one person felt after being subjected to rape. Rape is one of the most difficult offences that victims have to deal with. It brings with it a whole skein of tangled feelings, sometimes contradictory, which anyone who wishes to assist needs to understand. Anyone subjected to any crime will suffer some mental and physical reaction to it. This reaction obviously varies with the nature of the crime and with the threat it brings to the social world in which they live. For example, if your car is broken into in a car park and your radio is stolen you may feel annoyed and inconvenienced. If it is your handbag or briefcase which is stolen it may affect you much more in that you will have lost things which are very personal to your life and relationships. Consider then how much more intrusive is the burglary of your home where your own personal space has been invaded and your possessions have been handled and disturbed by the burglar. Many victims feel that they do not want to go on living in the house and live constantly in fear of it happening again.

Try then to imagine how much worse it can be for a victim of rape. Here, your social world has been violated in the most offensive and intrusive way. All the experiences and values which go to make up our normal lives have been turned upside down. Victims tell us that they often feel:

- *Helpless.* They often describe a feeling of powerlessness which cuts across every facet of their lives and can turn confident, outgoing people into introverted, nervous individuals. They constantly question, 'Why me?' A journal entry by an American rape victim describes the feelings:

    'I'm feeling so out of control, so depressed. My fears, my paranoia are overwhelming me, I can't focus. Run away – be strong. I'm caught. Uptight. I'm being torn apart. Inside out. Ripping away layer after layer. Coat after coat defences lost – strength to battle is being extinguished. Dying a slow, slow death inside. No energy to move. No energy to think. No energy to cope. No energy to work. I'm losing control. TOO TIRED – but can't stop.'

    (Katz, 1984: 29)

- *Guilt.* There is often a feeling of responsibility – with a questioning of the victim's own actions... 'It was my fault because I went back to his room'... 'It was my fault because I wore this dress'... 'It was my fault because I walked home alone'. This is often compounded by the fact that the perpetrator will tell them that it is their fault. This shifting of blame by offender to victim is a frequent occurrence reported by victims.

    June, who had fought off her attacker, who was married with three children, described the effect:

    'I do not wear make up, smart clothes, perfume, swimwear, a blouse unless it is covered with a big jumper. I keep myself and my body from view. I do not go out to a restaurant, as I would feel I would have to wear feminine clothes. To feel that you have no other function other than as an object to be used and thrown away completely destroys your confidence and makes you feel powerless, worthless, ashamed and guilty.'

(Lees, 1996)

- *Shame.*   Victims are often worried that other people will hold them responsible. This appears particularly true of male rape . . . 'I should have fought them off'. It is also a common feature when rape takes place within the family and the victim is trying to fit the experience (s)he has had into the context of a continuation of family life.

  'There is a constant battle with what others think – the people at work, the papers, passers-by, folk on the Tube who look at me as if I have no right to contaminate the air they breathe.'

(Saward, 1990: 137)

- *Anger.*   Victims often describe intense feelings of anger as the symptom of a whole range of conflicting emotions. Sometimes this anger is against the perpetrator but at other times can turn upon themselves or on those around them for lack of protection or for failing to understand.
  A young woman raped at home when her father and boyfriend were also badly beaten, wrote:

  'I am angry that he (her father) has not been able to protect me. All that hype about men being the protectors seems to have flown out of the window overnight.'

(Saward, 1990: 47)

- *Low self-esteem.*   Feelings of guilt, shame and anger coupled with a feeling of powerlessness are common experiences of people who have suffered rape. Often they report feeling worthless and of little value. The victim's own sex life is often dramatically affected; the victim may feel rejected and contaminated. The victim may feel spoiled and undesirable and unable to play a full part in a sexual relationship.

  'Because I had nobody to talk to about it, I continued to blame myself. It also did a lot of damage to my self-esteem, as I already had a low opinion of myself. The sad thing is that I felt worthless, so therefore I really became worthless and I am still working on that now.'

(Lees, 1996: 22)

- *Detachment.*   Victims sometimes report cutting all their feelings off – a kind of numbness which pervades all aspects of their lives. Alternatively victims often say that they go through a period where they purposely cut themselves off from people, places or things.

A woman who was raped by her husband said:

'I kept busy. I went to school and to work and to the gym and I walked four miles every night. I was physically and emotionally exhausted and I would fall asleep downstairs with the TV at night because I didn't want to go upstairs to bed.'

(Kennedy Bergen, 1996: 28)

- *Fear.* The feeling which is most constant in all these reactions is fear. Victims may be afraid to go out alone. They may be afraid to stay indoors on their own if the rape took place indoors; they may be afraid to enter large buildings alone; they may, like the victim in the poem, be afraid of any circumstance which reminds them of the offence. If the rape was by a stranger in the victim's own home it is the authors' experience that victims will rarely, if ever, go back to that house again.

'I think it's a state of shock you're in. All I can say is that after it happens you are so frightened. I was threatened not to say anything. I went back to an empty house and I spent about four or five days off work, shutting doors, locking doors after me, hiding in bed – and you know there is no way I would have communicated with anybody, any of it.'

(Adler, 1987: 12)

In recent years the major fear of victims is the prospect of getting AIDS. Rape victims of both sexes have also reported fears about their own sexuality. Male victims have reported fears of becoming or being seen as homosexual, whereas conversely, some female rape victims have reported enjoining in same sex relationships purely out of fear of relationships with men.

According to research in the US, some women are carrying condoms as a preventative measure so that in the event of an assault they can try to persuade the assailant to use protection (Lees, 1996).

Rape does not affect the victims alone – it also damages the world of the families and friends around them. For families who tend to feel the same effects as the victim initially this can be hard to understand. For them there is the acute aftermath of the rape itself but time may heal things more quickly for those around the victim than for the victim herself.

Burgess & Holstrom (1979) found that there were two specific phases of reaction to the crime. The first phase they called 'the acute phase – disorganisation'. Often the physical and emotional impact is so great that the victim will feel shock and disbelief at what has happened – displaying a wide range of emotions. They found that two main styles of emotion were shown by the victims – expressed and controlled. Victims also often try to block out thoughts of the rape from their minds but usually find they cannot.

They may think of how they could have avoided the assault, how they could have dealt with the situation differently and so prevented it from happening but they do not find any solution in this.

This acute phase, the researchers found, lasted from a few days to a few weeks. The way each person reacts to rape is related to many factors including the age of the victim, his or her personality, strength of character, cultural background, prior sexual experience and the environment (s)he lives in. Jill Saward, who was the victim of the 'Ealing vicarage' rape was a virgin who had had little sexual experience when she was raped by several men, faced just such difficulties.

'The police help enormously. They take time to be accurate and know exactly what they are talking about, even if I don't. Words like erection, ejaculation, buggery and oral sex are not ones I have used before. Until a few hours ago I knew very little about how the male reproduction organs work when excited – so I have a quick sex education lesson, much to my embarrassment. I feel so naïve, not knowing much about the mechanics or the right words to use. The police, male and female, take it all in their stride. I can laugh with them, they are sympathetic, caring, professional. A bit like concerned friends but without the emotional involvement.'

(Saward, 1990: 40)

The second phase of rape trauma syndrome Burgess & Holstrom called 'the long-term process – reorganisation'. They found that, not only did victims suffer disruption of their lives in the days and weeks after the assault, but suffered recurrence of this for many weeks and months afterwards. They found that the rape very often upsets the victim's normal routine of living. Some people, after being raped, try to carry on as normal. Having had control over their sexuality and their very being taken away from them during the rape, they try to hang on to what they can and refuse to be affected, carrying on at work or other normal pursuits, not talking about it to anyone. This may work for some – but the reality is that for many they cannot keep up the mask of normality and the result is behaviour such as that described in the section on fear above.

For the families and partners of victims this long-term effect can be catastrophic, leading to breakdowns in communication which can result in a vicious circle of misunderstanding. For families there must be as much communication and understanding as possible if they are to adjust satisfactorily. Victims often suffer flashbacks to the actual rape or the circumstances around it and partners can sometimes take on the aspect of the perpetrator.

'I blocked it out for about two years. But even in that time, it made me feel nervous around men. More recently I sometimes have flashbacks (usually during sex). Partly as a result I rarely have sex. I'm still dealing with the emotional and psychological effects.'

(Lees, 1996: 80)

Victims sometimes describe rape as being like a death in the family and they go through a grieving, mourning process. The difficulty is that those around the victim may not fully understand the depth of loss which the victim is going through.

One victim puts it thus:

'When I shared my experience with other friends, instead of support I would often receive a response of avoidance or denial. This would take the form of a statement such as, 'At least you're all right and survived'. No follow-up questions were asked. No sharing of their own feelings occurred. Different friends would assume that I was managing all right and would superficially note that it seemed as if I was getting my life back to normal.'

(Katz, 1984: 37)

What does the criminal law say?

The law says that rape is committed by a man who has sexual intercourse, whether vaginal or anal, with a person who, at the time of the intercourse does not consent and at the time the man knows that the person does not consent or is reckless as to whether the person consents.

Rape is regarded as one of the most serious sexual offences in the criminal law and this is reflected in the maximum penalty which the offence carries on conviction – life imprisonment. In reality this maximum penalty is only applied in the most serious of cases. This is a subject of much debate. The lawyer Helena Kennedy put it well in her James Smart Memorial Lecture in 1993:

'One of the problems in this debate is that hard lines are drawn. Women versus men. Feminists versus defence lawyers. Feminists versus other women. The characterisation of the debate in these terms can never be helpful. Justice is ill served by dogmatism. The definition of rape is simple. There is not "real" rape and other kinds of rape. However not all rape is the same. It is as unhelpful to hear women claim that no distinction should be made between the different manifestations of rape as it is to hear it claimed that all men are rapists. It is also quite silly, and alienating to those who are generally sympathetic to women's rights, for campaigners on this issue to insist that women do not make false allegations of rape. They do. It does not happen with the regularity that some newspaper journalists and legal commentators would have the world believe – but it does happen, and I have represented women who have made false allegations. There are different kinds of rape and this should be reflected in sentence. The attempted rape which led to the conviction of the solicitor, Angus Diggle, (who received two years imprisonment for attempting to rape a fellow solicitor after a dinner which he paid for) does not merit the same sentence as the violation experienced by Jill Saward, who was the victim in the Ealing vicarage rape. She was penetrated by several men, anally and vaginally, forced to provide oral sex and had a knife used in the process. In the aftermath, not surprisingly, there were times when she wanted to take her own life. However, the distinctions should be made because of factors about the crime. A difference in sentence is not justified simply because of factors about the woman. In 1991 Mr Justice Alliot passed a low sentence on a man who had committed a violent rape because the victim was a "common" prostitute, saying, "while every woman is entitled to complain about being violated, someone who for years has flaunted their body and sold it cannot complain as loudly as someone who has not".'

(Kennedy, 1996: 3)

Since 1991 a husband can rape his wife. Before that he could only be charged with indecently assaulting her, unless she had other physical injuries. This is a considerable shift, because when we examine the history of rape legislation we find that women were treated as property.

'Rape laws were originally enacted as property laws to protect a man's property (a daughter or a wife) from other men, not as laws to protect women or their rights to control their bodies, (R *v.* Pagelow, 1984). Thus, the penalty for rape was intended to punish a man for defiling another man's property. If a daughter was raped her father could be compensated for the loss of his valuable property – his daughter's virginity. A husband could also be compensated for the violation of his sexual property if his wife was raped by another man. However, as owners of this property, husbands could not be charged with the rape of their wives (R *v.* Dobash & Dobash, 1979).'

(Kennedy Bergen, 1996: 3)

The definition of rape states that it can only be committed by a man – but the law also allows for boys over the age of 10 to be charged if they have committed the offence and they knew it was seriously wrong. Until 1993 any male under 14 was held to be incapable of achieving sexual intercourse.

In order to prove the offence the prosecution has to be able to provide evidence of penetration by the penis either anally or vaginally. It is not necessary to prove that ejaculation took place.

One of the major difficulties with the offence of rape is the question of consent. Now that DNA analysis can tie semen down to an individual man, the most frequent defence put forward in rape cases is that the other person consented to the intercourse. For it not to be rape true consent must be given and frequent disputes arise over whether the other person consented or not. This is particularly difficult in cases where either (or both) of the parties had consumed alcohol or taken drugs and have only a vague recollection of what took place.

Equally the question of whether the alleged rapist was 'reckless' or not is one which often leads to courtroom debate or more frequently encourages the Crown Prosecution Service to withdraw the case before it gets to court on the basis that a conviction is not likely. Consent is clearly a difficult area but its effects can be negated – particularly by evidence of the victim making an immediate complaint to a third party.

The main problem is that there are no positive legal definitions of consensual sex, so that the burden of negotiated consent is not mutually shared and, instead, women are held responsible for giving or denying sexual access (Lees, 1996).

There are numerous other violent sexual offences which may have all the same effects as rape on the victim. The one most commonly charged by the police is indecent assault. This offence is committed when a person assaults another accompanied by any act of indecency. Unlike rape, the offender can be a man or a woman. Indecent assault can vary between simple touching on the outside of clothing to forcible penetration with an object. A kiss has been held to be an indecent assault. The maximum penalty on conviction for this offence is ten years imprisonment.

Police investigations of sexually violent crime

The police investigation of sexual crime has changed dramatically over the last 15 years. Following a 'fly on the wall' documentary by Roger Graef on the Thames Valley police in 1982, where an officer was shown bullying and hectoring a woman who was trying to make a complaint of rape, police practice changed dramatically. There was national outcry both within and without the police service and the result was a move away from treating the victim as someone who had to prove that the offence had taken place to a situation where the victim was treated as just that, the victim of a dreadful and serious crime.

The changes which have taken place have resulted in police investigations into sexual violence becoming non-judgmental and supportive. The police have recognised the necessity of choice for the victim in the gender of the interviewer and the doctor to carry out a medical examination. Victim support suites – away from the main parts of police stations – equipped with comfortable furniture and showers, baths and medical rooms, have been provided across the country.

A rape victim describes her experience:

'The rape suite at Brentford is a small unit away from the main building. I have some idea what to expect because it was shown on television about a month ago when it was opened. Even so, I am impressed by the relaxed atmosphere, which is totally unlike a normal police station. The interview room is very peaceful, tastefully decorated in subtle browns and creams. It is "user friendly", carpeted, with soft comfortable seats and pictures on the walls. There is even a coffee machine and kettle for making tea for those who actually like the stuff. I'm more interested in the bath/shower room which I am promised I can use later. The loo I make use of straight away. At long last my body is able to relax sufficiently, although blood is still coming from my hymen.'

(Lees, 1996: xviii)

The importance of involving other agencies in a healthy alliance to provide support and assistance in many different forms has been realised and acted upon. Many different agencies can be involved – but only in keeping with the victim's needs and wishes. Social workers, health professionals, Victim Support scheme volunteers, members of rape counselling services and even housing department staff can all help, depending on the needs of the victim. Unlike many other crimes, sexual assault has become client led, with as much information about the process of the investigation being supplied as possible to help empower the victim and try to redress some of the loss which has occurred. It is made clear that the victim is in control and that he or she dictates how far the investigation should go. It is about giving the victim the power to say 'no' – which is what was removed in the first place.

Helena Kennedy commented upon it thus in 1993:

'The role of the police in the field of sexual violence is no longer seen as purely investigative. There has been an acceptance of another role, a more supportive and sympathetic role of police working in collaboration with other agencies to enable women to recover from traumatic events. . . . I cannot emphasise enough the importance of that change.'

(Kennedy, 1993: 18)

Statistics on reported crime tend to support the view that the public and victims are aware of these changes because, while other reported crime peaked in 1992, rape and indecent assault have continued to rise at a steady rate. The number of rapes reported to the police more than doubled between 1985 and 1995. The Home Office Criminal Statistics for England and Wales 1995 state that:

'Since 1985 offences of rape have increased on average by about 11% per year. Much of the increase over this period is however thought to be attributable to both an increase in reporting by the public and changes in police practice.'

There is still considerable work to be done to ensure that victims of violent sexual crime come forward to report offences. The work of Victim Support and various other support agencies suggests that there is still a high incidence of women who have been subjected to sexual violence who do not report the matter to the police.

One more area where there still appears to be considerable work to be done is in the field of male rape. In 1995 there were 150 reported cases of rapes on males, but it is thought that many victims suffer in silence in the same way that women rape victims used to in higher numbers than they do now. Victims who do come forward say that they had fears about being believed, fears that they might be thought to be homosexual and fears about appearing in court. Part of this is cultural, stemming from the macho image of men in our society – but generally male rape victims suffer exactly the same trauma, loss and grief as females.

Police forces across the country now recognise the need to promote, not only good working practices, but to let the public know that they are doing so.

The police investigation of rape

The effects of the police investigation on victims can be profound. In some cases the telling and retelling of the experience can be cathartic and therapeutic. In others it can have the opposite effect, of making them relive a nightmare. Whatever happens it will always have an effect.

In one text, Ledray (1986) suggests:

'Telling the police does mean that you must describe the whole event verbally in detail, which will be hard to do. Survivors often find that talking about it helps desensitise them to the horrors. While it was bad, perhaps the worst thing you've ever been through, it's not so bad that another person can't hear the details and it doesn't make you an "untouchable" or "unclean" person whom no-one will accept or respect.'

(Ledray, 1986: 39)

The skill on the part of the police officers who work with victims is to gather the evidence in a way which helps the victim as far as is possible. The aim of the police investigation is to gather evidence about an incident so as to find out the truth of what happened. This will mean the taking of an extremely detailed statement from the victim. This requires the people working with the victim to very quickly build an environment of trust where all the elements required to ascertain the details of a traumatic event can be gathered in congruence. This process is about giving the victim permission not to know something and for the interviewer to feel able to ask very intimate and difficult questions which the victim knows he or she would not ask unless they really needed to know. The taking of the statement can sometimes take several days. The pace will be determined by the victim.

As well as gathering oral evidence in statement form from the victim it is critical also to gather external evidence. From the victim this will mean gathering the clothes that he or she was wearing. This means that other suitable clothing in which the victim will feel comfortable has to be available. Even more traumatic is the necessity to gather medical evidence to support the allegation. Many victims' first desire is to wash away the unclean feeling of being defiled. The aim of the police on the other hand is to delay that process so that a police doctor can gather forensic samples. This necessitates an intimate physical examination of the victim which will always be carried out with consent. No-one is forced to undergo this part of the investigation although it can make achieving a conviction extremely difficult without medical corroboration. During the medical the victim will always be attended by an officer of the same gender along with the police doctor.

This is always one of the most difficult areas of the investigation – no-one likes this process. Sometimes it can be very difficult. Jill Saward describes her experience:

> 'It takes me far less time to make up my mind about the doctor when he starts to examine me. The police had offered me a woman doctor, but I was prepared to go along with whatever would make it easier for them. I have swabs taken from my throat, skin, anus and vagina. My throat is already sore. Having someone poking around is agony and the doctor is not exactly gentle. He needs hair from my head and pubic area. One that has come out naturally and one that he has to pull. To him it is just a routine examination. He seems entirely unaware that any remaining shreds of self confidence are being chopped away as remorselessly as the samples he is now taking from my fingernails. Chop. Chop. Hack away. Don't worry about trying to keep a normal shape. One more little indignity won't make any difference.'

(Saward, 1990: 36)

Not all examinations are as bad as this and many forces employ specialist women doctors who are the antithesis of the doctor Jill Saward met.

While this is going on, other police officers will gather information at the scene or scenes of the rape. Others will work with anyone who has been accused of having carried out the crime. The accused will also have his clothes seized and will also be subjected to medical examination. The gathering of forensic samples will sometimes be carried out against the person's will with the authority of a police superintendent.

One of the improvements in the investigation of rape has been the follow-on support from the police and other agencies, such as Victim Support, to the victim during the sometimes lengthy phase between the initial investigation and the trial. Liaison is maintained and victims are kept informed of the progress of the preparation of the file and are told if the accused person is going to be released on bail and what the conditions of that bail are. Where an offender has not yet been traced and victims are in fear of a repeat attack the police can (and do) provide special panic alarms backed up by a rapid response.

As the trial approaches the victim is supported by the police and now more commonly by the Witness Service who can arrange visits to the court in advance of the trial and explain the process that the victim will have to go through while giving evidence. The trial is often a trial for the victim as well as the accused. The adversarial nature of English and Scottish law means that victims often feel pressured and accused by the barrister for the defence. This can be even worse if the accused person has exercised his right to defend himself and thus has the right to cross-examine the victim. Even though the environment of the court is strictly controlled and the defence have to abide by the rules of evidence, there is still the opportunity to make victims feel that they are to blame. When the accused is on trial for his freedom (for life in some cases) then every tactic to damage the prosecution case is used.

Judges are more aware now than they used to be of the need to protect the rights of victims. In the past the previous sexual history of the victim was often admitted as evidence and her character attacked. The law on this was amended during the 1980s and it is now much rarer for a victim's conduct away from the actual offence or offender to be admissible as evidence. Many people are not aware that this change took place so long ago.

The law also allows the victim anonymity. This applies not only throughout the case but also during the rest of their lifetime unless they consent to disclosure. The accused person's name can be and is published.

Fitting it all together

Being the victim of rape or other violent sexual offence changes your world forever. At the beginning of this chapter we said that everyone who is the victim of crime is damaged by it, but for the victim of a serious violent crime this damage is often much more dramatic. Individuals create their social world from a jigsaw of experiences they have throughout their lives. Rape can change that world utterly and create a jumble of broken pieces which look, to the victim, as though they will never fit back together again.

Those who intervene in the aftermath, be it police, Victim Support volunteers or health professionals, need to help the victim have the power, not only to put the jigsaw together again, but also to help them see that the picture will in some way be changed. For some it may be only slightly changed, for others it may be an entirely different picture. For many there will always be an area for which some pieces can never be found. Above all it takes love. Jill Saward put it perfectly,

'I have discovered that love is gentle, patient, ready to put itself in the other person's position and share the anger and the hurt. It does not expect the person to "snap out of it" and recover overnight or even after several years. Anyone recovering from the effects of rape needs a great deal of love. Rape is totally and utterly destructive striking right at the roots of a person's sense of self and worth. I can only thank God for all those who have helped in the healing, male and female. However unlikely it might once have seemed, this rape has most definitely been a love story.'

(Saward, 1990: 153)

Teaching and learning focus on the effects of sexual violence on individuals and families

Rationale

The rationale is to enable course participants to explore the feelings of the victim and to draw out the dichotomy between the need to gather evidence against the needs of the victim. The teaching focus is based on the classroom activities we have developed over three years. Whilst they look simple we caution facilitators to be prepared to support individuals and groups as this simplicity is misleading. Each stage of the exercise explores another layer of attitudes/beliefs. It is a powerful exercise.

Activity 1

You have been called to the home of a person who has just been raped. You have called the police at the request of the victim.

- What is your role?
- What do you see as the role of the police officers?
- Are there any possible areas of conflict?
- How can you promote a positive message to the assaulted person?

Students are asked to report back from their own professional or personal point of view depending on their backgrounds. They are then asked to answer the same questions in Activity 2.

Activity 2

You have been asked to accompany a person who has been raped whilst they attend a medical examination.

- What is your role?
- What do you see as the role of the police officers?
- Are there any possible areas of conflict?
- How can you promote a positive message to the assaulted person?

Students can be asked to report back in different ways depending on the size and nature of the group. The aim is to explore the feelings of the victim and to draw out the dichotomy between the need to gather evidence against the needs of the victim.

Activity 3

The third exercise focuses on the group's response to the police interview. Again members of the group are asked to accompany a person who has been raped while the police carry out an interview.

- What is your role?
- What do you see as the role of the police officers?
- Are there any possible areas of conflict?
- How can you promote a positive message to the assaulted person?

Again the focus is upon empathy for the victim and balancing this against the role of the police in evidence gathering and the painstaking detail which is needed if a prosecution is to be successful.

Activity 4

The final exercise aims to explore the feelings of student and victim in the following scenario:

You have been asked to support/counsel a person who has been raped and is awaiting the hearing of the criminal court case. You have also been asked to support them while they attend court.

- What is your role?
- What do you see as the role of the prosecution and defence counsel?
- What do you see as the role of the Judge?
- Are there any possible areas of conflict?
- How can you promote a positive message to the assaulted person?

Learning outcomes

The learning outcomes stimulated by the activities are for the course participants to:

- Become familiar with different methods of reporting back
- Unlock their own attitudes to rape and its victims
- Open their minds to the needs and pressures faced by the professional agencies who provide assistance.

Chapter 7
Suicide: An Exploration

Jackie Yardley

This chapter seeks to set out contemporary issues relating to suicide, the extent of the problem, the risk factors, the possible causal factors. It does this by taking an overview of suicide in the Health of the Nation *mental illness handbook, reviewing the targets and looking at how we can begin to improve prevention strategies within a number of health promotion settings. The chapter also attempts to explore how difficult life may be, and remain, for those left behind. It uses a metaphor, colour, as a way of looking at the grieving process in relation to suicide. Reference is made, throughout the chapter, to literature, poetry and case studies. Therapy techniques are explained especially those which the author has found helpful with clients.*

The perspectives from which this chapter is written are: phenomenological, professional, and empirical.

Introduction

The following discussion, whilst taking account of research findings and statistics, is not exclusively based on official data. The decision to take an alternative view is based on my belief that such data do not reflect well enough the reasons why people find there is no alternative way of managing life than deliberately to end it.

Progress in prevention will be limited until we understand the structure of suicide at an individual level. By this is meant a step-by-step understanding of what happens internally to a person as he or she prepares for an act of self-harm. The picture painted by researchers and statisticians is rather like knowing all the facts about smoking – but also knowing that people continue to smoke. All the knowledge and information we have, as professionals, about suicide, is of no direct use unless it relates in some way to that person's internal world.

The challenge is to allow many different perspectives to be integrated into one, like a jigsaw puzzle. The perspective which will be explored here is intended to complement the conventional approach, by trying to enter the psychological space of those who inflict self-harm and to work at an unconscious or preconscious level, see Epstein (1993).

Suicide in the UK

Sophie became so separated from her own purpose by succumbing to domestic pressure that she no longer felt she knew herself and she made a serious attempt at suicide. 'I had to burst out of the vise I was in', she explained.

'I felt as though I were absolutely somebody else, a terrible feeling. I took the risk of a suicide attempt because I wanted to be extricated, saved from the life I was living, to burst out of that stagnation.'

(Hancock, 1989: 116)

Sophie recovered from this attempt because her doctor husband was awoken early morning, by a phone call. He sent for an ambulance as soon as he realised something was wrong, that his wife was nearly dead. Sophie was admitted to a psychiatric unit where she was cared for by a young psychiatrist who resisted all the normal labels for a 49-year-old woman who had attempted suicide; for example menopause or depression and recognised instead, a 'lost soul'. He acknowledged, as she talked about the girl ('the inner soul of a person'), the neglect that had taken place. He treated her as Sophie, not a wife and mother, but a person. Sophie went on to reclaim that lost soul.

In the UK and Ireland up to 7000 people take their lives every year, which is 25% higher than the death toll from road traffic accidents and more than ten times the number of deaths by homicide. It has been estimated that more than 100 000 people attempt suicide each year (The Samaritans, 1996a). Deaths from suicide are about 6000 each year compared with about 4600 from road traffic accidents and 400 from homicide.

Annually, suicide accounts for approximately 1% of all deaths; since 1982 there has been a rise of 75% of suicides in young men aged 15–24 and in this group it is the second most common cause of death (Department of Health, 1993). There are two suicides every day in the UK by people under the age of 25 (Department of Health, 1993; The Samaritans, 1997d). Whilst there has been an overall decrease in women who commit suicide, the risk increases in women over the age of 75 to double that of women under 25 (Department of Health, 1993).

In the Samaritans Report (1996a), Armson states that suicide remains a taboo and if attitudes are going to change then we need to examine ourselves and those around us. Durkheim's (1897/1951) original study of suicide also makes such an observation; see also Horton (1997). He suggests that suicide is a social phenomenon and the solutions lie with society not only medicine.

Attitudes to suicide

The Samaritans' (1996a) research used a cross-section of the population for a telephone survey of 1000 adults. Twenty six per cent of the sample had known someone personally who had committed suicide and 60% agreed that suicide is not an easy way out. There was general agreement that depression is a side-effect of modern life and strong agreement that depression is a serious illness. However, one-third of those interviewed felt that people who are depressed should pull themselves together and one-third felt that depression is not a serious illness. Of the total sample, 42% strongly agreed that people who attempt suicide deserve more sympathy than they get, but one-third of those interviewed felt that people who attempt suicide are thinking only of themselves.

People are influenced by a number of factors in their attitudes to suicide and to those who have attempted suicide. In certain religions it is considered a sin to take your own life, therefore self-harm can be seen in a wholly negative light. Health workers, particularly doctors, play an important role and a patient admitted for attempted suicide would often be considered depressed and in need of some form of psychological or psychiatric treatment. Perhaps we should not always assume an underlying psychiatric condition, but look also to the individual's experience of social conditions, such as loneliness and despair brought about by poverty and unemployment (Pritchard, 1995).

Suicide can still be seen as a taboo subject (Scott, 1989) and news of death by suicide is more likely to attract morbid interest. Beliefs around suicide are reflected by words such as terrible, bad, tragic and sad about the incident and 'out of their mind', depraved, mad and selfish about the suicide. These paint a very negative picture, but beliefs are difficult to change, particularly those which are shared collectively, within cultures and social groups. It is possible that we have created a more dramatic and tragic scenario for suicide than for other forms of death. Death remains a topic that evokes discomfort in most people, whilst mental illness and depression remain topics we prefer not to explore. Outburst of anger, even as an appropriate angry reaction to a given situation, can be met with disapproval; the concept of death being more welcome than life creates conflict. These are components of suicide; are we afraid of the whole or the parts? This is not to minimise the devastating effects of suicide but to ask if, in our society, we compound grief by our own need to feel safe.

When examining the wider picture history is full of examples of suicide. Socrates committed suicide by drinking hemlock because he was found guilty of heresy and corrupting the mind of the young. In 73 AD at the siege of Masada, Josephus found the Jewish people drawing lots to identify the last three people to overview the mass suicide of the crowd when they knew the Romans were about to breech the wall (see Williamson, 1959: 395–495). Each man was responsible for killing his family by slitting their throats. In the Battle of the Alamo (1835–36) during the Texan war of independence, 185 Texans decided to die (fighting to the end) instead of submitting to the Mexicans. The act of seppuku (commonly known as hara-kiri) a ritual suicide committed by the Japanese was based on honour and a form of this was carried out by soldiers in war time. And in Jonestown, Guyana in 1978, Jim Jones, a cult leader of the People's Temple Christian Church, convinced his followers (914) to a mass suicide (including himself) but in the event some were coerced or murdered. It is even possible to consider acts of courage which result in death as a form of suicide. Captain Oates' words to Scott: 'I'm going out now and I may be some time' (Scott, 1989) were certainly considered an act of sacrifice as he walked out to his death in the South Pole. These examples illustrate the many and varied reasons which people have had for wishing to end their own lives.

Attempted suicide

There are many stated reasons as to why some may contemplate and even act out their intentions and these can range from relationship dilemmas, financial struggles, illness, pain, loneliness, anger, frustration and revenge. In England and Wales there are at least 100 000 attempts at suicide every year (Department of Health, 1993). Excluded from these figures are those who never present themselves for medical attention, those seen and managed by their GP and attempts made by patients in a psychiatric hospital. In 1994, a 22% increase of attempted suicide was recorded over a three-year period. Young females have been noted as the main group to attempt suicide but attempts by men are on the increase, especially in the 15–19 age group. More alarmingly, 1994 data show a marked increase in the number of children and very young adolescents who have attempted suicide. Every 30 minutes one adolescent attempts suicide (Department of Health, 1993). There can be negative reactions for those who make frequent attempts at suicide with onlookers becoming dismissive or irritated at such perceived attention-seeking behaviour. Yet 5% of the repeaters do in the end kill themselves. It is extremely difficult to be certain that someone has seriously intended to commit suicide. Fairbairn (1995) and Scott (1989) suggests that we should, therefore, err on the side of caution and take threats seriously. Attempted suicide is on the increase and the UK has one of the highest rates of attempted suicide in Europe (The Samaritans, 1997a).

Many people consider suicide at some point in their lives but the consideration is tempered by thoughts of family, friends, social and religious constraints. Some use it as a means of warning, an intention, and yet others complete the act by using a method which in its self speaks loudly as Fairbairn records for example, a man does not leap from a skyscraper with a plastic bag over his head having recently ingested a large quantity of sleeping pills and slit his wrists, with the idea in mind that he may be saved (Fairbairn, 1995: 10).

Attempted suicide is rarely as clear cut as that, however, and establishing intent remains a problem. Do people who do serious harm to themselves intend to die or do they wish to be saved, and are those who are found, glad to be alive or do they wish to be dead? Some suicides are not recorded as such by coroners because of the stigma attached and the difficulty of knowing absolutely that death occurred because of deliberate intent (Pritchard, 1995).

The suicidal person

It is reported that 40% of people who committed suicide consulted their GP during the previous week (Department of Health, 1993). Since 1993 there has been a 4% reduction in the suicide rate in England and Wales (The Samaritans, 1997b) but there has also been a change in the way deaths are registered and therefore it is more difficult to compare present data with previous years (The Samaritans, 1997c).

Men are more likely to commit suicide and favour hanging, car hoses and guns as a method of achieving their intention, whereas women primarily choose poisoning or overdose as a way of attempting suicide. The link between suicide and the misuse of alcohol and drugs has now been established (The Samaritans, 1996a).

The underlying causes for contemplation and action are numerous and variable and in the final analysis the word fear shouts out, fear of what will be if life continues. Is there a point when a person no longer belongs to him or herself or anyone else and the black nothingness leads to annihilation? (See Chapter 3.) At this point it will be useful to consider some emotional responses to such extreme fear.

Anger and depression

Most people, without realising it, recognise anger, not by the words spoken but by the changes in the physiology of the body. The breathing becomes more rapid and shallow, muscles will tense both in the body and face, with facial colour increasing. The tone of the voice will become sharper with an increase in volume and energy. Anger is one of the many emotions we all can experience from time to time. How we express the anger will depend on the individual. For many an outburst of anger is not acceptable behaviour, yet for others rage is sitting there all the time waiting for the right trigger and once released can often be uncontrollable (see Chapters 5 and 12). For most of us it will depend on the situation, what else is happening in our lives and how closely we are involved in the given situation before we release our angry response. For some, repression of anger is the only way to cope, they simply deny anything is happening. Others will lash out with their fists (sometimes using weapons), yet others will make 'cutting remarks'. For some the response is one of shutting themselves away, running away or refusing to speak. This is the only way they manage the internal turmoil and dialogue constantly battling away in their minds. Again another response will be to constantly talk to all and anyone who will listen, going over and over the scenario with no answers to the questions or statements made.

It is suggested (Scott, 1989) that anger is one of the main causes of suicide. Suicide is often perceived as an act of aggression both to self and to those who are left behind. This anger is often expressed in the chosen method of suicide; for example the use of guns, knives or hanging. The anger may or may not have been evident before the act of suicide. Many people consciously mask their anger, not being able to explain their frustrations because they lack social and verbal skills or they are unable to be assertive and bottle up their feelings until they can explain their emotions, often at an inappropriate time. At an unconscious level beliefs about how people deal with anger may create repression. Repressed anger can lead to depression.

In Great Britain one in seven adults has a diagnosable mental health problem (The Samaritans, 1996b), the most common form being anxiety and depression. Women will often talk about emotional problems they have but men are more likely to resort to alcohol or drugs. Stress and depression are the second most common self-reported reason for missing work (The Samaritans, 1996b).

Is depression a trigger for suicide or is it something deeper? Many people suffer from bouts of feeling down which is often labelled depression, whilst others suffer from a clinical depression which has been diagnosed, and yet individuals in either group may not consider suicide as a method of dealing with their condition. Is the depression linked, as it was in Sophie's case, to a loss of self or, as in the case of the interview given later in the chapter, with the loss of a loved one? Consider some of the following situations: the individual who has experienced years of pain and can no longer tolerate the unbearable circumstances; the teenager being bullied at school resulting in low self-esteem; the woman who has endured beatings from her drunken husband for all their married life; the man who has lost his job after years of loyalty and commitment only to find he is now virtually unemployable because of his age. It would be possible to write an endless list, the content may differ but the structure remains the same because at some level the internal and immediate external world is attacked and the individuals find they can no longer tolerate the situation.

An interview

Do people just wake up and say 'today'? The following account from a counselling interview highlights the emotional journey for someone left to cope with the effects of a close member of her family committing suicide.

On Jane's birthday the phone rang. It was her parents with the news that her grandfather had committed suicide. He was found in a barn, he had hanged himself. For the first few days Jane moved as if in a trance and spent most of that time in a blur where she went about tasks in a routine regimented way. She found it easier to manage the situation by disassociating herself so she could help those around her.

As I talked to Jane she informed me she was calm and felt rather selfish because her grandfather had been her 'rock' and she no longer had him to talk to about issues important to her. Jane's body shifted when asked if she was angry, yes she was angry because he went too soon, it was illogical to her, he was healthy. Jane's grandmother had died two years previously and before her death Jane's grandfather had said he would end his life. He could not accept his wife's death, he could not understand the purpose or logic of it all. His wife had always been the decision maker and after her death he just let other people make decisions for him. Though he lived on his own he had a cook, cleaner and gardener.

Soon after his wife's death he told his family 'I can't live without her' and there is 'no point – I want to take my life'. Jane did not believe he meant it, although six months prior to his suicide he had taken tablets and apparently there had been at least three previous attempts before that time.

On the day of the suicide he had dressed in his best clothes, had breakfast and walked out to the barn and hanged himself. He was 87 years old. Jane's brother found him.

Jane's grandfather was methodical. The letters found had been written in November and the letter with Jane's name on it had been written early December. (He died over the Christmas period.) He had made some form of contact with all his family, friends and colleagues by either telephone, letters or by having lunch with them.

Jane continued to talk about the anger. She felt some anger to other members of the family who appeared materialistic and greedy. She had wanted to show her grandfather that she had made changes in her life, mistakes made in the past now belonged to the past. She was angry because he had gone too soon. She felt no anger at what he did but sat and cried for the first time since his death. She asked, 'Do people just wake up and say "today"?'

Jane had seen her grandfather and lunched with him three weeks prior to his death. She made one brief phone call to thank him for lunch and that was to be the last time she spoke to him. She was not able to say goodbye. In her grandfather's diary was a reminder of Jane's birthday and a note saying 'lunch'.

Jane only released her anger when she felt she had been given permission and even then it was in a controlled way but she did describe the feelings of shock, the numbness and disbelief in those first few days after her grand-father's death. As if by order questions of 'why', and 'if only', as well as anger, self-pity, resentment, hate and love, and forgiveness all flood into the minds of those who are left to cope with the effects of suicide, with some experiencing all of these emotions to a greater or lesser extent. Anger and guilt are normal responses and the expression of such almost needs to be encouraged.

All death will create some response from elation to devastation. For some death has released either the dead person or those alive from physical and emotional pain. The suicidal person who has experienced a long painful illness has at last peace from that battle and in some way this can prove acceptable to those left behind and to society as a whole. Is the death of a person from suicide more devastating than the sudden unexpected death from a road accident, a cot death, a murder or a heart attack? Are these deaths more likely to cause more pain than 'nursing' someone through the long illness or the impact of sudden diagnosis, short illness and death? Is the death of a child less acceptable than the death of an elderly person? Is death in war less tragic than death in a country beset with internal strife? Are natural disasters and famine not just as painful? I provide no answers, only discussion, and ask the question again is suicide any more devastating, or have we constructed a kind of macabre image for it, which feeds the horror and stigma each time it occurs?

Suicide is not acceptable to most of society and most religious sects and yet certain acts of suicide are more readily received; for instance in the case of someone who is terminally ill. In certain conditions the taking of one's own life may even be heroic, such as in times of war. In these situations there is much more of a willingness to recognise the poignancy of the situation and still grieve and experience all the emotions described. However, those left behind after a suicide often have an overwhelming need to apportion blame, making bitterness and resentment much more the focus of their grief.

For many there is a sense of responsibility and guilt; if only they had listened more, taken some form of action, for example, informed the doctor, the vicar or physically moved in with the person. Maybe, just maybe 'they' would still be alive. Were signs missed and did that last row prove to be the last straw in the last hours of 'self-harm'? Is this part of the complexity when acknowledging the devastating effects for those left behind; the sense for some individuals of somehow being a part of the suicidal person decision-making process in that final act? Many people have difficulty in accepting the concept of responsibility of self and its resulting actions and these individuals constantly look to the environment for the cause of all that is not 'right'. Generalised statements such as 'it's society's fault', 'I told the doctor' mean not only are they not responsible but neither is the person who committed suicide. Equally if there is acceptance that each of us is responsible for our actions, why then do we berate ourselves for something over which we had no control? If suicide were not perceived as a stigma, a taboo subject, would the death initiate a normal grieving process with all its pain, anger, guilt, sadness and despair without the encumbering turmoil of personal liability? There are numerous practical aspects for those left behind; post-mortem, coroner's report, registration of death and funeral arrangements. Telling others about the death can be a painful process of repeating the same story over and over, coping with the rejection of some, anger of others and overcaring of yet others, can become overwhelming. At this stage, some people present themselves for therapy.

Therapy

As a therapist I worked for several years with cancer patients facing dying and death, patients and family and friends dealing with anticipatory grief and bereavement. Both within this work and other therapy sessions I have counselled clients coping with the aftereffects of suicide. Without their permission I cannot give detailed accounts, but observable reactions to the event were the disbelief at what had happened and even more noticeable the sense of self-deprecation in the client and the questioning of why and the sense of loss for their future.

Grieving can last from months to years and there are tasks to complete, from accepting the reality of death through to the letting go and investing energy in other relationships (Worden, 1991). As an eclectic practitioner I use a whole range of tools with which to help people with their grief tasks. One client found writing a 'once upon a time story' with all individuals represented as a fairy tale character was helpful. This technique gives the writer permission to write freely without guilt. Another was allowed the freedom to become very angry with the suicidal person; when she stepped into that person's shoes all the old excuses came out, she finally realised she had no reason to feel guilty and was able to put the responsibility where it belonged, on the 'self-harmer'. This approach was based on using perceptual positions from the technique known as neuro-linguistic programming (NLP) (Knight, 1995). Perceptual positions create a more balanced picture for the client, who, until then, has only been able to perceive events from one standpoint. Clients, in first position, stand in their own shoes and can express what they see, hear and feel about the situation. In position two clients stand in the other person's shoes and when they really feel like the other person, say what they see, hear and feel. Clients then step right outside in the third position and look on, rather like a fly on the wall, observing what they see, hear and feel about themselves and the other person. I have always found this technique to be powerful and effective, creating new understanding and change.

As reported in the interview account above, Jane and I worked on her time line (O'Connor & McDermott, 1996). When using the time line, the client is asked to indicate where the past is and where the future is located by pointing in that direction, then asked to imagine a line that joins past and future together. I asked Jane, with eyes closed, to imagine she could fly above her time line and to look at the past, the now and the future. This gave Jane a chance to step outside of the situation and she realised she was trying to please too many people, spreading herself too thinly and by overcaring for others, she had forgotten to care for herself. Jane had a sense of self-empowerment.

One client, outraged at the suicide of a close family member, found it almost impossible to get on with her life because of her anger. On exploration there were issues she had not dealt with and I asked her to write a letter to the suicidal person expressing her feelings and when she was ready, to destroy it. Once accomplished she was able to continue with the grieving process in a more constructive way. NLP can also 'fine tune' a picture held in the mind of those left. This is especially effective if the individual found the body. For example, if the picture is in vivid colour it can be made black and white; fast moving can become still; jarring sounds can be turned down; a picture so large it is blocking out the rest of life can be reduced. Suddenly the client has some control back; for most, being out of control is very distressing.

Questions asked in therapy reveal that the great sorrow around any death is about the individual experiencing the variety of emotions (anger, pain, loneliness, frustration, despair, guilt) and of course there is sadness at the loss of the person (even in cases where the individual is glad or relieved at the death) but the sadness for self is greater. The implications around the death may mean loneliness, financial constraints, unfulfilled dreams, a sense of life never being 'the same' and, above all, a void. The grieving person looks out and experiences a blackness, great pain in the solar plexus. The person who has died can no longer be relied on and trusted and the one left behind wonders, how can I do it all myself? At that point there is a nothingness. This is when people experience being out of control; an anger that asks 'why' and 'how dare you do this to me'. Couple this with the distress that in some way you may have been instrumental in that person's death and this highlights the turmoil most people have to cope with. Therapy can provide no answers but it can facilitate self-empowerment which in turn can create a future.

The future

It is said that the only way to challenge the taboo around suicide is by research which examines the public's perceptions and attitudes to suicide and depression and education programmes which increase awareness of the symptoms of depression and the importance of expression of feelings (The Samaritans, 1996a).

The Department of Health (1993) has highlighted the public's need for more knowledge and a better understanding of mental illness. Fear, ignorance and stigma will have to be addressed so that individuals can seek help without fear of labelling or feelings of failure. There is also a need for a more 'comprehensive' picture of incidence and factors related to suicide, for example age, sex, ethnic group. Interventions for reduction of suicide rates are as follows:

- Improved management of depression in general practice
- More community-based services which may reduce suicide levels; there is evidence linked with lower rates when services are in general hospitals and not psychiatric hospitals
- Changes: in the availability of lethal methods of injury, for example there are proposals for banning privately owned hand guns
- Motor vehicle exhaust fumes; in the USA (1968) new standards led to a reduction in deaths from exhaust fumes. Similar controls were introduced in 1992 in the UK, all new cars have been fitted with catalytic converters from 1 January 1993
- Availability of supportive observation, a person deemed at risk of suicide would have a named person on hand for support.

This document (Department of Health, 1993) also recommends the need for more bereavement counselling, a need for more collaboration with other agencies because the NHS and Social Services cannot achieve the *Health of the Nation* targets on their own. More support is recommended for voluntary organisations, such as the Samaritans and SANE, and more training and further education of primary health care teams. The Defeat Depression Campaign is developing training packages for use in general practice.

Finally

Jung (1954: 56–7) discusses secrets; how the conscious mind knows when we are concealing things. There are times when we repress certain issues so that even the conscious mind does not know, in fact we keep the secret from ourselves. People can develop suicidal tendency but because they 'reason' with their conscious minds they do not follow the thought through, but instead generate 'an unconscious suicide complex' (Worden, 1991). This unconscious part creates dangerous situations; for example driving too fast and taking risks when overtaking; standing too close to the edge of a cliff on a very windy day. Once made aware of what is happening, usually in a therapy session, the client can consciously avoid situations that can be regarded as self-destruction. I have witnessed this phenomenon with cancer patients, where an unconscious part of them wants death.

Working at an unconscious level can produce new meaning and management of the situation. Some therapists work with metaphor because metaphor allows the unconscious mind to find its own conclusions and understanding. We use metaphor all the time in our daily lives; for example in fairy tales, parables, proverbs, single words, stories and expressions. There is no denying that facts and figures, and training and campaigns are required for changes to take place in the reduction of suicide figures but what if the unconscious mind has not been acknowledged? I offer some metaphorical thoughts below.

Anyone who has ever gone shopping for a specific item of clothing and held to memory the exact colour they require to match the suit they left at home in the wardrobe, will know that sinking feeling of mismatch when they team the new item against the suit, only to find the colours jar instead of complement, though the colours by themselves are acceptable.

Colours can give richness to our lives: they can be dramatic; calming; give feelings of coolness or warmth; colours can act as a trigger for a memory of reaction (for example if you are driving, the colour red will elicit a certain response). We even use colour to describe our mood saying 'I feel blue' or 'I'm in the pink'. How dull our lives would be if it were colourless and yet almost without thinking about it, at an unconscious level, we surround ourselves with colour. We accept the difference and our only judgement may be that we favour certain colours more than another.

Suicide has many shades, depths and meanings and our reaction to this act can be as varied in response as it is to colour. Our judgement, however, may be much harsher and this can be directed to the person self-harming, other members of the family, friends or with the self. The pain of the act of suicide will be on the why, the anger, the feelings of failure, the blame; and not on the colours, the richness and appreciation for who or what that person offered. At that moment the feelings may be jarred but acceptability allows expression of love and compassion. Children, with no preconceived ideas of acceptable colour schemes, can mix colours of any hue because they pick what they like and not what is 'right'. Adult conformity means we lose this freedom of interpretation and expression. We also forget the wonderful inner resources we have. A potholer, deep in the cave, suddenly finds himself in darkness and the blackness becomes a trigger for fear, isolation and no direction but he remembers that he has knowledge, training, batteries and above all he can trust himself.

The person contemplating suicide forgets this.

Teaching and learning focus on suicide

Rationale

The rationale is that reflecting upon a past experience will enable course participants to better understand depression and lower mood and help them to a new perspective.

Activity

Invite the group to do the following tasks alone and then to discuss their thoughts in groups of two or three:

- Think back to a time when you have felt 'down'; what colour would describe that time and what would it be like if you changed that colour for your favourite colour?
- How would it affect that memory?
- Perhaps colour is not a metaphor you can work with. What other metaphor would you choose to describe your life right now?

Learning outcomes

The learning outcomes stimulated by the activities are for the course participants to:

- Examine their own feelings of sadness
- Consider an alternative way of understanding their feelings and memories.

Chapter 8
Job Loss

Celia Di Massimo

This chapter concentrates on 'how far our self-esteem is related to our work or work role'. It therefore links with Chapter 3 on the issue of personal identity. From the stance of 'identity and work' it then reviews what life would be like without work and how our identity might be enhanced or negated. This leads us to a review of the effects of unemployment and redundancy and the mental health and general health issues which could result.

The perspectives from which this chapter is written are: professional and empirical.

Introduction: a changing world

The Industrial Age has given way to the Information Age. Job loss either through retirement, redundancy or dismissal is increasingly more common as organisations try to survive in a rapidly changing world. As Drucker suggests:

'As recently as the 1960s, almost one-half of all workers in the industrialised countries were involved in making (or helping to make) things. By the year 2000, however, no developed country will have more than one-sixth or one-eighth of its workforce in the traditional roles of making and moving goods. Already an estimated two-thirds of US employees work in the services sector, and "knowledge" is becoming our most important "product". This calls for different organisations, as well as different kinds of workers.'

(Drucker, 1996: 1)

Communication technology has radically changed the speed of passing information around the world and this, in turn, has speeded up the pace of life for everyone. As people are changing jobs and careers faster than ever before it is necessary to accept ambiguity and uncertainty in our working lives because resisting change can ruin careers and prevent re-establishment. We need to become more resilient now that jobs are no longer for life.

There is a tendency to look for someone to blame for the new conditions. We may imagine faceless people in the boardrooms of organisations around the world reducing people to statistics, hiring and firing to bolster the profits and shareholders' dividends. But in reality, many organisations are fighting for survival too. The public sector has to streamline as budgets are reduced and private sector companies have to avoid losses, hostile take-overs and bankruptcy. They all have to maximise profit and become or stay competitive in order to remain viable. The survival rate is not high. Only 32 out of the top 100 industrial companies that were listed in *The Times* in 1965 could still be found in the top 100 by 1995 (Pritchett, 1996).

In the midst of this change, those made unemployed seek to make sense of their place in the great plan and often end up blaming themselves instead of understanding that they are chess pieces in a greater game. Loss of job or career, the inability to find other employment and the turmoil caused to personal relationships can all lead to a sense of powerlessness and ineffectiveness. When this happens, self-esteem suffers and depression can take over. This can result in a person being left bewildered by the strong emotions that are engendered. They can find themselves grieving for the loss of a major part of their lives, the emotion compounded by not comprehending why it has happened. They can become frozen by the experience in a block of anger, bitterness and guilt, preventing the activity needed to secure further employment.

This chapter explores the components of the experience of job loss with a view towards effecting a more successful transition.

United Kingdom perspective

Government figures in *Social Trends 27* (Church, 1997) assure us of declining rates of redundancies:

'The general trend in redundancy rates has been downwards in the 1990s. In Spring 1996 the redundancy rate for men was more than twice that for women: 13 per thousand employees compared with 6 per thousand. The highest redundancy rates occurred among people in the craft and related occupations and plant and machine operatives where 14 employees in every thousand were made redundant. Both these occupations have had high redundancy rates throughout the 1990s. People in the construction industry are more likely to have been affected by redundancy than those in any other industry group, with a rate of 26 per thousand employees in Spring 1996. On the other hand employees in public administration, health and education experienced a redundancy rate of only 3 per thousand employees and were the least likely to have been made redundant.'

(Church, 1997: 87)

However, those affected will not be comforted by the figures and may still be inclined to blame government policies for the prevailing conditions. But economic factors, such as inflation, technological changes, the inability of educational institutes to respond to changing requirements, and world economics, all play a major part. Closer to home are the social engineering factors of living in depressed areas and being caught in the home ownership and negative equity trap which prevent the mobility needed to move in search of further work.

Unemployment affects all of society. The seasonally adjusted figures for March 1995 showed that 2.256 million were unemployed in the UK, 8.3% of the total estimated workforce (Central Statistical Office, 1995/96). Sinfield, in Haralambos & Holborn (1991), argues that unemployment devalues or debases the standard or quality of life in society in the following ways:

(1) Those remaining in work feel less secure and may have their standard of living threatened. This is partly because of short-time working and reductions in the amount of overtime, and partly due to the reduced bargaining power of workers which leads to downward pressure on wages.
(2) The workforce becomes less willing to leave an unsatisfactory job because of the fear that they will be unable to find new employment. It becomes less mobile and the number of frustrated and alienated workers increases.
(3) Divisions within society are likely to grow. The unemployed and those in unsatisfactory work may blame weak groups in their society for their problems. Male workers accustomed to full-time work, for example, may attribute their unemployment to married women entering the labour market. Immigrants and ethnic minorities may be used as scapegoats with the result that racial tensions increase.
(4) High unemployment reduces the chance of equality of opportunity being achieved. With a surplus of labour, employers need no longer make an effort to recruit women, ethnic minorities, the young, the old, the disabled and handicapped, or former inmates of prisons or mental hospitals.

So called 'full employment', on the other hand, can lead to 'marginal' labour, i.e. those who are barely suitable for the job being recruited, leading to higher costs, inefficiency, inflation and 'don't care' attitudes as evidenced in the business cycle statistics from the 1970s and 1980s. There are no easy answers.

Attitudes to work are changing. Being made redundant or taking early retirement no longer carries the same stigma that it did ten years ago. Increasingly, people are looking forward to their working life ending in their mid-fifties and not perceiving it as personal failure. Some younger people consider their careers to be more mobile. They do not think that they will be in the same job for life but consider it in terms of the next two to five years. Work contracts are increasingly drawn up for much shorter periods in both the private and the public sector. More and more people opt to become consultants or self-employed, no longer depending on the salary and pension systems of organisations; becoming financially responsible for their own pensions. Arguably, long-term employment is now at risk because organisations have found that the costs of providing pensions and employee support are now prohibitive in a competitive market when the watchwords are 'lean and mean'.

The individual's perspective – 'A view from the bridge'

Apart from the financial aspects, employment provides other social functions that, when lost, increase the feeling of deprivation. Work provides according to Archer & Rhodes (1987: 211):

(1) The imposition of a time structure
(2) Regularly shared experiences and contacts with people outside the home
(3) Linking a person to goals and purposes which transcend those of his or her own
(4) Defining aspects of personal status and identity and enforcing regular activity.

Work is a social activity. Karl Marx believed that a person who is unable to express their true nature through work becomes estranged from self and others. Durkheim, in *The Division of Labour in Society* first published in 1893, identified that division of labour and rapid expansion of the industrial society contained threats to social solidarity creating a state of 'anomie' or 'normlessness' (Haralambos & Holborn, 1991). Anomie is present when social controls weaken and the moral obligations that have controlled behaviour in the past no longer function properly, indicating a normative breakdown characterised by rapid social change. Parallels can be drawn with the present time and the increasing rate of suicide, marital disharmony and industrial conflict which Durkheim identified in the nineteenth century. In his opinion, belonging to an organised workforce was the strongest protection against suicide.

Models of change and job loss

Not all find the loss of a job negative. Stressful events can spur some to reassess their lives, retrain or develop new directions and turn the negative into a positive force (Schlossberg, 1981; Sheehy, 1981 cited in Latack & Dozier, 1986). However, avoiding long-term unemployment can help to prevent the downward spiral leading to loss of motivation and depression which, in turn, inhibit the goal-setting tasks that can promote the psychological growth necessary for a successful transition.

The element of control often affects the outcome of the experience (Rotter 1966; Abel & Hayslip, 1986). There are many studies highlighting that when individuals perceive that they have little or no control over events, they suffer greater psychological and physical distress (Pearlin *et al.*, 1981; Suls & McMullen, 1981; Latack, 1984).

In circumstances of compulsory redundancy it is not difficult to imagine the assault to personal dignity and status. Or the feelings of guilt, shame and anger that can accompany the experience, contributing to increased stress, loss of self-esteem and even, possibly, illness.

A job or career is more than a weekly wage or salary. It can define a person's existence in providing status and a purpose to life. It can furnish social support, friends, colleagues, team work, etc. If the job is taken away, the loss can be just as acute as being bereaved. Marris describes the typical signs of grief at bereavement as:

'... physical distress and worse health; an inability to surrender the past – expressed, for instance, by brooding over memories, sensing the presence of the dead, clinging to possessions, being unable to comprehend the loss, feelings of unreality; withdrawal into apathy; and hostility against others; against fate; or turned in upon oneself.'

(Marris, 1986: 26)

All these emotions can be experienced by those who have been made redundant, especially if 'sensing of the presence of the dead' can be interpreted as a fixation on the past career.

'Unemployment is a form of crippling that can be expected to have the same psychological effect as other forms of loss.'

(Parkes, 1971; cited in Archer & Rhodes, 1993: 396)

Although the models of Kubler-Ross (1969) and Bowlby & Parkes (1970) 'phases of grief' have been questioned on the grounds that not everyone goes through the stages in this way, they do, nevertheless, help us to understand the process of dying and grief (see Chapter 1). These can also be applied, as a loose framework, to the loss of a job. Eisenberg & Lazerfeld (1938) proposed a model of bereavement that was applicable in situations of unemployment – shock; optimism and active job seeking; pessimism and active distress; and fatalism and adaptation to the unemployment role. In the research it was shown that at 3 months after redundancy, mental health was at its lowest but reached a plateau at between 9 and 12 months after the event (Owen & Watson, 1995). Comparisons can be made with this and Parkes' model of four stages of grief which appear appropriate to the loss of a job and which is described in Chapter 1.

Research identifies that the grief and anger generated during the job loss transition must be resolved before positive growth can be achieved and individuals can 'let go' and move on successfully (Adams *et al.*, 1976; Stybel, 1981 cited in Latack & Dozier, 1986; Archer & Rhodes, 1987). This may differ from the bereavement experience. There is much discussion on whether a bereaved person ever actually 'lets go' of the deceased (Archer & Rhodes, 1993; Walter, 1996a), and many would argue that some never do and neither do they wish to (see Chapter 9). Neither do people necessarily go through all stages in a linear progression but may find themselves swinging between stages, returning to former phases or finding that they are 'stuck', in the depression phase for example (Kubler-Ross, 1969; Adams *et al.*, 1976; Weiss, 1976 cited in Latack & Dozier, 1986; Jones, 1979; Schlossberg, 1981; Stybel, 1981).

Stybel (1981 cited in Latack & Dozier, 1986: 384) observed

'Managers who actively job hunt before resolving the anger stage often take jobs exactly like the one they lost in an attempt to "show those SOBs" they made a mistake'.

This may not be in their best interests and could be destructive, culminating in a failed opportunity to investigate a more worthwhile career path. Training prior to the event highlighting the transitional phases could make this less likely to happen.

Additionally, Archer & Rhodes (1993) identified four aspects that are likely to have direct and indirect psychological effects on a person suffering job loss and may evoke a reaction similar to the grief process that follows bereavement:

(1) Lack of money, accentuated by living in a consumer society
(2) The restricted social network of the unemployed compared with employed people
(3) The social representation of being unemployed, both as they affect the person's self-esteem and how others react to them
(4) The impact of losing a central aspect of their personal world, which often forms an important part of self-definition.

Many are able to identify themselves in the stages mentioned in this review of models but there are things that can be done to lessen the impact and shorten the time needed to adjust.

Factors affecting the transition

Heron (1961) recommended that on approaching retirement, the use of a framework (here paraphrased) can help to bring into focus the areas that need to be considered:

- Health
- Finance
- People
- Environment
- Activities
- Philosophy.

However, this structure can be adapted to any job-loss situation even if the order is changed and it is used here to focus attention on the factors that can influence the transition.

Health

Good health helps the coping process. Health is often negatively affected by job loss but there is a problem of linking unemployment and health directly which Smith, after analysing many studies from the UK and the USA summarises thus:

'I concluded that we could not be certain, although we could be fairly confident, that unemployment caused extra and premature deaths. Similarly, we cannot be certain that unemployment causes extra physical illness, although the best evidence suggests it does. As a group, the unemployed are, however, more unhealthy than the employed and clearly the unhealthy have a higher chance of becoming and staying unemployed.'

(Smith, 1987: 124)

However, the experience of redundancy and long-term unemployment can be associated with the same emotional responses that occur in bereavement and loss. Physiological theory and research have shown that bereavement and loss do lead to an increased risk of mortality and morbidity. Kim & Jacobs (1993), and the empirical research of Irwin & Pike (1993), show there is a relationship between bereavement, the depression that can follow and changes in the immune system that can lead to ill health. Moreover, the more attached a person has been to their employment, the more severe the course of grief experienced at the transition is likely to be (Miles, 1983; Warr, 1983). This parallels the findings from the grief literature that grief is more pronounced for a closer relationship (Archer & Rhodes, 1993). It is not difficult to see how those who consider work to have been their 'whole life' will feel the loss more than someone who has a range of hobbies, interests and supportive relationships to fall back on (Coleman *et al.*, 1993).

Many studies have confirmed the association between suicide or attempted suicide and unemployment. For instance Hawton & Rose (1986):

'... one study found that in each year since 1977 the unemployment rate in Great Britain had been positively and significantly correlated with the total suicide rate (Kreitman & Platt, 1984). A study in Edinburgh during 1968–82 found that the unemployed had a much greater risk of attempted suicide than employed men – of the order of 11:1. The risk ratio increased sharply with the length of the spell of unemployment... Similarly, a study in Oxford found that the attempted suicide rates for unemployed men were twelve to fifteen times higher than those for employed men, and again were particularly high for the long-term unemployed.'

(Hawton & Rose, 1986; cited in Townsend & Davidson, 1988: 239)

Many argue, however, that the positive correlation is influenced by external variables (financial or marital worries, home being repossessed, etc.) and is not due to unemployment alone (Platt, 1984 cited in Owen & Watson, 1995: 64). The greatest relative increases in suicide rates were found to occur in areas of low unemployment (Owen & Watson, 1995) due perhaps to the increased stigma attached to the event. There is also a greater vulnerability to suicide among unemployed men, to the extent of needing preventive hospital treatment (Crombie, 1989; Renvoize & Clyden, 1989). The figures only apply to men; women do not show up in the unemployment and suicide figures to the same extent.

Platt *et al.* (1992) found a negative relationship between unemployment and suicide in women and even went as far as to suggest that for women unemployment works as a protective mechanism against suicide (Owen & Watson, 1995: 67–8). Although women may be less prone to suicide they still experience a sense of grief at being unemployed.

Analysing grief as an emotional reaction can help one understand the symptoms people experience after loss and the effects that this can have on physical and mental health. There are similarities in the research done by Selye (1956) in which he identified personal stressors and the effect that failure to adapt and loss of homeostasis could have on health; Holmes & Rahe's (1967) social readjustment scale and the accumulation of points awarded to different stresses which could lead to a deterioration in health; and, Seligman's theory of learned helplessness (Hall & Lindzey, 1985), that point to the depression that can develop from the emotional disruption that is experienced when a person has no control over unpleasant events. All show that stress and emotional disease are closely linked with ill health. However, associating unemployment with health can be problematic if the grief experienced at the loss is seen as a disease that should be treated medically.

Those drawn into the medical model of health, may look to medicine to 'cure' the pain of the experience but this could eliminate the coherence and meaning that can follow the conventional grief process (Averill & Nunley, 1993). The grief process is a period of adaptation which is dependent on personal autonomy. Medical intervention is a counter to autonomy and should be kept to the minimum (Illich, 1977). This does not deny that there are some who will need medical help from time to time but when medical support is withdrawn, the individual will still have to come to terms with the loss. Activities that help people to prepare themselves for an event, on the other hand, can lead to experience and growth.

Keeping oneself as fit as possible during the transition is a positive aid. Exercise can be seen to affect all levels of psychosocial health.

'A positive association has been found between exercise and a decreased level of mild to moderate depression, and it may also be useful as an adjunct to professional treatment of severe depression. Regular, particularly rhythmic, exercise has been found to reduce anxiety, with the greatest reductions seen in people who were both unfit and highly anxious.'

(Whitehead, 1995: 11)

Making sure that enough exercise is taken will help manage the harmful effects of increased stress levels. So will adequate relaxation, either formally through relaxation techniques or informally through activities and hobbies that will absorb and enable people to 'switch off' from the stressful experience.

Finance

Townsend, in Haralambos & Holborn, defines poverty as:

'Individuals, families and groups in the population can be said to be in poverty when they lack the resources to obtain the types of diets, participate in the activities and have the living conditions and amenities that are customary, or at least widely encouraged or approved, in the societies to which they belong. Their resources are so seriously below those commanded by the average individual or family that they are, in effect, excluded from ordinary living patterns, customs and activities.'

(Townsend, 1970; cited in Haralambos & Holborn, 1991: 200)

Those living on a reduced income after being made redundant; the retired person with no or a small occupational pension; or the widowed or divorced, dependent on the basic State Pension would fit within the above parameters of poverty. The British Government is currently trying to persuade people to take care of their own pensions in the future because of the demographic changes taking place. People are living longer and there are less young people in the workplace; who then is going to support the increasing pensions bill?

It is true that supplementary benefits can be claimed but with each passing year benefits are being cut. To the unemployed, the erosion of these benefits is even more severe. Previously, the unemployed were able to claim benefit for up to one year before being means tested for income support paid at a lower rate. But now the Unemployment Benefit has been replaced by the Jobseeker's Allowance which is only payable for six months and then only under strict conditions.

Coyle (1984) comments that women who lose their jobs additionally suffer because they are not even properly recorded in unemployment statistics. It is assumed that they are absorbed back 'into the family'. Women are more likely to be called 'economically inactive' in official counts rather than unemployed (Martin & Roberts, 1984). Financially, older women are among the most disadvantaged in society because even though they have worked, state policy still insists in treating them as dependents of male workers (Arber & Ginn, 1991). The scale of benefits relative to wages is also falling and those who have to rely for their income from state benefits are amongst the largest groups of the poor.

Poverty can isolate, increasing the trauma of unemployment. The grief felt at the loss of a previous way of life is intensified. This can and does affect individuals and the whole family unit so organising finances to the best advantage is imperative and may help relieve some of the anxiety. It can be worth while to talk to the Citizens Advice Bureaux who help people with debts to organise a reduced schedule of payments whilst out of work. They are used to assisting people who have lost their jobs for whatever reason and will help an individual to consider the implications of living on a reduced budget whilst looking for another job, as well as how to safeguard existing insurance, mortgage, and ongoing payments, etc.

For those who have been given a lump sum payment when taking early retirement or a redundancy payment, it is important to make sure that the money is put to work to provide income and growth for the future, and to protect against inflation as much as possible. An independent financial advisor can be useful in this situation although it makes sense to see more than one to compare the advice given. Budgeting should be the first step, to make sure that basic living costs are covered before locking money away in investment vehicles.

People

The tensions and conflicts that arise within the family at times of job loss are often forgotten. Support of partners is frequently assumed but, on the contrary, job loss can split families apart. Several research studies have shown that an influencing factor is how adaptable people are in their family roles. It has been shown that the more inflexible they are, the more likely it is that the family will disintegrate at the transition, especially if there are financial problems as well (Cavan & Ranck 1938; Marsh 1938; Bakke, 1940; Angell, 1965; Leventman, 1981 cited in Latack & Dozier 1986).

Grief is felt by all the family when a member is made redundant. Previous relationships are reassessed and perspectives can and do change. The effects of the emotions experienced can be very difficult to handle and can influence the whole communication process between partners. Women have told me that they felt more bitter and angry about the situation than their partner appeared to be:

'He just became silent and refused to discuss anything, he kept telling me "just leave it alone", but I wanted to hit out at them. I couldn't believe he was taking it lying down like this. He had given them nearly 30 years of his life, he loved that place, and after all that loyalty, that was the way they treated him. I was all for taking them to court.'

Whilst understandable, this reaction is unlikely to help the situation or assist her partner in helping him come to terms with the situation. Partners and family have to work through the transition for themselves and at their own pace. Their experiences will not necessarily overlap, and this just adds to the stress.

Family support can be an important factor in whether an individual succeeds in getting another job (McLellan, 1985). It is not unknown for a person made redundant to continue to leave home each day as if going to work rather than tell the family. Where family support is missing the availability of social support via colleagues and outplacement organisations become even more necessary.

Environment

Work environmental factors can influence the transition. The Institute of Personnel and Development recommend that the negative effects can be reduced by sensitive handling but the reality is often very different.

It is interesting to note the terminology used to explain the phenomenon of job loss by both sides: 'downsizing', 'right-sizing', 'rationalising', 'restructuring', 'outplacement' and 'outsourcing', are all euphemisms that mean a person's job is being taken away from them. Compare these somewhat sterile metaphors to the more direct language used by those affected by the process: 'sacked', 'fired', 'chopped', 'legs cut off', 'shafted', 'walking the plank', getting the axe', 'on the scrap-heap', etc., and you become aware of the severity of the psychological trauma experienced. Listening to people's images and words can be a harrowing indication of their hurt. Stein (1996) in a paper exploring *Death Imagery and the Experience of Organizational Downsizing* goes as far as subtitling his paper *Or Is Your Name on Schindler's List?* To support this view he quotes a meeting with a member of a planning committee in a hospital downsizing who described it this way:

> 'I'm planning a funeral for somebody who's going to die but doesn't know they're going to die ... I as a manager feel it's like World War II. The Nazis have come in and tell us "Point out all the Jewish people so we can get rid of them. Then tell us the Gypsies, then the Poles ..." That's what it feels like. ....'

(Stein, 1996: 10)

This graphically demonstrates that the anxiety, guilt and pain is not only felt by those losing their jobs but is experienced by those who have to give the unpleasant news. The message often appears communicated in a manner that seems designed to dehumanise but can arise because the bearer of the tidings is embarrassed or does not know how to cope with the situation themselves. They may also be experiencing the fear of wondering when their own 'number will be up'. Organisations need to consider not only those leaving the organisation but also the effect this can have on those remaining.

Research has shown that the stress of the situation can be moderated providing that the information is transmitted by an immediate superior who is willing to provide explanations and reasons for the termination decision. Preferably the news should not come as a surprise but should have been flagged up as a possibility much earlier so that people can get used to the idea. It may even be discussed in relation to work performance feedback at an earlier assessment interview.

> 'If the explanation includes accurate performance feedback, it may lead to either a better person-job match in the next position or to development of new competencies through training. Finally, if the decision is handled professionally by the immediate superior, there may be less anger to resolve before redirecting one's efforts toward career growth.'
>
> (Latack & Dozier, 1986: 384)

The Institute of Personnel and Development (1997) recommends that managers need to be trained to handle redundancies with sympathy and clarity. Common faults are that the news is given too abruptly or the information can be too vague. 'Notice of redundancy' and 'consultation' should be handled in two separate stages with discussion about alternative work and practical support given at the consultation phase.

Apart from the psychological benefits of communicating the news in advance, it gives those affected time to start looking for new positions whilst still employed when it is easier to get another job. Latack & Dozier (1986) make the recommendation that an office be set aside for those identified as leaving, where they can search for another job whilst still on the pay-roll. They can then take advantage of the office facilities and, hopefully, have access to outplacement agencies, courses, and the support of their colleagues in the same position. This may help compensate for the loss of self-esteem and stigma that could affect the positive view necessary for the job-search phase.

Activities

Hepworth (1980) proposed that another important factor in reducing the stress of the transition was the activity levels of the victims. Those who occupied their time productively in job search and other activities experienced the least stress. Other studies reviewed in Latack & Dozier (1986) confirm the importance of productive activity and proactive job search. Setting up a strategy at this time can help by giving structure and purpose to the day. A plan helps to make sure that the individual is constantly updating and following up procedures. Lethargy can be a by-product of having 'all the time in the world'. Thought must be given to establishing a routine that works for the person involved. All coping strategies are based on choices of what is right for the individual, but planning is the first stage.

Although not many would choose to lose their jobs in the first place, it does offer an opportunity to re-evaluate who you are, your needs and wants as well as your dreams and hopes. It is worth refocusing at this time and redefining your value system. By doing this, an individual is more likely to choose a career path based on self-knowledge and a belief in one's self, or even decide whether another route completely should be chosen. This may include opting not to work at all, or becoming self-employed, or retraining and developing other latent skills.

Handy (1990), the management consultant, suggests that it is worth considering building 'portfolio' careers – bits and pieces of different types of work that combine as in a portfolio instead of a single job. All this can lead to a more flexible, rewarding life where the individual can be more in control of his/her destiny. It is a way of incorporating many different interests and hobbies. This can apply to those who choose to take full retirement who also need a full range of interests to ensure fulfilment after full-time work has finished.

Two strategies are proposed by Pearlin & Schooler (1978) which may help the individual to become more proactive at the transition stage. These are:

• Problem-focused coping
• Symptom-focused coping.

Empirical evidence was found by Leana & Feldman (1990) that problem-focused strategies, i.e. self-initiated job search activities, relocation, retraining, etc., were more likely to lead to re-employment than depending on symptom-focused strategies, i.e. asking relatives and friends for support, joining community groups, borrowing finances, etc., although people may use a combination of the two methods.

Bennet *et al.* (1995) conducted a longitudinal study of people involved in a layoff in the USA testing Pearlin and Schooler's theory amongst others. The study found that of the two methods, problem-focused coping was more effective for both the men and the women involved but it also found, surprisingly, that contrary to common belief, the perceived 'fairness' of the organisation during the layoff did not encourage problem-based coping.

> '... the findings of the current study suggest that being fair to victims may also be harmful to them. Specifically, by being fair the organization may reduce victims' willingness to seek speedy re-employment. Perhaps as stated by a respondent in an earlier investigation, "the unfairness of the situation" forces layoff victims to "take the initiative" and turn the job loss into an opportunity ...'
>
> (Bennet *et al.*, 1995: 1037–8)

In this instance, perceived unfairness acted as a spur. It was also found in this study that when the intensity of the emotions declined, there was greater problem-focused coping by victims, supporting the view that the sooner the anger is worked through, the quicker will be the recovery (Pearlin & Schooler, 1978; Leana & Feldman, 1992). There are similarities in this problem-coping approach to the force field analysis technique developed by Kurt Lewin (Spier, 1973). This technique helps an individual analyse the major obstacles that are working against them in any situation and looks at ways of reducing these whilst also identifying the resources available and how these can be increased.

Assertion skills can help build self-esteem and the confidence necessary to take a positive view in which 'selling yourself' to future employers will be a major factor. Role-play techniques can give a chance to practise interview techniques in a safe environment as many will not have experienced an interview in many years. Feedback on performance either verbally or through CCTV can be useful in refining techniques and body language when under pressure.

Counselling can help, especially if people find that they are stranded at any particular stage and cannot see their way forward alone. Counselling can help a person move from the present to the preferred scenario by implementing a plan (Egan, 1984). This counselling may be informal; talking things through with friends, colleagues or relations. Or, formal through the professional help of counsellors, social workers, ministers, psychologists, psychiatrists, and doctors. Or, through agencies specialising in job loss, redeployment and outplacement.

Philosophy

For some, losing their job has been the spur to realising their full potential. They may have been unhappy in their past occupation for some time but felt that they had to remain at their post because of their personal commitments. When the decision has been taken out of their own hands, it has given them the impetus to try out that new idea for a business or a new direction, etc.

All transitions offer the opportunity for growth and development even though it is not perhaps appreciated at the time. Attitude and past experience can affect the mind-set necessary to see the transition as a challenge and not a crisis. It can affect a person's perception of whether they have any control over the event.

An understanding of the transitional experience is extremely important to final outcomes. Adams *et al*. (1976) suggest that consideration of the following points can encourage those affected to see the challenge of change:

- Know your new situation
- Know people that can help
- Learn from the past
- Look after yourself
- Let go of the past
- Set goals and make action plans
- Look for the gains you have made.

Planning affects the adjustment time necessary to work through the experience. In a recent survey undertaken by the author of people who had retired, taken early retirement or been made redundant it was found that planning was an important component in helping people cope with the transition. The data revealed that 61% of the 805 people who had replied to the survey had planned towards retirement and 55.15% had adjusted to the new way of life within 3 months.

For many, redundancy and early retirement may have given them little time to plan. Thirty four people in the study who were made redundant reported that they had not planned towards retirement with only six of this group saying that they were able to adjust within the first 3 months. Interestingly, there did not appear any difference in gender. For most who were made redundant, it took longer, with ten saying that it had taken them over 18 months to 2 years and two admitted that they had been unable to adjust.

Of the 45 people who took early retirement who also had not planned, a higher proportion had adjusted in under 6 months, the fact that they had had a choice in the matter might explain the easier adjustment reflecting Rotter's locus of control theory (1966). However, 14 took up to 18 months and five took up to 2 years. Four had been unable to adjust at all.

From these figures it can be seen that planning was an influencing factor with 419 (52.14%) of people who had planned showing positive feelings about retirement. Of the people who had not planned, only 11.10% had positive feelings (Di Massimo, 1997). Therefore it is indicated that advance planning can help the transition supporting Parkes (1971) and Adams *et al.* (1976).

The other influencing factor is learning. Erikson (1963, cited in Hall & Lindzey, 1985: 75) identified that 'creativity comes from an individual constantly adapting to the world around them'. An individual can adapt and learn from transitions by combining inner strengths with social and cultural factors (Hall & Lindzey, 1985).

Kelly (1955) saw everyone as scientists, constantly forming hypotheses and testing them out and believed that a person's behaviour and personality is determined by how they perceive and understand the world. He maintained that anxiety arises when personal construct systems are inadequate to cope with the events that are presented. But learning helps people to cope and change.

'Learning is not a special class of psychological processes; it is synonymous with any and all psychological processes.'

(Kelly, 1955: 46)

Conclusion

Ideally, planning and learning should take place before the event. Understanding models of change in loss, bereavement and transition can help people to prepare in advance. It can help them anticipate the future and build on strengths gained from past transitions. New frameworks and constructs can be built, based on the changed view of the world and a person's place in it. But education should start from an early age and in a preventive framework.

Training begins in the home in childhood. Giving our children the language to express their emotions and to encourage them to talk about their losses, their anger, frustrations and fears will help them cope with future loss. Education starts in schools by helping to build self-esteem, confidence, problem-solving and assertion skills. Loss as a concept should be explored and related to all life stages and seen as a necessary part of transition and development.

Existing courses in the workplace, stress management, life skills and pre-retirement should be expanded to encompass a wider understanding of bereavement, loss, change and transitions.

Courses in the workplace should be encouraged, specifically on coping with change, incorporating the effects of bereavement and loss, and promoted as a way to help staff adapt. There are gains for organisations in this strategy. An understanding of the models of change encourages a more flexible attitude and would help employees to accept change more readily, and help protect them from the emotional fragmentation that can occur.

Teaching and learning focus on job loss

Rationale

As identified in the chapter, the inability to let go of the anger, bitterness and self reproach that can accompany the job loss experience can prevent or slow down the adaptation process. Failure to come to terms with the situation can impede future progress and effective job search. Thoroughly recommended for anyone who is contemplating future career development is *Build Your Own Rainbow: A Workbook for Career and Life Management* by Hopson & Scally (1984). This book takes the individual through the transition in an analytical and constructive way. It is designed to help people understand themselves and their motivation and to come out with personal and career objectives with action plans.

Activity

Thinking about your current life situation, write down the ways in which you may have become trapped in a lifestyle, unable to contemplate changes because of assumptions made of what you *must have* before life is worthwhile and how you may be holding onto a way of life that is not in your best interests. Ask yourself:

- What am I currently valuing in life?
- What could I gain if I let go?

- Are there other things to value?
- Are there other places where I can find what I value?
- What is holding on to what I value costing me?

Learning outcomes

The learning outcomes stimulated by the activities are for the course participants to:

- become more aware of attachments, particularly those associated with work, that may be impeding their own personal growth;
- understand the origin of those feelings that emerge when people have important work attachments suddenly and unexpectedly severed through redundancy.

Chapter 9
Portrait of Family Grief

Pamela Elder

This chapter tells the story of Kate Elder's death and explains, personally, the grief process of her mother, Pamela, her Father, Tom and her sisters, Nancy, Helen and Alex. Alex shares her poems, which she wrote throughout the period following Kate's death, with us. It is autobiographical and raises many issues about our expectations of the police, the medical profession and the support/caring agencies. It illuminates the needs of each family member and the many problems and difficulties they face. The account also shares with us the way the family ensured that they had the funeral they wanted for Kate and themselves and how they have integrated her into their lives now.

The perspective from which this chapter is written is: autobiographical.

Kate's mother, Pamela

This is an account of the death of a child, as experienced by me and my family. Each member of the family has told their story as they know it. It is intended to be a story of hope and understanding. 'We cannot prevent the birds of sorrow from landing on our shoulders', begins a Chinese proverb, 'we can prevent them from nesting in our hair'. My daughter Kate is not here any more but one can still be grateful for what is here. Despite her death the skylark will still be singing.

The essential component of our internal computer, the inseparable link between the brain and the spinal cord is how Jean Dominique Bauby (1997) describes the brain stem in his moving account of how a massive stroke took his brain stem out of action. Our daughter Kate's brain stem death was caused by a fall when she stepped off an open platform London bus as it was moving quickly away from her stop. The conductor refused to signal the driver to stop the bus. Left lying in the road, she was then hit by one or more cars, none of which stopped.

The telephone woke us at 1:45 AM. My husband, Tom, answered it.

'Are you Dr Elder, the father of Katherine Elder?'
'Yes.'

The caller, having mistakenly assumed that Tom's doctorate was in medicine (it is, in fact, geological), explained that Kate had been admitted to the Royal Free Hospital following an accident and launched into a complex medical description of her condition.

Little of what Tom was told made any sense. We were only able to establish the fact that Kate was in a serious condition in hospital and we needed to get there as quickly as possible. We arrived at the Royal Free in Hampstead around 4 AM and immediately met the man, a minicab driver, who had found her. He kept apologising for not getting to her sooner.

'I thought it was just a black bin liner in the middle of the road, until I saw blonde hair.'

Kate had been dressed all in black that evening. We were taken to the intensive care unit, but were not allowed to see her. Meanwhile, two police officers came to talk to us to ask if we could identify her things. I was overwhelmed by the need to have physical contact with my child. I didn't want to see her things – just her.

Eventually we were allowed to go to her – lying in a hospital bed attached to a life support machine. She looked pale, almost translucent, but her face was not marked in any way. Gentle tears of blood occasionally rolled down her cheeks. I sat beside her and willed her to live. I watched the blood pressure monitor rise and fall and felt hope. I could nurse her back to health. I would give up everything to look after her. I wiped the tears from her face, as did Tom. We were then taken to meet the consultant. I suppose it is difficult to combine scientific expertise with compassion but the clinical manner and detailed medical terms left me floundering. I only understood five years later about brain stem death and what it meant. I did understand that different consultants would come to examine Kate again, but that there was little hope.

Kate's tutors from her college, Queen Mary and Westfield, London University, were tremendously supportive and arranged for us to rest at the college. We returned to the hospital and waited. The second series of tests was negative. As we walked towards the intensive care ward, Tom vividly remembers how the nurses were removing Kate's charts from the wall outside her room. It was as if Kate had already become a number, a statistic. And yet I continued to believe that I could challenge what I had been told and a miracle would happen and I'd be able to take her home with me.

We were told that we could stay with her as long as we wanted. The nurse then gave me a lock of her shining blonde hair. She looked just the same as when she was first born – eyes closed, full cheeks, peaceful. We had nearly lost her then due to a very long and difficult labour. She came through that trauma, but not this one.

Sudden, unexpected death leaves so much unfinished business. I tried to tell her all the things I wish I'd told her when she was alive. We still wiped her tears, tenderly but fearful, and watched the machines. Eventually we knew we had to leave her. I still feel as if it was the ultimate betrayal – to leave my lovely daughter in the hands of strangers, knowing that her life support machine would now be turned off.

Kate's heart, lungs, kidneys and both corneas were given for transplant operations. As a family, we believe in this and indeed Kate had been impressed by the fact that her father carried a donor card. However, the meeting with the person who came to discuss organ donation with us was blunt, mechanical, and unfeeling. No help or information was offered at any time. Indeed it was only a year later when, at my insistence and through the intervention of a friend, we found out anything about the subsequent operations. Despite what one reads or hears, the decision to allow the organs of your child to be used for transplants does not necessarily bring any comfort, nor does it help in assuaging grief. 'If all her organs are perfect, why isn't she alive?' was the thought constantly going round my head at the time.

We finally got home later that day. We sat in the hall together, with Kate's triplet sisters and my parents, and told them Kate had died.

The next trial, and indeed it felt like one, was the visit to the police in London. They wanted to talk to us about the accident. It felt like an interrogation and when they asked if there was any reason to suppose Kate might have been trying to commit suicide, I didn't know whether to leave the room or scream. In the end I babbled that Kate had passed her first-year exams, had a new boyfriend and was in love. Tom quietly saved the situation and calmly answered the question. Why was there no warning beforehand of the line of questioning that takes place in cases of sudden death? To infer suicide without warning is surely unnecessary to bereaved parents. We needed a clear, if brief, explanation of the accident as far as they could ascertain at the time. We needed to be informed about what action, if any, they intended to take and the subsequent results of their enquiries. We left the station deeply disturbed and angry at the total lack of sensitivity.

We were determined to make Kate's funeral our service for our child. This meant taking our hi-fi system into our local church. Tom then spent hours recording the music we wanted for her. The Reverend Tony Hogg, who had taken Kate on a school trip to Egypt, agreed to take the service. It included readings in Spanish of Lorca poems, music by Dire Straits and Jacqueline Du Pre's playing of the Elgar Cello Concerto. I read the wonderful passage on death by Canon Scott Holland (1910).

Everyone tried to persuade me not to do this but I knew, instinctively, as a mother, that I had to do it for my daughter. I did not break down. It was as if I was talking to her hoping that somehow she was listening. 'Play, smile, think of me, pray for me. Let my name be ever the household word it always was.'

The church was packed. Old friends from Spain and Portugal came, as well as many of Kate's friends. Together we acknowledged what Kate's life had meant and still means to us. It was a lovely June day, bright and sunny like Kate. I remember thinking as I moved around in the gathering afterwards that an outsider might have thought they were witnessing an ordinary garden party. People were chatting animatedly and there was even some laughter.

The inquest came much later. We had no idea what to expect. I remember very little about it. I closed my mind to the details of her injuries, partly because I didn't want to know and partly because I could understand little of what was being said. The bus conductor and his solicitor were present. He didn't look at us at all. His solicitor seemed to be guarding him, almost as if they thought we would attack him. I found it deeply unnerving. The bus conductor was later fined £100.

Words are not adequate to describe the devastation I felt at the loss of my daughter. You do not expect your child to die before you do. It is a complete reversal of the natural order of things. It was the sudden, unexpected waste, of a young and vibrant girl that was so terrible. Her life had only just begun. And yet death is an inherent feature of the human condition that requires people to develop the means of coping with it. As a family, we did not talk much about Kate's death. Rather, we each found our own cocoon in which to exist, knowing there was love and support from each other when needed. I kept thinking of the trivial decision I made that totally altered my life; that of asking Kate to stay on in London so my parents could have her bedroom. I thought of how we teach our children many things; the importance of saying please and thank you, how to cross the road. We do not teach them how to step off a bus.

The press were keen for us to campaign against hit-and-run drivers. The police were keen for us to take out a civil action against the bus driver. I didn't want to do either. For some people, all the grieving energy locked up after a major bereavement is turned into very effective public campaigns. Diana Lamplugh, whose daughter Suzy disappeared one day never to return, has established The Suzy Lamplugh Trust – The National Charity for Personal Safety. She has worked tirelessly to raise public awareness of personal safety, violence and aggression in the workplace and awareness of the victims, for whom the Trust is setting up 'Victims Voice'. After the death of their son, Tim, Colin and Wendy Parry campaigned for peace in Ireland, there was the 'Snowdrop' petition to ban handguns after Dunblane, and Frances Lawrences's moral crusade after the murder of her husband. This demonstrates how grief can provide a catalyst for action, thereby giving back a sense of purpose, and a feeling of control to those involved. Such a course of action was not right for me. I threw my energy into work – smothering the pain in frenetic activity. It seemed to me at the time a good defiant way to 'rage against the dying of the light' (Dylan Thomas). I felt it imperative to cook wholesome meals for everyone and to make sure that our home was clean and warm. It was as if all the nurturing I could no longer do for Kate, I had to do twice as much for everyone else.

At times, I was suspended with shock, then raging with anger, at the injustice of it all, followed by periods of great calm. There were days when I felt perfectly normal, as if nothing had really changed, but then I worried about whether I was a cold, uncaring mother. Kate had been so vital, so filled with joy and confidence in living. Yet she was dead, and I had had no power to save her. And so began the everyday business of living with grief.

I did not want counselling, nor antidepressants, although I was persuaded to try both. I think there is a conviction that counselling is a good thing for everyone, but it may not be. I can appreciate that the instinct to do something to help the bereaved is very strong, but rushing in where people have been shocked and disorientated may not be appropriate, and could be destabilising. Is professional help always needed? Some recent research, carried out in Oxford at the Radcliffe and Warneford Hospitals, (Hobbs *et al.*, 1996), suggests that counselling and debriefing might work better for some than for others. Dr Michael Hobbs, the lead author, makes the point that for some people tea and sympathy might be more effective.

In personal tragedy some people will choose to talk. Colin Parry (1995) freely admits in his book, *An Ordinary Boy*, that he had to talk about Tim with as many people as he could. 'I'm damned if I will ever stop talking about our Tim, an ordinary boy.' I chose silence, solitude and introspection. 'Small tragedies are outspoken, but real tragedies are mute' (Lucio A. Seneca). It was as if I wanted to keep Kate's death to myself, to mourn her privately. I started writing a journal to Kate at this time. I needed to talk to her, to tell her things, and I imagined that some sort of telepathic communication with her was possible.

Over time, the entries in the journal changed. They became more about exploring my feelings. I wanted to analyse my experience of losing a child, in an attempt to make sense of it, to give Kate's brief life, meaning. I could re-read my words and although it wasn't easy revisiting so much unhappiness, it did enable me to make a conscious effort to focus my thoughts and my writing on more positive aspects of my life and Kate's. Brian Keenan (1992) describes, in the preface to his book *An Evil Cradling*, how the book is both a therapy and an exploration. Perhaps this is what I was trying to do. In retrospect, writing did help me find a way forward without really thinking about it.

In my darkest moments, art has been healing – pictures, music, poetry and things people have written to explain what the anguish of living can be. Reading about how other people coped with their tragedies diminished the desolate isolation grief can bring. Diana Lamplugh's profoundly moving account of how she and her family coped with 'no body, no accident, no murder that we know of' brought me comfort and strength.

There are many theories of grief in contemporary bereavement literature, the dominant model being that of working through and coming to terms with a whole range of feelings; denial, anger, depression, guilt and sadness, culminating in detachment from the deceased. Whilst I respect that this conceptual framework may be suitable in some cases, it did not work for me. As my account demonstrates, I did not experience emotions in serial stages, rather my own individual mixture of emotions together and simultaneously. I dipped in and out of grief, sometimes coping, sometimes not. I did not feel that I 'worked' through my grief, rather that 'it' worked through me.

By analysing my own and my family's experience of loss, it is possible to suggest there is no right way of coping with loss. The 'stages of grief' theory is frequently interpreted as a normative standard. Whilst there may be some advantages for individuals to see their feelings expressed as part of a normal range of feelings or behaviour, to judge their own experience by the rules of a model might lead the bereaved to perceive their own responses as inappropriate and abnormal. Alternatively, bereaved people may respond in certain ways because it is prescribed or expected of them. Do we really want people to conform? I would argue that each individual and each family's experience of loss is unique and unpredictable in its consequences. Equally, different individuals grieve in different ways and we must respect this diversity.

The construct central to many bereavement programmes, that of working through grief to enable the bereaved to move on and 'let go' of the deceased, I would also challenge. I was advised to let go of Kate. Why? Remaining connected to Kate helps me cope with her loss. Often we are told, as I was, that dealing with bereavement involves putting the past behind us, letting go of the relationship in order to get on with our lives. My relationship with Kate has changed, but it hasn't ended. I do not think it has to. This does not mean that I live in the past, only that I recognise that this past relationship will affect the rest of my life. I am still Kate's mother, even though I have lost her.

Walter (1996a) also challenges the importance of letting go as the ultimate solution for adjusting to loss. He makes the point that grief has a purpose, that of finding a way of not letting go of the deceased; this is done through the process of talking openly and honestly with others who knew the deceased. I used my writing, those internal conversations I had with Kate, to help me acknowledge that Kate was gone, to help me find, 'a secure place', as Walter describes it, for her in my life and thus maintaining my bond with her.

Grief has no fixed formula. Kate's younger sisters, five years her junior, Alex, Helen and Nancy, are identical triplets yet as you can see their stories are quite different. I believe that we need to take people's experiences at face value, thereby validating whatever the bereaved person feels. We cannot make assumptions about people's emotions, neither can we expect or impose patterns of grief upon them. We need to allow individuals to make their own meaning, their own peace.

Kate died on 15 June 1988.

Over the intervening nine years this subjective view of her death, always uncertain, has shifted and changed. There has been a continuing process of reassessment and reconstruction of the experience in order to enlarge the understanding of it. We have, as a family, reached the point when the concentration on the past, on Kate's death, has moved so that we all feel able to live in the present and invest in the future. The intensity of feelings has lessened. Tears are no longer so upsetting. However, the past, is always there and we are always working with it, but it no longer dominates every waking moment. A part of our life has gone, a part that won't ever come back. I will always set out five plates on the dining table, not six and I will always wonder what she would be like now. We have learned to live with

Kate's death. We have reached an accommodation with it, by accepting that we won't 'recover' from it. For this implies we can go back to being the family we were before Kate's death. Losing her changed everything.

My feet will want to march
toward where you sleep
but
I shall go on living

Pablo Neruda (1972: 107–109)

Together with the Department of Hispanic Studies, at Westfield College, London University, we set up the Kate Elder Prize, awarded annually to the best first-year Honours Spanish student, and the Kate Elder lecture series. The lecture is an annual event for students past and present whereby leading authorities on Hispanic Literature are invited to speak. The lectures are subsequently published by the University.

The following extract is taken from the opening of the first Kate Elder Lecture, written by Professor Robert Pring-Mill, University of Oxford.

'Kate seems to have been a lovely mixture, behind that cheerful face which first stared out at me from the photograph in that sad press report: romantic, yet with a nicely dry sense of humour (which could, however, be quite cynical when appropriate); nicely headstrong (would do anything – within limits – for a dare); had enthusiasms and took up causes, would go on demos with the best of them: choosy in her friendships but loyal to those she had accepted (one of a close-knit quartet of Westfield girls who went about together and could, or so I was told, "perhaps get rather wild at times"); wide-eyed yet clear-sighted, occasionally perhaps a bit mixed up – aren't we all? – yet with her own priorities mapped out (though open-minded enough to know they would have been subject to revision had she lived). Above all, perhaps, a fun person to know, to be with, to teach.'

A lovely epitaph for our daughter Kate.

Kate's father, Tom

At about the time the triplets were born and Kate was 4 years old, while we were living in Rome, there was a car crash involving the teenage children of American neighbours of ours. Everyone in the car was badly injured and one of the youngsters, a girl of about 19, killed. I recall being profoundly moved at hearing this news and thinking to myself, Heaven forbid that such a thing should ever happen to us . . .

Kate had been adorable as a baby; placid, sunny disposition, a real treasure. Thinking back, I can only wonder at how marvellously she coped with the transition from being the centre of attention herself, only to be abruptly sidelined completely as Pamela and I struggled to cope with triplet babies. There is a particularly poignant scene in a home movie of the period when Kate enters the living room to find me filming the year-old triplets and hurries to remove herself from sight. Why, I wonder to myself now, did I not encourage her to get back into the shot?

My relationship with Kate, the teenager, had been strained for years and only in the last year before her death did things improve. Problem areas had included smoking, singularly ill-chosen boy friends, lack of effort at school (she got ten GCSEs but not enough As and Bs!) treating home as a hotel. The usual stuff. But at university, she seemed suddenly to find herself and became, for me, the loveable kid she'd been when she was little.

Pamela has described the actual events surrounding Kate's death. What of the days, months and years which have passed since?

I hold no religious beliefs; as a geologist I simply cannot accept the concept that God created the universe and then waited around for more than 10 000 million years for a creature to emerge who could appreciate His efforts. But I did, for a while, fervently hope that Kate was not lost to me forever, that I would see her again somewhere, somehow if only to express regret at the home movie episode.

Regretful feelings of guilt form a major element in the emotional turmoil which followed Kate's death. Of not having shown adequate appreciation when she was good, and of having been over-critical during her difficult years.

The rest of the early grieving amounted to 'why go on?' This event had been of such overwhelming significance, so unexpected, so much against the natural order of things, that everything else in life became utterly trivial and meaningless. In organising Kate's burial, we bought two adjacent plots, the second for ourselves. In my blacker periods, I seriously contemplated choosing the right sort of sufficiently freezing night and lying down on the plot next to Kate. I'd have been found the following morning having died of hypothermia and would have joined Kate to make amends for past failing her as a father.

Such thoughts don't occur any more, though the regrets remain. Life does indeed go on. The mistakes of the past have to be lived with and thanks given for the time we did have Kate with us. The grave is still my most important link with Kate, lying as it does on a peaceful downland hillside overlooking the small town where she spent her last years. I like to start my week by spending a few minutes at her graveside on Monday mornings. Not so much to communicate with her, as I tried to do in the early days, but rather to remind myself about what is important in life.

Nancy

The strangest thing about writing about Kate's death, nearly nine years after the event, is that my recollection is hazy. My family can recall vivid details that I can't. I know how it is now and that is all I seem to know. I don't even remember my first reaction. Alex told me. We were never given many details. I remember finding out she had been run over by three cars because I read it in the paper.

I know that as far as grieving is concerned we all went in our own solitary directions. I think it was about two years later that Alex and I discussed it. In fact, it wasn't a discussion because we did it through writing. I'm not sure if I have ever talked to the others about it. I'm not sure I would want to. I desperately wanted to talk to her friends, people who knew her.

I remember people being surprised that we could still act normally. It was like they expected you to be crying all the time! There is no pattern to grief. I don't believe in stages you go through. I believe that the individual's pattern of grief depends largely on the relationship they had with the deceased. It is basically a myriad of emotions that intermingle and surface at any time. In my case, it was a difficult situation. Kate and I hadn't spoken in nearly a year. We were very alike, therefore we clashed.

Like Helen, I felt no real inclination to talk. I wrote a lot of letters, but I never sent them. I wanted answers to a lot of questions. But there seemed to be no-one to answer them. I don't remember if I was preoccupied with trying to figure out what death was. I think I just felt that I hadn't had the chance to really get to know my sister and I wanted to know from everybody; 'what was she like?'

I would say it took about seven years to really come to terms with what had happened. I think, looking back, I put dealing with it on hold. We were so young. I think I preoccupied myself with looking after the others. Mainly Alex. She had fallen to pieces. Helen and my father were very alike. They kept whatever it was they were feeling to themselves.

Its funny how although something like this invariably brings you closer together it can also divide you. Family visits to the cemetery were something I didn't find particularly comforting. My time at the grave was my time alone.

Now? We still don't talk much. Writing this was something I wasn't keen to do. I know deep down that what happened had a profound effect on my life. I know that the person I am now has been shaped to a large extent by the effect of losing Kate. Looking back, I think maybe I should have tried harder to deal with it sooner but how was I to know how to? Dealing with unexpected and painful events in your life is not something you are taught how to do! Life went on and I just lived for the day knowing that one day her loss would not be such a negative part of my life.

She changed us all in our own way and I believe I will see her again someday. But recalling those first few days, those first few years, is very painful. Christmas will never be the same. I think we try to avoid it. If I were to give advice I would say that you never really lose the pain of losing someone you love, but you can be happy again. You can look back and smile and you get used to not having them around. Time heals only in the respect that you realise that life is a cause for celebration and, no matter how long the one you love has been with you, their life is to be remembered and celebrated. I don't feel pain anymore just peace. I cannot help but smile when I think of her. I cannot help but laugh as I recall the enormous arguments we used to have! She will always be my older sister and I will always cherish my memories of her because they will always be alive within me.

Helen

The first reaction was incredible shock. I refused to believe what I had heard and insisted that my father admit to me that he was lying. It had never occurred to me that someone in my family could die, particularly Kate – my invincible big sister. After the initial shock came a period of numbness before the next outpouring of emotion. A pattern that progressively repeated itself. During the periods of numbness I would try and make sense of the whole event. The biggest problem was this – I didn't understand death and needed to figure it out. I was 14 at the time. But thinking and analysing were not always possible and there were times when I just had to follow my emotions no questions asked – the crying, the anger and the frustration, and just let them be.

Even though I was living in a house where every member of the household was suffering from immense pain, dealing with the grief was very personal. I don't remember ever talking about it except for when I had to and indeed found this process extremely uncomfortable. Neither did I find any comfort in crying or talking together with other members of my family. I wanted to be left alone when it came to the bereavement. I think that each one of us – although aware of each other's presence and distress – had to deal with Kate's death in our own way.

More or less from day one I went about trying to understand what it was that had happened. Obviously I was aware that Kate was not coming back, but the yearning for it almost made me believe in the paranormal, such as time going backwards like in a *Superman* film, meaning that the accident could have been avoided. Endless hours were spent exploring this daydream. I also swore I would sacrifice various parts of my body if it meant that she would return, half hoping that this would be possible. One thing I realised almost immediately was that I needed to see her again. I was not particularly thrilled with the prospect of facing her dead body, but at the same time every thought or emotion I felt came back to the same point – I needed to have proof, without this, I knew that I would latch on to the hope that perhaps someone, somewhere, had made a mistake and it would be all right. A process of thought which I felt was destructive as it distracted me from the reality that in actual fact, she was not coming back. I also needed to answer the perpetual question – What on earth was death? By seeing her I hoped to further my understanding and also, as I saw it, help me to cope. So I went to see her and there she was and an end was put to all my hopes of a mistake. I won't deny that this was extremely traumatising, and I'm sure it would not be beneficial to everybody, but for me it was a huge step towards accepting her death. It also brought home the fact that, yes, it was true people did die and, yes, people in my family died too.

After this event, I confirmed what I had felt from day one of life after Kate.

This feeling was that the real Kate, not the one in the funeral parlour, was in the sky. I had never had any real inclinations towards any religion and still don't. Indeed I had certainly found no comfort in a visit from the local vicar shortly after her death, as I was more concerned about saying something that might offend him than listening to what he had to say. I was, however, grateful for his attempt. What I had decided was not a religious revelation to me, it was a Helen belief, a personal belief, and the more I thought about it, the more I decided that Kate was definitely 'in the sky'. I was reluctant to call it heaven because of its religious connotation, and this new idea was very comforting. To me she was not lying six foot under the ground, but above me in the sunshine and the warm breezes and in the clouds. I derived such comfort from this thought that I stayed with it. Indeed, on the very first hour after the news of her death I had walked out and spent a long time lying in a field looking upwards. It's not that I believed that she was looking at me or even seeing me but that somehow amongst the clouds she was in a very nice place. This meant, however, that visiting the grave and seeing people talking to the Kate that was in the ground was extremely difficult to bear. For the first few years I detested visiting the grave as it had absolutely no significance to me and yet I did find an overwhelming pressure to do so. Not from anyone in particular, just a feeling that it is something you should do. It's not that I dismissed a grave at all – it was certainly very important to me to have some sort of recognition of the event for all to see – but further than that it remained for me simply a symbol of her death rather than Kate herself. However, I could understand how talking whilst by the side of a grave could provide the same comfort that I felt whilst looking at the sky, I did visit her grave at times of my own accord but not until much later.

With regard to my emotions there was no particular pattern. There were times of utter pain and so much crying that I became exhausted, followed frequently, though not always, by a period of numb calm or a time when I smiled or even laughed at something. I found that there was a certain feeling of guilt attached to the times when I didn't cry – when I thought instead about what I was going to treat myself to that day or I laughed at a comedy programme on TV. It was as if I couldn't possibly have a happy thought, because of what had happened, and it was only much later that I realised that this negative thinking was simply a form of punishment which only served to increase the anguish. The fact is that I did smile and laugh and that the dreaded expression 'life goes on' was in fact true. At other times there was extreme anger and frustration that this had happened. Frustration that this should happen to us when surely someone else deserved it more. Frustration at seeing my family in such pain and not being able to do a damn thing about it. Frustration at not being able to talk to Kate, to just have a quick moment with her so that she could tell me where she was and what she was doing and tell me that I would be OK. Times when life without that person was an utter waste and why the hell carry on. I remember writing a sentence down that I remembered again and again in times of anger – the pain of losing someone is too high a price to pay for having loved them. But there were other times when I remembered other people that I loved and that loved me, times when I realised that death was an integral part of life and was not supposed to halt my life forever. For me grief is a cyclical process of many emotions, thoughts and feelings whose intensity gradually lessens over time. The pain became more bearable and the first day that I spent a few minutes thinking of nothing but positive thoughts about Kate was, I felt, a real change because these were of accepting death and being able to remember her life rather than regretting her death. This, to me, meant that I was healing. There was no specific time for this however, it didn't happen in the third month or in the fifth year after her death. It came and went and intermingled with every other emotion. There was no right or wrong answer. I also realised that there was no specific place you should be or any certain emotion you should feel at any given time, I think that grief works the way your body and mind decides that it is going to work and you just have to ride with it.

The Passage of Grief by Alex Elder

Introduction

I wrote the first of these poems almost a month after Kate died. I had never written a poem before in my life. It marked the beginning of what I call my 'Passage of Grief' that was to last for three years. Throughout this time, I wrote many poems, normally when I was feeling particularly down. Sometimes, I wrote four or five in a week and perhaps not another for a month or two. They express exactly how I felt at the time, sometimes I felt positive and at other times, negative. Needless to say they do not show a chronological pattern with regard to the emotions they express.

I spent the first year following Kate's death in shock. I couldn't even begin to think about her death and what it meant. I imagined it as an enormous apple that I was unable to take a bite out of because of its sheer size. I had not experienced bereavement before, so it was completely alien to me. I also felt that if I did come to terms with her death, then I would lose her completely. My reaction then, was to block it out. I couldn't keep this up forever however, and I spent the second year following her accident trying to come to terms with what had happened, trying to adjust to a new life without her.

During this time I became deeply depressed. I suffered from insomnia and horrific nightmares; some about death in general and others where I would reach out desperately to touch Kate but simply couldn't. I began to think and hope, that I would simply die of grief.

For many months, I was convinced that I was suffering a slow and gradual demise. I began seeing a counsellor and although it helped me to talk unreservedly about my feelings, it did not stop the pain. I was just waiting to die.

About half way through the third year following Kate's death I felt myself beginning to recover. My nightmares were less frequent and I was sleeping better. Instead of letting myself be immersed in my own sorrow, I began to

crave happiness and to realise that I had a future ahead of me, and of course
my family to think about.

One day in August just over three years after Kate's death. I was walking with one of my sisters down a street in Spain and I felt a strange sen-
sation. Quite simply, I felt happy. I had almost forgotten what happiness
felt like. I realised that my 'Passage of Grief' had come to an end. Some
time after this I was looking at a wonderful picture we have of Kate
smiling. I still felt a deep sadness but, for the first time ever, I smiled back
at Kate.

Kate

(Part One)

So many words left unsaid.
So many things left undone.
So abrupt;
here then,
gone now.

The future drags on;
life so painful.
Nothing is understood.

Memories cling
Tight.
Fresh tears fall,
cries of pain,
desperate
for the answer of one word:
Why?

A bad hour passes.
New strength...
Until the next hour
when you fall again
into sorrow.

A quiet sob.
A scream, a thump.
Frustration.
Pounding on the wall,
crying, No, No, No!

Visiting the grave,
fresh flowers
for a body six feet below...
soul in heaven?

Questions asked,
never answered.
New hope;
'She's in Heaven.'
Forcing to believe it.

Climbing a steep hill,
the top is near
but a sudden slip,
a fall,
And the climb begins again.

Songs remind you,
words remind you,
memories ... only good,
bad things are forgotten.

People around you
try to help forget;
but even a word
brings fresh.
Hurt so strong,
other's understanding weak;
awkward smiles quiet mutterings
'Should we say something to them?'

A Six has become Five.
A part of everyone has gone.
But not forever,
just around the corner,
over the hill,
very soon,
Five will become Six again;
A whole unit
A whole heart,
beating strong.

Until then,
only one healer:
Time.
Pain lessens,
memories fondly remembered
And the girl, who will always be
beautiful,
will stay in our hearts,
Forever.

'Til we meet again,
Kate.

(Part Two)

We won't forget you.
We'll never leave you.
You'll always be with us.

Brave faces,
cover tear stains.
'Life must go on' –
but it's very hard;
an awful struggle.
Concentration falls,
problems get worse.
But there's always a light at the end of the tunnel.
Always a brighter sun,
...greener grass.
Then we'll look back at you
and smile,
no hurt,
no pain,
no tears.

Until that day,
hope must be strong,
faith must prevail,
Love never dies.
'Til we meet again.

9–10 July 1988

When you think of me

When I have gone,
don't think of me as having taken my life.
Don't think of me as having died in pain.
Don't think that I didn't love you.
Don't think that I didn't want to live every passing day next to you...

Think of me as a star in the sky,
with no strength to shine anymore.
Think of me as a river,
with no water flowing.
Think of me as a candle,
with no fuel left to burn.

Don't think of me with sadness in your heart...

Think of me as a free spirit,
floating in the wind,

caressing the leaves on the trees as I pass.
Think of me as a free soul,
riding on the crests of waves,
reaching out to touch the shore.
Think of me as a free bird,
flying without a care in the world,
gently touching the clouds.

Think of me as having liberated myself from my endless pain,
my unbearable pain,
of being without my precious love.
Think of me as now being where I truly want to be.
Think of me as being happy,
finally, after so many tears.

Think of it as my only way out.
Think of me as having died quietly,
with a smile on my face.
For I shall be with whom I have been waiting to see for so long
because now
she is the only person in the world that can make me happy...

Never forget how much I love you.
Never forget how much I care.
Please don't be sad.
Please don't cry.

I just couldn't handle my life the way it was,
the way it was always going to be.
Most of all, take care
and I'll see you all again,
Some day.

9 April 1990

The Struggle

I know,
OK?
I know
She won't come back
(she will never come back)
What I feel when I see her in the photo
is how much I miss her
(it is only the gentle passing breeze
that makes me think that she sees me too)
because she won't come back.

The future that I see
(yes I know she won't be there)
is without her.
The photos I will take will be of five people,
not six.
I know that I shan't be able to hug her
(you don't need to tell me, I already know).

I am even used to the pain!
I put up with the loss that I feel.
For goodness sake, I feel it every day!
I feel it when I wake,
I feel it when I dress,
I feel it when I go out onto the street,
and I know she won't come back
(no one needs to tell me).

There's just one thing, explain to me,
Why do I still not understand it?
Someone explain to me,
Why does it still not seem real?
Someone explain to me, please
Why is it at times as if she never existed?
Why is she lost in a world that I do not know?
Why do I still search for her, whilst walking along the street?

I've already told you, I know!
she will never, never return
(but I search for her ...)
She will never return!
(but I am searching for her ...)
SHE WON'T COME BACK
(but ...).

The Passage of Grief

Grieving for the loss of you,
streams of angry, agonised tears,
are wrenched from my heart.
The shrouds of memory
enclose all that is within
all that will remain within,
carried like Hercules and his world
with the weight of grief on its shoulders.

What stirs within,
directs, controls,

the life without.
Silent, angry screams in the night,
dark hours of solitude
mourning a lost soul.

I stoop, I bend,
I stumble, I fall,
I readjust the weight,
but the gravity is always there,
is ever felt.

The blondness of that summer afternoon,
filters my thoughts and penetrates my heart.
The hint of a smile
lost.

The dim memory that will fade
only to recoil and lash out again
burning like the torrid sun of grief
alone in a sweltering sky.

Estrangement.
The story of a life cheated before it begins,
the intolerable pain
conquers even the strongest heart.

The dreamlike images of reunification
are crushed at the dawn of reality
boxed in by a corporeal frame
that lays waste to hopes and dreams.

A face, a love
preserved.
The soul of one
mingles with another;
the fierce passion of life
is not forgotten,

You went on your journey without saying
'Goodbye'.
You were here for one
brief
shining moment.
And then gone forever
like the gleam of a star before its
eclipse by a passing cloud.

What is death but a passing cloud?
Drifting slowly
but always travelling
Ready to enter and depart
taking one
and leaving those behind to drown in their sorrow

But I will live to tell your tale
you will remain within my heart for all my days
I will strive, fight,
love, laugh,
with you beside me.
we will march through life together
strong.

I will never lose you.
I will never
ever
stop loving you.
I will never
ever
ever
forget you.

The memories of my childhood days
will forever shine brightly in my sky.
Your smile will remain on my lips.
I will carry you on my shoulders.
I will hold you in my arms.
You shall be alive within me forever.
WE WILL MARCH THROUGH LIFE TOGETHER.

8 December 1992

Epilogue

The notions of 'acceptance' and 'letting go' are difficult ones. I don't know that I have accepted that Kate is dead, or that I am simply used to her not being around. Death is as much an enigma to me as it always has been. Not having any definite religious beliefs I can't be assured that I will meet her again in the event of my own death. But it remains a hope.

Organ donation is another difficult subject. How *do* doctors find the fine line between being compassionate to the newly bereaved and retrieving the organs in time to be transplanted? I'm glad Kate's organs were used, because I strongly believe in organ donation myself, but it is of no comfort to me. Her death will always be in vain.

Death is a transition in life over which there is no control. The bereaved are forced to reconstruct the reality of the world around them. The security of life as you know it is nothing less than smashed to pieces. Nine years on I remain acutely aware that nothing in life can be taken for granted.

Literature was very important to me. Henry Scott Holland's 'Death is nothing at all', W.H. Auden's 'Funeral Blues', Shakespeare, P.B. Shelley, Keats ... anything I could get my hands on that seemed to me to express exactly how I was feeling.

A friend of mine once said about me that I carried Kate around in my heart like a promise. He had never met her but had almost got to know her through me.

A lot of friends in the months following Kate's death told me that Kate was still 'with me'. I tried to believe it but I couldn't, and after a while I wanted to shout at anyone who said that to me 'NO SHE ISN'T AND SHE NEVER WILL BE SO STOP TALKING RUBBISH!' I ached for some sort of 'spiritual' presence of Kate but it never came. In my lifetime I will never 'feel' her with me. I will always feel great pain when I think of her and I will always feel her loss. (Even now nearly nine years on, I still lock myself in my room from time to time to cry and scream.) However, she is 'alive' within me. Wherever I go, her pictures, her memory come with me. There is no-one who gets to know me well without to some extent getting to know Kate. I smile with her when I look at the photograph, and I often imagine just what she'd say at some of the things I say and do, (laugh I suspect!). She is not just a sad part of my past but a relevant part of my present, my future and most importantly, of me.

Teaching and learning focus on portrait of family grief

Rationale

The rationale is that by sharing our own reactions to a poetic expression of grief we can thereby appreciate the individual and complex nature of the grieving process.

Activity: poetry

This activity uses the poems written about Kate's death by her sister, Alex. The poems are exactly as Alex wrote them. Some have headings, some have not. They can be used in a number of ways, both by individuals and groups.

Ask participants to:

- Read the poems (one at a time, or as a whole, or selected poems)
- Consider what the poems say
- How do they communicate feelings and emotions?
- How can they further our understanding of personal grief?

- Acknowledge how the poems have made them feel – how can we cope with such feelings?

Note: The group can explore and lead the session as it wishes. It can also decide how it wishes to conclude the session and what it wants to record.

Learning outcomes

The learning outcomes stimulated by the activities are for the course participants to:

- Be more aware of their own personal reactions to a moving expression of grief
- Appreciate how varied individual responses can be to such an experience.

Chapter 10
Changing the Emphasis on Death: Issues Surrounding Organ Donation

Graham E. Watkinson

This chapter outlines the current evidence for brain stem death, organ donation and support of grieving relatives. It explores the views of family, the medical team and nursing team in relation to this complex issue.

The perspectives from which this chapter is written are: phenomenological, professional and empirical.

Introduction

A different kind of loss, where decisions have to be made for the potential benefit for unknown others, surrounds donating organs.

> Sorrow touched by love grows bright
> with more than rapture's ray;
> and darkness shows us worlds of light
> we never saw by day.

(Miller, 1980: 17 August)

As a student nurse, during the autumn of 1979, the author cared for a young man involved in a road traffic accident. He was a rear seat passenger in a car and died the victim of 'brain stem death' (BSD). This pathological insult occurred three days following his head injury. Two other people in the car including the driver escaped serious injury. Ironically, the driver had swerved to miss a rabbit and lost control of his vehicle.

The diagnosis of BSD is a catastrophe no matter what aetiology has led up to it. The effects are widespread and devastating, not least for the patient, but all those who care for, know and love them. These patients bring very real challenges to the nursing and medical team, whose role may change from aggressive resuscitation, to be radically refocused on the salvaging of organs for potential transplantation.

As many transplantable organs require a viable blood supply up until the moment they are removed, the donor's heart has to be kept beating. This involves caring for the donor in an intensive care facility and the diagnosis of BSD whereby all functions of the brain have permanently and 'irreversibly destroyed' (Pallis, 1987).

There is an incongruous situation surrounding the brain-dead patient. Although they are legally dead, their heart still beats, they may remain warm to touch, pink in colour and look as though they are sleeping. Fresh urine dribbles into their catheter bag. Each heart beat dependent upon the ventilator breathing oxygen-enriched air into their lungs enabling their chest to rhythmically rise and fall. A plethora of monitoring and supportive technology usually surrounds them. Their cardiac monitor shows an electro-cardiographic trace, whilst nurses continue to record and chart all their 'vital signs'.

If this person, an individual, who becomes a patient, the victim of a cerebral catastrophe, is the one you love most dearly, then perhaps you can begin to glimpse the pain, the stress and the turmoil that families in this situation face. The immediacy, suddenness and shock of the situation wrenches away any locus of control once enjoyed. It may seem that hi-tech machines, which display a 'digital handle' on the patient, have perhaps dominion over them. On the one hand, an acute event leading to a bereavement, whilst on the other, the chance to improve or even save some distant person's life. Perhaps in the back of your mind you may wonder, are they really dead? How can the medical and nursing staff be so sure?

The aim of this chapter is to introduce the reader to a range of issues concerning potential organ donation following death. The purpose of which is to enable an informed decision to be made regarding the potential donation of one's own organs. The chapter concludes with a teaching and learning focus that staff working within the intensive care unit may like to do to tease out pertinent issues surrounding the management of loss that these patients inevitably bring. How this may affect the caring team and what strategies may be utilised are discussed within the chapter.

Background

The creation of intensive care facilities in the second half of the twentieth century has brought about an ongoing revolution in technology and patient support. The notion of 'life support systems' is frequently perpetuated by the media when reporting about hospitalised critically ill patients. More often this consists of a number of differing supportive devices carefully orchestrated by the physician and nurse to maintain some sort of home-ostasis. Certainly, as the turn of the century rapidly approaches, society as consumers of care expects more from the health care providers than ever before.

Organ transplantation has benefited enormously from improvements in bio-medical technology, and immuno-suppressive pharmacology. This has pushed forward transplantation from an experimental state, to what has become acceptable medical treatment for end-stage renal, heart, lung, liver and pancreatic diseases (Stoeckle, 1990). Transplantation may improve both quantity of life and quality as measured by the recipient (Koostra, 1988). These advances according to Borozny (1988), have had at least one major effect on today's health care system; that nurses in intensive care units are required to provide physical care to dead patients. Pallis (1983) suggests that this is one of the more macabre by-products of modern intensive care technology. It is a paradox that advances in resuscitation techniques enable a ventilated corpse to become a potential 'beating heart organ donor'. Organs from unrelated brain-dead donors are essential to the transplantation enterprise.

Fundamental to the UK Governments' health strategy, indeed it is at the very core of the *Health of the Nation*, White Paper (Department of Health, 1992) is the notion of 'adding years to life and life to years'. A philosophy shared by those involved in transplantation. Although it must be pointed out that in the context of tertiary care this was possibly not considered to be of strategic importance in what is becoming a primary care led National Health Service.

Transplant Support Services Authority

The United Kingdom Transplant Support Service Authority (UKTSSA) in Bristol, England coordinates all of the transplant units in the UK and Republic of Ireland. It is responsible for the matching and allocation of organs and maintains a data base of all patients awaiting an organ transplant. This data base also includes clinical data on recipients, their donors and the outcome of transplants. It provides evidence-based data to inform clinical practice and is a special health authority of the National Health Service.

Cumulative data for the period 1 January 1996 to 31 December 1996 (UKTSSA, 1997) show that the total number of people on the waiting lists for transplantation was 6275, whilst the total number of organs donated from cadaver donors was 2614. It must be appreciated that some donors donate more that one organ. Also hearts from recipients who receive a heart and lung may become available for another patient known as the 'domino' donor. Twenty-one such hearts were transplanted during 1996, even so, demand always exceeds supply.

What is brain stem death (BSD)?

Brain stem death was not invented by neurologists to satisfy the demands of transplant surgeons. It came about as a consequence of mechanically ventilating patients with irreversible structural brain damage, who could no longer breath for themselves (Pallis, 1983; Allan, 1988). Whilst the ventilator 'breathed' for them, enabling the body to be oxygenated and carbon dioxide removed, the heart would continue to beat for a few hours or days at the most. The first description of this phenomenon was termed 'coma depasse' by the French physicians Mollaret and Goulon in 1959 who identified a condition 'beyond coma'.

The brain stem is situated at the base of the brain linking the spinal cord to the higher centres of the brain. It is divided into three parts: the mid-brain, pons varolii and medulla oblongata (see Fig. 10.1). Information coming into, or out of the brain must pass through the brain stem. The centres that control our cardiovascular function, heart beat and respiration, together with the level of consciousness, are also sited here. The brain stem therefore provides more than just a vital link, it is the centre of life. Irreversible damage to this link will result in the heart stopping and death.

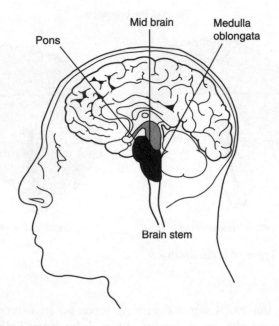

Fig. 10.1 Brain and brain stem.

A diagnosis of death of the brain stem or death of the whole brain is required before proceeding to donation. Types of brain death are shown in Fig. 10.2. Brain stem death will always be followed by cardiac arrest. The fact that the function of the heart can be briefly extended by mechanical ventilation should not be allowed to cloud the issue, that is, 'permanent functional death of the brain stem constitutes brain death' (Conference of Royal Colleges and Faculties, 1976). This was updated in 1979 (Conference of Medical Royal Colleges and their Faculties, 1979), when the colleges added:

'Brain death represents the stage at which a patient becomes truly dead, because by then all functions of the brain have permanently and irreversibly ceased.'

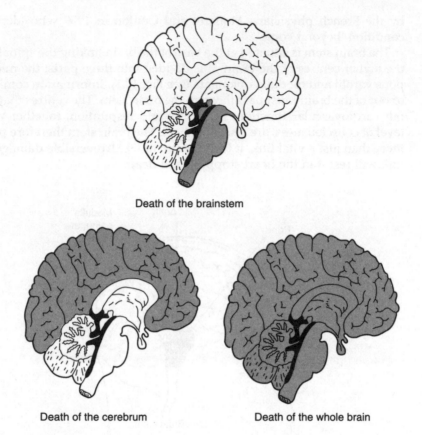

Fig. 10.2   Types of brain death.

During the 1970s when decisions were taken to ventilate these 'dead' patients until the heart finally stopped beating, Pallis (1983) reported, '... that the plight of the relatives was pitiful: they became emotional hostages to uncomprehending machines'.

Toole (1971), commenting on medical training (though this equally applies to nursing), suggests that until the last heart beat there is life and hope. All this changed dramatically with the first successful human cardiac transplantation on 3 December 1967. The transition from life to death of one critically ill patient, who is subsequently medically diagnosed as brain stem dead, may give new life and hope to others, through the giving of relevant human organs.

Relatives often ask are there any clinically documented cases where a patient has been diagnosed as brain stem dead and later wakes up. There are none. When the media has reported this in the past the cases referred to were not brain stem dead. They were either in a deep coma or a vegetative state with their brain stem still functioning. The potential outcomes of coma are shown in Fig. 10.3.

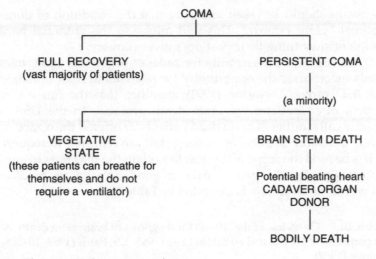

Fig. 10.3 The potential outcomes of coma.

Causes of brain stem death (BSD)

Causes of BSD are:

(1) Bleeding into the brain or blockage of a cerebral blood vessel denying the brain stem oxygenated blood and nutrients. This is the result of some forms of stroke.
(2) Head trauma.
(3) Lack of oxygen reaching the brain, 'cerebral hypoxia' due to failure of the patient to breathe or the heart not pumping blood or smoke inhalation/carbon monoxide poisoning – starving the blood of oxygen.
(4) Cerebral tumour – as the tumour grows there is no room in the rigid skull to allow for expansion. As the pressure within the skull increases it will eventually result in force pushing the brain stem through the hole in the base of the skull (foramen magnum) irreversibly damaging the brain stem. This is often referred to as 'coning'. Because primary malignant brain cancers do not metastasise or spread the patient may be come a donor without fear of passing on cancer to recipients.
(5) Drug overdose.
(6) Intracranial infection.

In 1993 McCullagh (1993: 9) stated that the purpose of diagnosing brain death was to, '... release patients from the imposition of further treatment which offered them no possible benefit'. He goes on to suggest that once diagnosed as brain stem dead, the contemporary potential donor paradoxically will have a whole range of treatment imposed, for the benefit of the recipient(s).

Within the UK, the Code of Practice for *Cadaveric Organs for Transplantation* (Department of Health and Social Security, 1983) states; that all practicable measures should be taken to ensure that the condition of donor organs is optimal before removal. This will minimise the potential hazards to the recipient smoothing their post-operative recovery.

Since BSD is a pre-requisite for cadaver organ donation, many UK hospitals incorporate the opportunity for relatives to offer donation as part of the BSD protocol. Norton (1992) identifies that the nurse caring for the patient often initiates the brain death protocol. In the USA federal law requires all families of brain dead patients be offered the option of organ and tissue donation. Medical or nursing staff are required to request this.

It is beyond the scope of this text to explain the BSD tests in any detail. This information can be gained from a good nursing or medical textbook. However, an overview is provided in Table 10.1.

Table 10.1   Overview of the criteria for diagnosis of brain stem death. Adapted from Department of Health and Social Security (1983: 12), Pallis (1983: 10–20) and Davis & Lemke (1987).

Harvard criteria 1968

- Irreversible coma
- Apnoea
- Absence of cephalic reflexes
- Absence of spinal reflexes
- Isoelectric EEG
- Persistence of condition for 24 hours
- Absence of drug intoxication or hypothermia

Current accepted USA criteria

- Absence of cerebral function
- Absence of cephalic reflexes
- Inability to maintain normal vital signs without artificial support
- Absence of sedative drugs, including alcohol
- Absence of hypothermia
- As yet there exists no universal acceptance of a specific length of time for the condition to persist

British criteria 1976

- No brain stem reflexes
- No pupillary response to light
- No corneal reflex
- No vestibular ocular reflex
- No motor response within the cranial nerve distribution in response to adequate stimulation of any somatic area
- No gag reflex or reflex response to bronchial stimulation
- No respiratory movements occur when the respiratory centre is stimulated (apnoea in the presence of $PaCO_2$ above 6.66 KPa)

In the UK the following preconditions are essential, prior to the tests being performed:

- That the patient is comatosed and on a ventilator
- Positive diagnosis of coma (irredeemable structural brain damage) has been made.

If any of the following exclusions prevail, then testing cannot be performed:

- Hypothermia (core temperature <35°C)
- There must be no drug intoxication or metabolic or endocrine disturbances which can be responsible for, or contribute to, coma.

The time before testing equals the time it takes to satisfy the preconditions. The British guidelines state that the examination and testing is carried out by preferably the consultant in charge of the patient, and another consultant or senior registrar clinically independent of the first. Both shall have expertise in this field and neither must be a member of the transplant team (Department of Health and Social Security, 1983).

Re-testing ensures that there is no observer error and, as Pallis (1983) suggests, that non-functioning of the brain stem has persisted. The interval between tests is at the discretion of the medical staff, usually taking into account the feelings and circumstances of the next of kin. For the patient, once the second set of BSD tests are complete, proving no brain stem function, they are certified dead.

Matten *et al.* (1991: 165) suggested that:

'The rights of the donor, the desires of the family, and the needs of the potential recipient must be balanced and protected by the professional nurse.'

What happens after the potential donor is declared dead?

For the potential organ donor the nursing care continues, as does the psychological and social support for the family. On the one hand, the nursing and medical team is concerned with maintaining the potential of the cadaver for organ donation, whilst on the other, helping and supporting the bereaved family to come to terms with their tragedy. Hospital chaplains very often play a tremendous supporting role to the family and friends of the dead patient as well as to all those involved.

Bidigare & Oermann (1991: 24) identified that nurses possessing greater knowledge and positive attitudes:

'... will be better able to provide comfort, and support the donor's family in the decision making process, thereby increasing the family's self-care agency.'

Before donation is enacted and as a safety measure to the potential recipients of organs, blood samples are taken for the matching process. In the UK this will include screening for the antibodies of HIV. The logistics involved in organising the donation have given the process an undeservedly sinister image. This is perhaps due to the non-availability of operating theatres during normal working hours so that organ retrieval often takes place at night. Time waiting for theatres, or the transplant team to arrive, is precious for the family as they prepare to say their goodbyes. The nursing and medical team should do all that they can to enable and facilitate the family, relatives and friends to do this. A short religious service often marks this ultimate 'rite of passage'.

For the organ donor supportive care continues up to and including the operative period when 'healthy' organs are removed from the cadaver donor. This is undertaken in the operating theatre like any other major surgery, except that the patient (cadaver) requires no anaesthetic because they are already dead. The surgical wounds are sutured and dressed and the body 'laid out' prior to being taken to the mortuary. This should not cause any delay with the funeral arrangements. The circumstances and aetiology that led to the diagnosis of BSD will determine whether the coroner is involved and he is often consulted. A post-mortem examination may also be required.

For those brain stem dead patients who are not going to become donors their care ends at the completion of the second set of BSD tests when the diagnosis is made and they are declared dead. Life-supporting equipment is withdrawn and the patient 'laid out' prior to being taken to the mortuary. Since the patient is already dead, the withdrawal of support is not euthanasia.

The donation process

The donation process is supported and underpinned by the society in which we live and die. Figure 10.4 identifies some key elements which need to be in place to support and facilitate this. This is a complex process which the diagrammatic conceptualisation simplifies. Nevertheless, there is always an expectation on behalf of the potential recipients for an organ or organs to become available. Many patients die waiting. The process requires inspiration, motivation and effort to be successful. There are also three sets of 'gate keepers': the donor family members, the critical care professionals and the transplant teams.

According to the UKTSSA (1997) the donor card was first introduced in the UK in 1971 as a kidney donor card only. Some ten years later it changed to a multi-organ donor card. Since the mid-1980s an estimated 115 million cards have been issued by the Department of Health. Complementing this is the Organ Donor Register. By 1996 the NHS Organ Donor Register had over 3 million people wishing to donate their organs should they die.

A study by Watkinson (1995) examined the lived experiences of intensive care nurses (n = 103) caring for actual and potential organ donors. Many of

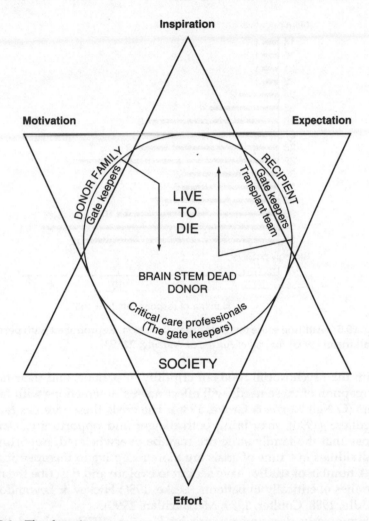

Fig. 10.4   The donation process.

these nurses had cared for over 20 donors and their families. Their attitudes scores can be seen in Fig. 10.5 (a series of statements were scored, the scale ranged from 7 points = extremely negative to 35 points = extremely positive towards organ donation).

According to the theory of reasoned action (Ajzen & Fishbein, 1980) typically an individual will perform a behaviour if they evaluate it positively, and when they believe that significant others think it should be performed (Fig. 10.6).

Potential donor family needs

The family in its many guises, forms the critical intervening variable between the individual and society. Nursing requires nurses to intervene

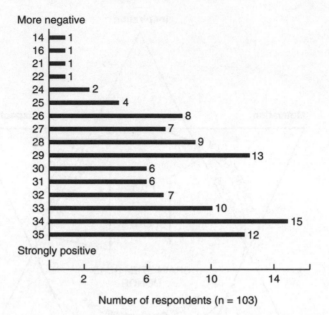

More negative

Strongly positive

Number of respondents (n = 103)

Fig. 10.5 Attitude score towards organ donation. Reproduced with permission from Watkinson (1995) *Journal of Advanced Nursing*, **22**, 932.

with the psychosocial needs of critically ill patients and their families. The perception of these needs will affect nurses' interactions with family members (O'Neil Norris & Grove, 1986). The crisis these families face, suggests Aguilera (1990), may bring both danger and opportunity. Danger in the sense that the family structure may be overwhelmed, opportunity in that individuals in a time of crisis are more receptive to therapeutic influence.

A number of studies have set out to explore and describe the needs of the families of critically ill patients (Leske, 1986; Hickey & Lewandowski, 1988; Liddle, 1988; Coulter, 1989; McLauchlan, 1990).

Some early descriptive work by Hampe (1975) explored the needs of spouses of terminally ill partners and provided an empirical basis for further studies. All eight of the following major needs were expressed by 93% of the 27 spouses interviewed.

The need to be:

(1) With the dying person
(2) Helpful to the dying person
(3) Assured that the dying person is comfortable
(4) Informed of the person's condition
(5) Informed of impending death
(6) Able to ventilate emotions
(7) Comforted and supported by family members
(8) Accepted, supported and comforted by health professionals.

Building on Hampe's work, in what has perhaps become a classic study,

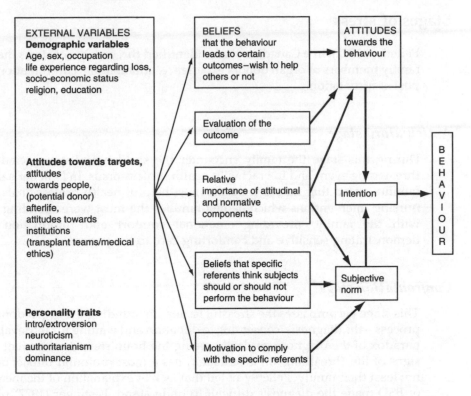

→ Possible explanations for observed relations between external variables and behaviour

→ Stable theoretical relations linking belief to behaviour

Fig. 10.6 Scheme representing possible explanations for observed relationships between external variables and behaviour regarding organ donation. Adapted from Fishbein's model (Ajzen & Fishbein, 1980).

Molter (1979) identified felt and expressed needs occurring in the families of critically ill patients. Relatives need to feel that there is hope and have their questions answered honestly, with explanations given in terms that they understand. Studies by Leske (1986) and O'Neil Norris & Grove (1986) substantiated Molter's findings. Nevertheless, O'Neil Norris & Grove found incongruent perceptions between critical care nurses and families over the needs of families. Critical care nurses perceived that the normative needs of giving information to the family, and demonstrating that health professionals cared about the patient, were the important family needs. However, offering hope to the families of potential brain stem dead patients would not always be honest. There is perhaps, some hope in the initial acute period, when the certainty of diagnosis still hangs in the balance of time.

Further studies have examined the feelings of donor families: Bartucci, 1987; Bisnaire *et al.*, 1988; Buckley, 1989; Perez-San-Gregorio *et al.*, 1992; Sque & Payne, 1996).

Stages of stress

Pelletier (1992), in a Canadian study, identified three stages of stress that the family members of organ donors experience: anticipation, confrontation and post-confrontation.

Anticipatory stage

During this stage the family encounter the sudden and unexpected life-threatening event and interact with health professionals. In Pelletier's study families noted that nurses were the most helpful health professionals. The nursing interventions which helped families the most were spending time with the family, providing emotional comfort and information and demonstrating sensitive and comforting care to the patient.

Confrontation stage

This stage encompasses the stressful issues surrounding the organ donation process – the diagnosis, consenting to donation and waiting for retrieval. The paradox of the diagnosis of death, seeing the brain stem dead patient with signs of life, 'breathing' on a ventilator, has a most profound impact on all, not least their family. Pelletier noted that lack of explanation of the meaning of BSD made the diagnosis difficult to understand. Festinger (1977) postulated that the presence of dissonance motivates the individual to reduce it in order to achieve consistency. The notion of cognitive dissonance may be very strong during this stage. During this acute grief-stricken state, families are at their most vulnerable. They need well-educated and skilled nurses to support them.

Families that were not approached, or approached too late to donate, found this very stressful, similar findings were reported by Bartucci (1987).

Once permission to donate was given, waiting for the retrieval was reported as the most stressful time. The waiting for the donation to take place and parting with the loved one, saying 'goodbye', may generate questions and doubts about death.

Post-confrontational stage

The impact of death on other family members may affect their emotional, physical, spiritual and social well-being. In spite of this, Pelletier (1992) found that organ donation had given positive meaning to the tragic loss that families felt. Silvey (1990) found that the family suffering bereavement remembers compassionate acts clearly, the same may be true for uncompassionate acts. Hence the importance of an empathetic nursing approach by knowledgeable nurses.

Working with donor families

Wolley (1990) advocates the use of 'crisis theory' as a paradigm to working with families. Adapting this tripartite framework, the following could be achieved:

- A cognitive understanding of BSD
- Providing appropriate situational support for the family
- Enabling the family to establish effective coping strategies.

This paradigm may provide the basis for restoration of their emotional equilibrium, and indeed, may also help those intimately involved in the process namely the nursing and medical teams.

Sque & Payne (1996), in a study which explored the experiences of 24 donor relatives in the UK, construct a model of conflict resolution around the issues of dissonant loss. Seven key experiences are reflected upon:

(1) Recalling – the last time of being together
(2) Informing – discovering something is wrong
(3) Hoping – waiting for the diagnosis with expectations
(4) Realising – things are going wrong and the likelihood of death
(5) Deciding – confirmation of BSD tests
(6) Parting – saying 'goodbye' and confusion
(7) Coping – dealing with grief and donation.

Peplau (1969), with great insight, suggests that the nurse is required not only to observe the patient and their family, but also their own participation in this relationship. With the plethora of monitoring and supportive equipment that surrounds potential and actual brain stem dead patients, this compassionate role is perhaps even more important today.

In a study by the author into the perceptions and experiences of critical care nurses caring for actual and potential organ donors, Watkinson (1995) found that the close involvement of the nurse can often help reduce family stress. Where time enables a good rapport between nurse and family to be established, sharing the experience was found to be mutually beneficial. Indeed, when nurses were unable, or had failed perhaps due to the speed of events, to establish a good rapport with the patients family, breaking news of the patient's death was considered stressful. This was mainly because of the uncertainty of the families reaction. Figure 10.7 depicts the possible ways that dissonance may affect carers.

One staff nurse highlighted the fact that:

'...your attitude very much will make the difference on whether the relatives will donate or not, and how you approach them...So you are in a very honoured position really. Because you are making all the difference to the patient as well as giving them a dignified death and helping the relatives.'

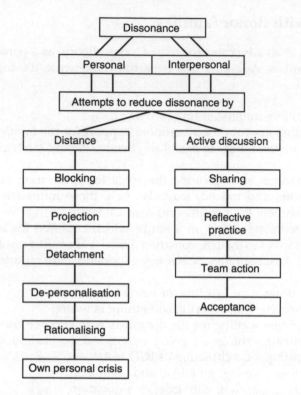

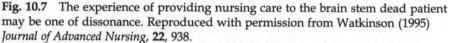

Fig. 10.7 The experience of providing nursing care to the brain stem dead patient may be one of dissonance. Reproduced with permission from Watkinson (1995) *Journal of Advanced Nursing*, **22**, 938.

Making sense of the experience is something that many relatives and hospital staff grapple with. For the health care professionals this is something that perhaps can be left at work, though frequently, and not surprisingly, invades their personal lives too. However, for the family it is something that they will perhaps carry for the rest of their lives. Getting the support right is therefore crucial to aid their understanding and enable the grieving process to be worked through. There are no short cuts or easy fixes.

Why relatives may refuse to donate

Following a two-year confidential survey a report on the relatives' refusal of organ donation, by the same title, was produced (UKTCA & BACCN, 1995). Over a two-year period the survey recorded 1991 cases of BSD which resulted in the data given in Table 10.2.

From the intensive care unit staff the main restriction to organ retrieval seems to be the dislike of adding to relatives' distress, followed by lack of training on how to approach relatives, a finding supported by Malecki & Hoffman (1987). Fear of expressing their emotions, being blamed, not

Table 10.2   Why relatives refuse to donate (UKTCA & BACCN, 1995: 19).

1214 (61%) cases where the offer of donation was made
 515 (26%) cases of relatives' refusal
 239 (12%) case of non-approach (usually due to medical unsuitability of any
                potential organs)

Factors that the report suggest are likely to increase donation:

(1)   Presence of a parent at the time of request
(2)   The patient being aged 15–24 or over 65 years
(3)   A plan for cremation of the body
(4)   The request being made after the second set of brain stem death tests
(5)   Situations where more than one hour elapses between the two sets of brain stem
     death tests

The five most common reasons for refusal were recorded as:

(1)   Relative(s) did not want surgery on the body (24%)
(2)   Patient had stated in the past that he/she did not wish donation to take place
     (21%)
(3)   Relative(s) felt patient had suffered enough (21%)
(4)   Relative(s) were divided over the decision (19%)
(5)   The relative(s) were not sure whether the patient would have agreed to organ
     donation (18%)

knowing all the answers, or how to cope with relatives reactions, may compound this.

Conclusion

This chapter has set the scene regarding what may happen in the intensive or critical care unit when a patient has been diagnosed as brain stem dead. The causes of BSD and the importance of the brain stem have been discussed. Some of the services of the UKTSSA have been highlighted. What has not been mentioned is the crucial role of the transplant coordinator who works very closely with donor families, the intensive care staff and the potential recipients of organs. Their role is one of supporting the family through the donation process and giving information on how the recipient is progressing following transplantation. The normative and expressed needs of donor families has been detailed.

It is important to state that grief does not diminish through or because of organ donation. Families often report that the donor achieved something through their untimely demise. That part of them, 'their kindness and caring' live on (Sque & Payne, 1996). What organ donation does do is change the emphasis on death. It has become a watershed in the relationship between Judeo-Christian ethics and scientific advancement. As Moran (1986) states the option of organ donation gives Christians a concrete opportunity to act as 'people of the resurrection' by passing on life-giving organs when they are no longer required.

Teaching and learning focus on changing the emphasis on death

Rationale

The rationale is to enable course participants to examine the UK brain stem death criteria and strategies of interaction with the potential organ donor family.

Activity

Read carefully through the following scenario:

Mr and Mrs Brown live in Whiteley with their two children, Michael aged 9 and Catherine aged 7 years. Mr Brown is a coach driver in his mid-fifties, his wife is about ten years younger. Times had been hard for the Brown family. Mr Brown had had several poorly paid jobs over recent years, his low wage supplemented by his wife's income as a part-time cleaner. Mrs Brown also cared for her mother who lived just around the corner from their three-bedroomed terraced house. Holidays were a luxury they could not afford.

Michael enjoyed all the fun and games that 9-year-old boys play, and had been pestering his mother for some weeks about going on a Church Youth Club camp. Finally she relented and agreed to let him go on the last day that names had to be in. It would be the first time that Michael had been away from home. To 'earn' a little extra pocket money, Michael helped his father clean his coach at weekends. Excitedly he left home on a Saturday morning for six nights away in Cornwall.

The following Friday 1.15 PM:

On the intensive care unit (ICU) a telephone call from the Accident and Emergency Department (A&E) warns of the imminent admission of a child in need of ventilation following a drowning accident. A few minutes and one cardiac arrest later, Michael is admitted to the ICU for elective ventilation and continued resuscitation. He is cold, wet and unresponsive.

Earlier that morning he had been on a beach-combing expedition. Michael and the rest of the children had been told not to go too close to the sea. Unfortunately Michael had found a ridge of shingle which jutted out at right angles to the beach. He slipped and was quickly carried out of his depth. A supervising adult entered the water but it was too late. Michael was nowhere to be seen. Just at that time a search-and-rescue helicopter passed overhead on a training flight. An observant crew member saw the shore-side commotion and found Michael some 15 minutes after he had slipped into the water. He was deeply unconscious and cold.

2 PM:

Neurological observations reveal a fixed and dilated left pupil. Full resuscitation continues to prevent Michael's brain swelling and causing further cerebral damage. The police are contacted to bring the next of kin into hospital. However, Michael's father is away on a long distance coach trip on the continent.

6 PM:

Michael is now warm and has a good circulation, though he remains deeply unconscious. He has an intravenous infusion (IVI), going into his arm. A urinary catheter ensures that his bladder remains empty and monitors his renal function, whilst an endotracheal tube is in situ, (this is a tube to enable Michael to be ventilated). It maintains his airway allowing oxygen enriched air to inflate his lungs and carbon dioxide to be removed by the ventilator. To a lay person he looks as though he is sleeping as the ventilator takes each breath for him.

Plan:

It is decided to ventilate Michael for 48 hours before full neurological reassessment and possible brain stem death tests are performed. His mother and grandmother arrive and are in the ICU waiting room.

Now consider the following questions:

- What information do they require?
- How will you convey this?
- Hope is something we cling on to. How will you handle this?
- Should the family be involved in the care of Michael? If so how, when and why?
- What other agencies would you involve and why? What is their role?
- How will brain stem tests be explained to the family?
- Can they be present for the tests if they wish? How would you facilitate this?
- What strategies can be used to reduce a conflict of interests between the nursing and medical staff should they arise?
- How could the family be given the opportunity to donate Michael's organs?
- How may the team ensure that the family's needs are met?
  - During their bedside vigil
  - Preparing to say goodbye

- Risk taking/appropriateness
- Following the second set of tests and the diagnosis of brain stem death how will the team debrief?

The key issues raised through the activity are:

- The importance of allowing the bereaved family time to react and reflect
- The positive use of silence and therapeutic touch appropriately utilised may help to facilitate a sharing relationship
- The caring team being honest and consistent throughout
- The dangers of avoidance, rushing and protecting from the truth
- The need to engender a culture of care.

Learning outcomes

The learning outcomes stimulated by the activities are for the course participants to:

- Explore the values and attitudes that surround death
- Examine and clarify their own beliefs about brain stem function tests
- Qualify the importance of teamwork when communicating with a grieving family, through the use of a life and death scenario.

Chapter 11
Mass Disaster

Anne Eyre

This chapter documents case studies and personal accounts from those who have been involved in a disaster. It then goes on to look at key issues which face survivors and the relatives and friends of those who died as well as the emergency services. It brings together very recent knowledge and experience of coping with disaster.

The perspectives from which this chapter is written are: phenomenological, professional and empirical.

Introduction

'Knowing that I was totally unable to help myself or, indeed, anyone else around me, and having seen no signs of encouragement in front of me, I had accepted the fact that soon my pain and suffering would stop and that I would not feel anything at all.

At that time, my sense of panic seemed to disappear as it merely seemed futile. Instead my thoughts turned to my family and my girlfriend. I could see their faces in my mind but the images were blurred. I felt desperately sad as I thought of how distraught they would be. I just wanted to be with them again, so that I could say goodbye "properly". I tried to bring their images into focus so that I could be with them in spirit, but they merely faded.'

(Rob White, Hillsborough survivor in Taylor *et al.* 1995: 66)

Mr Shinto was in bed when the earthquake struck:

'I remember waking up and thinking at first that this was just another small earthquake, then the wall behind my bed collapsed on to me. Luckily our water boiler is next to the bed and it stopped the wall falling right on me. Even so, I was totally trapped. I knew my wife was up. I called to her but got no reply and was afraid she was dead.'

Mrs Shinto had gone to use the lavatory at the back of the house.

'I felt the ground move, sort of round and round, and the plaster from the ceiling came down. I had to kick the door to get out. Our house had collapsed. It had actually moved down the street a few metres.

I called for my husband but there was no reply. I could see the corner of the bed sticking out of the rubble. Then I heard his voice. Some of my neighbours came round and together we pulled him out, but it took us two hours. The survivors were all out in the street, hugging one another and crying with relief. Most people were barefoot as they had escaped straight from their beds, and this was midwinter so it was really cold.

After a few weeks we moved into this temporary house – it's OK, but small. It is right out on the edge of the city. It's a 20-minute walk to the nearest metro station from here and then half an hour by metro into town. We don't really need to get to town but it is really tough for the younger people who have to go to work.'

(IFRCRCS, 1996: 67)

When we think of disasters we tend to conjure up a range of images in our minds and perhaps remember recent tragedies with which we are familiar. The whole notion of mass disasters conjures up large-scale tragedy on an uncontrollable scale of panic and disorder; indeed many definitions of 'disaster' are based on such notions of chaos, uncontrollability and unpredictability.

Disasters such as famine, drought or civil war tend to be things that happen to 'other people' in communities or societies we would prefer to think of as somehow more vulnerable and prone than our own. Yet when technological or humanly caused disasters happen to 'ordinary people' like ourselves travelling on a plane or train, working in a factory or watching a football match, we suddenly become aware of our own frailty and vulnerability. Perhaps this is one of the reasons why news of disaster so appals and frightens us; we know that we might be equally as powerless and vulnerable as those presented to us through distressing pictures and images.

It is emotionally easier for us to conceive and think of disasters from a remote perspective – to think of victims as 'them' rather than 'us'. However, as Hodgkinson & Stewart point out:

'... disaster survivors are basically very ordinary people – the only thing that distinguishes them from the reader of this book is that they happened to be in the wrong place at the wrong time.'

(Hodgkinson & Stewart, 1991: 1)

Today we are increasingly in close proximity to many disaster situations as they happen through the technology and immediacy of live media broadcasts. Although we are at a physical distance from the tragic scenes unfolding in front of our eyes, some suggest that society's fascination with disaster reflects our desire to enter into the emotion of disaster. We can do this vicariously through a process by which we remain in control. Thus we can switch off the television, we can know the outcome of a disaster movie and in the comfort of our imagination we can ask ourselves whether we would be a hero and save others; but at the end of the day we know this is fantasy.

The quotations above highlight the graphic reality of disaster experience from survivors' points of view. The first, from a survivor of the crush at the Hillsborough football stadium, demonstrates an extreme point in his experience during which the feelings of panic and horror started to fade away as if he were a bystander watching his own demise. He goes on to describe the feeling of coming out of the trance he let himself fall into and facing the glaring reality of the horrific experience he was in at the moment of rescue.

The extract highlights that there may be a whole range of emotions and experiences gone through in experiencing disaster. The Hillsborough quote has been chosen because, as a televised disaster, many of us are familiar with it and the images which are frequently played back of spectators in a state of panic and frenzied activity. Yet this is only part of the Hillsborough story and its victims. There are also the experiences of those rescue workers who struggled to make sense of the pandemonium and confusion both at the time and in the months and years after, and there are relatives and friends of direct victims who watched the disaster on television knowing their loved ones were present. Others knew that as football fans they had stood on those same terraces or were faced with the sudden realisation that they might have been equally vulnerable any time they went to a football game. The emotional effects of a single disaster extend like ripples to these primary, secondary and tertiary level victims.

As in the example above, a primary victim involved in a disaster situation may, throughout the event, go through a range of emotions and behaviours from activity to passivity, from anger and pain, to lethargy and numbness. Although the portrayal of disasters often simplifies the experiences and behaviours of participants, we tend to underestimate the time it takes to recover. We must be aware of this complex range of emotions and behaviours and the fact that they will vary at different times and stages of the disaster experience and rehabilitation.

The second quotation is an account from two survivors of the 1995 Kobe earthquake. It has been chosen to reflect the contrast with Hillsborough in terms of the type, time-scale and scope of disaster and so warns against generalising about disaster experience. It also focuses on the severe nature and scale of disaster experience which is likely to be almost beyond the conception of most readers. It is impossible for those who have never experienced earthquakes and their aftermath first-hand to be able to fully empathise with Mr and Mrs Shinto's experiences. This highlights the importance of listening to and giving credence to survivors' voices and interpretations.

This sort of approach – which gives priority to the experiences of those involved in disaster, particularly survivors as victims – is one reflected throughout this chapter which focuses on the psychological and social aspects of disaster and the longer term emotional effects of experiencing loss and bereavement on a large scale.

Defining 'disaster'

Before we go any further it is important to have a clear understanding of what we mean by disaster and the nature of the definition being employed in this chapter.

> 'A disaster can be defined as the impact of a natural or man-made phe-
> nomenon happening on a vulnerable population to cause disruption,
> damage and casualties.'
>
> (Davis & Wall, 1992: 89)

This definition highlights the range of disciplines which form part of the field of disaster management ranging from those focusing on the structural causes and consequences of disaster (engineering and geology, for example) to those embracing the human or social dimensions of disaster (including development studies, legal and political studies, and sociological studies). The latter approach embraces a qualitative approach in terms of including the psychosocial aspects of disaster, that is the beliefs, feelings, attitudes and experiential dimensions of those involved.

Sociological definitions of disaster reflect this emphasis on the social dimensions of tragedy. Quarantelli, for example, highlights how sociologists have been able to shift from primarily physical referents of the term 'disaster' to definitions of a more social nature (1978: 3). Such definitions imply that there will be a social response to the social disruption, whether by individuals or societies. Such an approach to disaster studies complements the more technical contributions to our understanding of why disasters happen and how we can better plan and prepare for them. Indeed some writers, such as Turner (1978), highlight how both disciplinary approaches are important given that disasters can often be thought of as 'socio-technical' events, products of a combination of human and/or engineering factors.

Different types of disaster have been distinguished within this field of study, for example natural as opposed to humanly caused or technological disasters. Those caused by natural hazards have been classified in terms of being either 'slow onset', for example a slowly developing and foreseeable situation of drought or flooding or 'fast impact' such as volcanic eruption, cyclone or flash flood. Humanly caused or technological disasters include civil disturbances, transport, industrial and crowd-related incidents.

In studying examples of disaster it is useful to employ the concept of the 'disaster cycle' which addresses the different phases of disaster. Although the media tends to focus on the impact and shorter term consequences of disaster, researchers adopt a much longer term perspective and recognise that disasters can be better conceived of and understood in terms of the following phases: preparedness (the degree to which communities have planned and prepared for coping with hazards), the event itself, relief and rehabilitation and reconstruction (responding to the immediate and basic needs of survivors, restoring basic services and longer term recovery), and longer term mitigation (vulnerability reduction) which brings us back to the preparedness and planning stages (Davis & Wall, 1992: 102).

It is helpful to explain these basic concepts and ideas which form part of the field of disaster management because they show that a range of approaches is important for a fuller understanding. However, within disaster management there has tended, until recently, to be a dominant emphasis on a technocratic approach (emphasising engineering and scientific perspectives) and a neglect, and even resistance, to the contribution of the psychosocial dimensions. This anomaly is thankfully now being addressed through a greater understanding of, and interest in, psychological and sociological studies which highlight the importance of the longer term emotional impact of disasters, phenomena such as post-traumatic stress and the need for interdisciplinary research.

Part of the reason for this gap in our understanding and emphasis has been the difficulty in measuring phenomena which cannot be physically seen and hence easily quantified. There is also the feeling that disasters are relatively rare events which, by the sort of definitions mentioned above, are unlikely, cannot be planned for and hence do not merit the degree of preparation and attention that more common everyday situations deserve. However, more forward looking professionals and those dealing with the longer term impact and effects of disasters on victims do recognise that there are some similarities and mutual lessons to be learned from those working with victims of large-scale tragedy and those dealing with loss and bereavement on smaller scales.

The extent of disaster

Some practitioners define situations of disaster in numerical terms (for example where more than a 100 people are killed or seriously injured). Such measures have been the basis for tabulating the number and impact of disasters over time, type and region. The *World Disasters Report*, which gives an annual breakdown of trends in the number and impact of disasters, acknowledges the difficulty in producing accurate and meaningful data. With this in mind, however, it shows how the number of people killed by disaster has risen in the past 25 years or so (FRCRCS, 1997: 116). Citing statistics from the Centre for Research on the Epidemiology of Disasters (CRED), it states:

'While in Africa and Asia this partly reflects an increase in population and hence people exposed to disaster, in Europe the upward trend reflects both the rise in traffic-accident deaths and the wars and civil unrest of the last decade.'

(IFRCRCS, 1997: 116)

In terms of type of disaster, famine remains the biggest killer with an annual average of over 73 000 between 1971 and 1995 and has also affected the greatest number of people, an average of over 60 million between 1971 and 1995 (IFRCRCS, 1997: 119). While flooding also affected similar numbers, fewer have been killed as they were able to move away from the danger. Other disasters with a natural trigger, such as earthquakes and volcanoes, affect much fewer people, but kill a far greater proportion of those affected (IFRCRCS, 1997: 119).

While a quantitative approach such as this helps us to appreciate the vast numbers of people affected by disaster worldwide it has its limitations. It does not give us the sort of personal insight detailed in the quotations at the start of this chapter. Also, in terms of qualitative effects for example, we would need to take account of the ripple effect on different levels of victims (direct survivors, rescue workers, friends and relatives, etc.) as discussed above. While we can more easily give a figure to the number of people killed or physically injured, it is much harder to quantify the psychological impact of disasters.

Psychological research into disaster

Part of the psychological research into disaster focuses on the behaviour of individuals in the impact phase and how and why people respond differently to life-threatening situations. It has been observed that while some people 'freeze' in the face of danger others become activated, a response which in many cases can make the difference between life and death. The testimony of some survivors suggests that they instinctively experience a heightened sense of perception and physical response in the face of danger which enables them to channel important bodily resources into survival efforts. These responses have even been found to confound scientific predictions and expectations about the human body's ability to respond to such extreme situations of physical challenge.

Part of the explanation for such remarkable accounts of survival has been based on biological studies of the 'fight v. flight' response seen in animals. Biological explanations also focus on neurological responses in the brain and the production of chemicals which can help to activate the body's response. With humans, however, it is suggested that the ability to reason and to feel fear, guilt and emotion can become either an asset or a liability in such situations. Perhaps the conflict involved in choosing between saving oneself and saving others can help to explain why some people become paralysed in the face of emergency situations.

This sort of research is still in its infancy but may have important implications for the selection and training of those involved in rescue work or other occupations likely to involve encounter with situations of personal danger and survival. What is of interest to health workers is the longer term effects of personal survival from such conditions and the relationship between the particular experiences of disaster survivors, the sense they make of those experiences and the longer term processes of mental and emotional recovery.

Grieving loss through disaster

Grieving loss through disaster shares many of the symptoms of more 'normal' grief, but also includes some special features. It comes under the category of sudden deaths, those which occur without warning and which, as Worden (1991) stresses, require special understanding and intervention. He summarises the common conclusion of various studies that sudden deaths are more difficult to grieve than other deaths in which there is some prior warning that death is imminent.

'A sudden death will usually leave the survivor with a sense of unreality about the loss. Whenever the phone rings and one learns that a loved one has died unexpectedly, it creates this sense of unreality which may last a long time. It is not unusual for the survivor to experience nightmares and intrusive images after a sudden loss, even though they were not present at the time of the death. Appropriate counselling intervention can help the survivor deal with this manifestation of sudden death and heighten the reality of the event.'

(Worden, 1991: 98)

If we apply the above quotation to a situation of losing someone through disaster we get some insight into the potential experiences and feelings associated with sudden loss. One may first be alerted to a tragedy through a newsflash and start to become concerned about a relative or friend. The media arrive at the scene of a tragedy much more quickly these days, though reliable information takes time to process. Hence the combination of uncertainty and the exposure to emotional, unedited images may be immensely distressing for those who know people at the scene. The recollection of graphic images may persist as part of the process described by Worden above, particularly as details of disaster and tragic death are recounted by the media in the days after.

Many survivors who have been present at an event and have experienced scenes first-hand find that television coverage later can be one trigger for flashback experiences and memories. Hodgkinson & Stewart describe the intrusion of the 'death imprint' which

'... comprises a condensation of the entire experience – images of the impact such as the sight of bodies dismembered or crushed, the sounds of screaming, or the smell of burning flesh. No details are spared the survivor who may appear to have a "spellbound fascination" with the events.'

(Hodgkinson & Stewart, 1991: 3)

One way in which the media can trigger flashbacks is by drawing on photographs which become symbols of a particular disaster or film footage, either of which are projected on an anniversary or when a similar tragedy occurs. The sudden appearance of these images can be distressing particularly when viewers are unprepared for the portrayal and are still trying to come to terms with the reality of the event. The imagery need not be directly related to the actual event itself. Hodgkinson & Stewart (1991: 3) cite the experience of a survivor from the Piper Alpha disaster in 1988 for whom flashback was triggered by a film about the Korean War. Many disaster survivors find that having experienced a disaster first-hand makes them more sensitive to later disasters since they can identify with the feelings of the new victims.

Survivor guilt

As well as the lack of prior warning, a second feature associated with sudden death is the exacerbation of guilt feelings. Worden (1991: 98) states that although guilt feelings are common following any kind of death they may be strongly present in cases of sudden death, for example as stressed in the form of 'if only . . .' statements. The apparent arbitrariness of when and how disasters strike does not lessen the employment of 'if only . . .' sentiments and may only confound this sense of guilt.

For those directly involved in a disaster and who survived when others did not, this sense of 'survivor guilt' may be particularly heightened. It may take the form of general guilt about why the individual was spared or focus specifically on aspects of behaviour, on what one did or did not do or could and should have done. Hodgkinson & Stewart state that such guilt may be particularly intense where parents survive their children or where there is competition for survival (1991: 4). They suggest that survivor guilt presupposes the presence of choice and the power to exercise it which in reality may not have been actually possible. In this sense the guilt may be understood as an unconscious attempt to deny or undo this sense of helplessness (1991: 6).

Part of the healing process here includes enabling the survivor to acknowledge the reality of their helplessness and the fact that they were not responsible for it. In discussing post-traumatic stress, Hodgkinson & Stewart state that for those bereaved by disaster, the helplessness associated with guilt may be paramount. Treatment involves exploring the conflicts related to the parting and decisions that put the person in the position in which they met their death. The process of catharsis is described as follows:

'The person must be encouraged to identify what the feelings are related to, or what the conflict is that they are attached to – this is what emotional processing is all about, the working through not merely of feelings, but also of their significance.'

(Hodgkinson & Stewart, 1991: 166)

Blame is a further feature associated with sudden death. 'Related to the guilt is the need to blame, and in the case of a sudden death, the need to blame someone for what happened is extremely strong' (Worden, 1991: 99). In situations of mass tragic death, finding a scapegoat and allocating blame may be a way of helping to make sense of the scale of the unbelievable and inexplicable. The media are often influential in this respect, focusing in the first few days after an event on perpetrators and innocent victims, importing a well-rehearsed narrative which polarises the 'heroes' and the 'villains', regardless of the appropriateness of these constructions. This may be quite unhelpful for survivors who are still in shock and trying to make sense of the event itself. The potential for survivor guilt among these victims may be increased in an accusatory environment allocating blame and accountability before the full facts are available and a proper process of investigation has begun.

Post-disaster legal processes

This links with a further feature of sudden death which is particularly significant after disaster, namely the involvement of medical and legal authorities and processes. There may be a series of inquiries and investigations associated with disasters and legal proceedings which may continue for a number of years. A feature of judicial systems is that they are long, drawn-out and the bureaucratic procedures have little regard for the emotional trauma they prolong. Worden outlines both the positive and negative effects of legal interruptions:

'The delays can serve one of two functions: they can delay the grieving process; that is people who are grieving may be so distracted by the details of the trial that they are kept from dealing with their own grief on a first-hand basis. However, there are times when these legal interruptions can play a positive role. When there is some adjudication of a case and the case is closed, this can help put some closure on their grief.'

(Worden, 1991: 99)

Worden's quotation focuses on situations involving a trial. Not all public inquiries into disasters lead to prosecution and it is rare for individuals or companies to be found culpable and prosecuted. This is a cause of continuing distress for victims of disasters such as Bhopal, Hillsborough and others where calls persist for further legal action. Meanwhile, although inquiries into the tragedies such as the Dunblane shootings and the Oklahoma bombing may have established who the perpetrators were and where the blame lies, this does not necessarily ease the sense of loss or anger for relatives and survivors.

In some situations survivors and family members may attend and even contribute to inquests set up to inquire into the circumstances in which deaths occurred, to establish the medical cause of death and present a verdict reflecting the circumstances of death. From their detailed study into such legal processes, Scraton *et al.* (1995) suggest that this is problematic due to the nature of the British inquest system which they describe as 'both a dishonest and inadequate process':

'In most cases the coroner promises a thorough and searching inquiry, guaranteeing that the bereaved will have their questions fully examined and, wherever possible, answered. This rarely happens. The coroner conducts and directs the preliminary investigation and gathers evidence. Families have no right of access, or disclosure, to that evidence. The coroner decides from that evidence who will be called as witnesses. Families, or any other 'interested parties', have no right to call witnesses. The coroner organises the presentation of evidence, the order of cross-examination, the style and content of questioning by legal representatives and the broader conduct of the inquest. Families have no access to legal aid and the costs of representation, particularly in complex cases, are prohibitive. Only the coroner can address the jury, both summing-up the case and providing legal direction. Families or their lawyers cannot sum up the case or challenge the coroner's direction before the jury. And it is the coroner who puts the acceptable verdicts to the jury, directing them to the verdict which is closest to his or her interpretation. Jurists cannot add riders, nor can families ask for words to be included.'

(Scraton *et al.*, 1995: vi)

In their analysis of the various investigative and inquest procedures following the Hillsborough disaster, Scraton *et al.* (1995) highlight how the procedural processes and insensitive treatment by officials made for a particularly distressing experience for families and survivors. Although their experience was particularly conflictual given the role of the police as being both themselves under investigation and the agents of investigation for the inquiries and the inquest in this case, the authors' conclusions have clear implications for others who may experience post-disaster inquests:

'For them the process was traumatic. They were survivors of a major disaster, many had lost family and friends, and they were well aware that they could easily have died. Some suffered injury, others lost consciousness and all had endured mental suffering. Recounting events to investigating officers and going through the process of giving evidence, demanded that survivors relived the events of the Disaster. For those revisited by investigating officers or those who gave evidence, their statements and deeply personal experiences, were repeatedly exposed to scrutiny, cross-examination and doubt. It remains a matter of considerable concern that such lengthy proceedings appear to neglect the long-term suffering and trauma which they inflict on those who have survived such tragedies. While lawyers swap jokes, score points and make inappropriate asides, the survivor stands before the court publicly vulnerable, personally traumatised and without protection. It is a reprehensible process in which pleasantries and platitudes are exchanged while the feelings of people, whose experiences will live with them for the rest of their life, are treated in a cavalier manner.'

(Scraton *et al.*, 1995: 140)

It is hardly surprising then that many feel victimised by 'the system' in the aftermath of disasters and angry when the processes they feel should help them have the opposite effect. An inordinate significance may have been placed on inquiries and the legal process as part of the very real need associated with sudden death to understand why the deaths happened. Worden sees this search for meaning as related to the need for mastery when a death has been traumatic (1991: 100).

Feelings of helplessness

Linked with this is a sense of helplessness on the part of survivors as a further feature of sudden death. Worden explains that this is because this type of death 'is an assault on our sense of power and on our sense of orderliness' (1991: 99). The helplessness is also associated with the loss of certainty. Hodgkinson & Stewart expand on the nature of disaster-related loss:

'In disasters people lose loved ones, relatives and friends, and they lose property, but above all, in psychological terms, they lose faith – not religious faith, but faith in the fact that B follows A – the faith that life has a certain consistency or predictability. Once something of this nature has happened to a person, it is very difficult for them to believe that life can ever be the same again.'

(Hodgkinson & Stewart, 1991: 1–2)

An incredible sense of rage and anger may accompany this helplessness which may be expressed verbally and physically. Worden thus stresses that counsellors should be aware that the desire for retribution may be a defence against both the reality and the pain of the death. He suggests that the expression of rage may help to counter the helpless feelings they are experiencing. In some circumstances anger may be positively channelled into the creative efforts of action groups addressing political and legal issues arising from disasters as shall be discussed later.

Post-traumatic stress disorder (PTSD)

Much emphasis is now being placed on post-traumatic stress disorder (PTSD) as a significant aspect of disasters. In Britain discussions about the definition and measurements of PTSD have started to revolve around complex legal, social and political debates. For our purposes it is important to establish here the nature and symptoms of post-trauma stress and of PTSD and ways of addressing them.

Writers on PTSD emphasise that it is 'a very normal human response to a very abnormal situation' (Kinchin, 1994: 2). This is because these situations are associated with sudden, shocking and terrifying events which bring into stark relief the uncertainty, unpredictability and insecurity of human vulnerability. In this sense it should be recognised that a stress reaction is to be expected in anyone who has gone through a traumatic experience. In other words they are likely to experience post-trauma stress. For some a more persistent and intense form of post-trauma stress may occur leading to a diagnosis of PTSD which requires special treatment.

Post-traumatic stress disorder is characterised by the development of a set of specific symptoms. Hodgkinson & Stewart discuss the nature and degree of trauma with reference to:

'... an event that is outside the range of usual human experience and that would be markedly distressing to almost anyone, e.g. serious threat to one's life or physical integrity; serious threat to one's children, spouse, or other close relatives and friends; sudden destruction of one's home or community; or seeing another person who has recently been, or is being, seriously injured or killed as a result of an accident or physical violence.'

(Hodgkinson & Stewart, 1991: 11)

Post-traumatic stress disorder was first given official recognition as a diagnostic category in 1980 in the third edition of the *Diagnostic and Statistical Manual of Mental Disorders* of the American Psychiatric Association (DSM-III). This was the culmination of various initiatives examining traumatic stress in victims of various types of circumstance including war, the Holocaust, hostage-taking and armed crime. In this respect, PTSD itself was not new in 1980 only its formal identification and classification. Thus what in previous generations was labelled 'shell shock', 'battle fatigue' or 'cowardice' might well today be diagnosed as symptoms of post-trauma stress.

An important feature of PTSD is that the experiences either are or are perceived by the sufferer to be life threatening. In 1994 the definition of PTSD was revised in recognition of the significance of perception and interpretation in determining a traumatic event. Post-traumatic stress disorder is now seen to comprise a set of symptoms that may follow the experiencing, witnessing or confronting of an event involving actual or threatened serious injury or death, or a threat to the physical integrity of the self or of others. The victim's perception is important here as opposed to an outsider's rationale of the reality, or not, of the threat. Kinchin states:

'The event only has to be perceived as traumatic by the victim. In reality the incident might not pose a serious threat to life, but as the incident is

genuinely considered to be life-threatening, then the victim has experienced an event outside the range of normal human experience.'

(Kinchin, 1994: 2)

There are a number of symptoms of PTSD which have been listed under
three main groups of symptoms: re-experience phenomena, avoidance or
numbing reactions and symptoms of increased arousal. According to DSM-
III R (a revised edition of DSM-III) five criteria need to be met before a
diagnosis of PTSD can be made. They are as follows:

'(1)   The person must have witnessed or experienced a serious threat
       (real or perceived) to his life or physical well-being
 (2)   The person must re-experience the event, or part of the event, in
       some form
 (3)   The person must persistently avoid situations associated with the
       trauma, or experience a numbing of general responsiveness
 (4)   The person must experience persistent symptoms of increased
       arousal or "over-awareness"
 (5)   Symptoms must have lasted at least a month.'

(Kinchin, 1994: 5)

For further discussion of the symptoms of PTSD see Hodgkinson &
Stewart (1991), Parkinson (1993) and Kinchin (1994). It is important to note
that the symptoms of PTSD may not appear immediately and instead be
delayed for days, weeks or even years. A distinction is also made between
acute PTSD, where the disorder is successfully treated within three months,
and chronic PTSD, persisting for more than three months. In the latter, more
exceptional cases,

'...the "trauma beliefs" have become less susceptible to influence,
repeated avoidance behaviour is well established, and sufferers are far
more likely to default from counselling. Consequently the chronic condition is often compounded by feelings of depression and anxiety, and
treatment becomes more difficult.'

(Kinchin, 1994: 51)

Most people experiencing a traumatic event are unlikely either to
experience the extremes of PTSD or to be so diagnosed. It is estimated that
the number of people suffering from PTSD at any one time is equal to about
1% of the general population, (though Kinchin suggests that the survivors of
a major disaster stand a 30–60% risk of developing PTSD (1994:11)). Having
said this, it is very difficult to quantify the extent of PTSD or other forms of
post-trauma stress in terms of the number of sufferers. Victims may not
recognise the symptoms; if they do acknowledge symptoms they may not
recognise them as being sufficiently serious to merit addressing; even then

they may not visit a doctor (especially given the traditional stigma attached to mental illness). Further, not all GPs are sufficiently knowledgeable about PTSD and its diagnosis and so may not refer patients on. For a whole host of reasons, then, it is difficult to give accurate statistics on trauma-related stress.

Despite this it is possible to identify which types of people and experiences are more likely to be vulnerable. Significant factors here include the degree of exposure to an event and losses, dimensions of the trauma, personality type (neuroticism being causal), any previous history of psychiatric disorder and dimensions of the recovery environment (Hodgkinson & Stewart, 1991: 19–20). High-risk groups include survivors of particular types of disaster (such as shipwrecks, bombings, air crashes and hijacks), victims of rape, abuse or combat and emergency service staff.

Research into social welfare after disasters has also highlighted the potential for significant stress among counsellors and social workers and other volunteers who increasingly are expected to provide treatment and care in the aftermath of disaster. A common experience among social workers and others who have been part of such a response is a tendency to overwork, to be reluctant to take breaks and to labour under a strong sense of urgency and emotional strain (Newburn, 1993: 134). As well as this having implications for those responsible for staff care, workers themselves need to be aware of their personal welfare and coping abilities. Their own needs should not be stigmatised and regarded as evidence of professional ineptitude as has historically been the case:

> 'Social workers appear to be just as reluctant to admit that they cannot or will not be able to cope with everything that confronts them in their jobs as are policemen and firemen, if not more so.'
>
> (Newburn, 1993: 137)

Attitudes are rapidly changing in this area which has resulted in a range of further complex legal and political issues. These have been highlighted by the case of certain police officers at the Hillsborough disaster who have since pursued claims for compensation from their employers. This case and its resolution has implications for all those working in potentially vulnerable environments and for their employers in terms of preparing for, training and protecting their staff.

Responding to post-trauma stress

One of the recurring findings of research into post-trauma stress is that early intervention can significantly mitigate its effects and thereby prevent the development of PTSD. One of the most useful ways in which those involved in trauma can be helped is through being given the opportunity to talk through what has happened in an environment of mutual support and caring. It is suggested that informal processes of 'defusing' have tradition-ally happened within the emergency services, though the extent to which personal experiences and feelings can be expressed and worked through in detail is likely to be somewhat limited in this context. In recognition of this and the need for more to be done, greater emphasis is now placed on psychological debriefing in organisations such as the emergency and armed services.

Psychological debriefing has been defined as:

'A meeting with one or more persons, the purpose of which is to review the impressions and reactions that survivors, helpers and others experi-ence during or after a traumatic incident such as an accident or disaster.'

(Dyregrov (1989) cited in Parkinson, 1993: 150)

Parkinson describes the aim as being to provide an opportunity for people to talk and share their experiences and feelings, to reduce any effects and to lessen the possible development of PTSD. It is the focus on talking through personal experiences and how one feels about it that is crucial and the aspect of post-incident response that has traditionally been neglected. According to Parkinson, psychological debriefing differs from counselling in that rather than involving a series of sessions, usually for an hour at a time, debriefing involves one or more sessions set within a formal structure within two to three days of the incident and with an open-ended time frame (1993: 153). The process involves an introduction and explanation of ground rules, after which members of a group are invited to talk about their expectations, facts, thoughts, impressions and emotional reactions. The role of the leader is to emphasise that the reactions and feelings are entirely normal, to explain post-trauma reactions and the effects that these may have on victims and others and to discuss the possibility of further help and support as appropriate.

Parkinson recommends this type of debriefing as a normal response for all those who have been involved in a traumatic incident, either as survivors, helpers, rescue workers or carers, and calls for further recognition of its advantages:

'Those in authority should ensure that it is not viewed as an optional extra, but is included as a normal part of the response to accidents and disaster. It should be standard operating procedure and written into the rules.'

(Parkinson, 1993: 162)

Furthermore he calls for greater coordination and resourcing:

'There should be a nationally recognised and funded body to provide teams of debriefers who can be called upon when needed and who can give advice and help. This team should be multidisciplinary and the personnel selected and trained.'

(Parkinson, 1993: 162)

Were this to be available it is not only likely that awareness of post-trauma stress in general would be increased, but the need for longer term more extensive treatments would be reduced. Instead a response to the symptoms generally tends to be neglected until a diagnosis of PTSD is made whereupon various methods of treatment may be available. These include behavioural treatments, cognitive therapy, psychotherapy, group therapy and medication (see Hodgkinson & Stewart, 1991, for further discussion).

An important final point to be made with regard to survivors and post-trauma stress is that not all responses are entirely negative. Many survivors refer to positive effects of survival on their lives and outlooks which suggests that there can be room for hope and optimism alongside the despair and hopelessness of the bleaker moments:

'Quite simply, the confrontation with death can reveal the importance of many aspects of life. This may be one of the most positive outcomes of cognitive completion, the giving of meaning and inner form to the experience, and to life thereafter.'

(Hodgkinson & Stewart, 1991: 24, citing Lifton, 1993)

An examination of the social dimensions of disaster also suggests that there can be positive outcomes as well as the more obvious negative ones.

Social responses to disaster

Sociological research into disasters complements our understanding of the psychological dimensions by analysing collective social responses to disaster. Many of the ways in which people behave in the short and longer term of disaster, that appear at face value to be irrational or out of character, can be seen to be fulfilling important social and psychological functions, and are often part of the positive rehabilitative process for individuals or communities in the rehabilitation and reconstruction phases of disaster. This point is supported by the fact that there are some common patterns across communities and societies in the face of collective tragedy despite their different situations. This suggests that some common fundamental needs are being addressed.

It is useful for those health workers planning for and responding to the mental effects and needs post-disaster to be equipped with understanding by learning the lessons of others in the form of case studies. Such behaviour highlights some of the positive outcomes of disaster, such as increased altruism. Case studies are also important for countering the numerous myths about the behaviour of people after disasters which tend to persist and be reinforced by the media in the aftermath of disaster. These are not only particularly unhelpful to the victims of disaster but may be positively unhelpful in guiding those wanting to help.

The myth of anti-social behaviour

One of the myths about disasters that sociologists have challenged is the association between anti-social behaviour, such as looting, and disasters:

> 'Disaster research has fairly well destroyed the myth of anti-social behaviour in disasters... There is very little anti-social behaviour in disasters, if by that is meant panic behaviour or hysterical breakdowns.'
>
> (Taylor, 1978: 253)

This is an important point to make because notions of looting and other anti-social behaviour still persist in the public mind and are often inflated by public rumour and media coverage of disaster events. A classic example of this was the *Sun* newspaper's reporting of the Hillsborough disaster (on the front page, 19 April 1989) in which it alleged that fans had picked the pockets of victims, urinated on police officers and beaten up a police constable. These allegations were later found by Lord Justice Taylor, in his official inquiry, to be unfounded and untrue. However, the apportioning of blame and misconduct by survivors on that day continues to add to their deep distress.

What appears to be more significant in the event and aftermath of disasters is the increase in more positive altruistic reactions in the form of helping behaviour and extensive volunteering by individuals and groups in such crisis situations. Indeed Taylor states that 'the question of pro-social behaviour is a much more meaningful one to address in disaster studies' (1978: 253–4).

There are plenty of examples of different types of pro-social behaviour both in the impact phase and longer term. In the village of Aberfan, South Wales, where a coal tip became unstable and slipped onto a primary school killing 116 people in 1966, the villagers spontaneously participated in rescue attempts and bonded in common identity afterwards in the face of collective grief. In more recent examples too, where an incident has occurred, neighbours in an impacted vicinity have opened their homes and hearts to immediate victims and relatives. The community of Lockerbie billeted American relatives visiting the site of the Pan-Am air crash in 1988; in Sheffield 1989 neighbours of the football stadium took distressed Liverpool supporters into their homes and a bond between the two cities developed after; in Oklahoma City, after the bombing of a federal building in 1995, volunteer rescue workers and counsellors turned up within hours to help counsel and console relatives; and when an IRA bomb alert disrupted the Grand National Race at Aintree in 1997 thousands found refuge in homes within the community.

A number of these initiatives and links between affected communities endure long term. Miller (1974) discusses the development of a strong community association in Aberfan and other community-based activities which endured, serving both practical and therapeutic functions and symbolising reconciliation and hope for the future. A marked feature of human

behaviour in these situations is a spirit of outreach and altruism, in contrast
to the sense of short-term riot, looting and other anti-social forms which are
more likely to make news headlines.

Altruism and activism after disaster

Sociologists have commented on how an observable feature of disaster is
often increased altruism amongst disaster-stricken populations, a remarkable trend in view of the increasing individualism and anonymity which has
become a feature of contemporary societies. In the face of a common threat
or outcome, social divisions may become less important than the sense of
mutuality. Fritz (1961: 684) argues:

'Culturally derived discriminations and social distinctions tend to be
eliminated in disaster because all groups and statuses in the society are
indiscriminately affected: danger, loss and suffering become public rather
than private phenomena... The widespread sharing of danger, loss and
deprivation produces an intimate, primary group solidarity among the
survivors, which overcome social isolation and provides a channel for
intimate communication and expression and a major source of physical
and emotional support and reassurance.'

This statement by Fritz is a rather general one which may apply more to
some situations of disaster than others. There are other situations where the
opposite is quite clearly the case, for example where disasters arise out of
and are inflamed by culturally derived conflicts as in the former Yugoslavia
and Rwanda. The nature of community dynamics during and after disasters
is an area requiring further research in order to improve our understanding
of the conditions under which harmony or social conflict are likely to thrive
and endure.

The public social response to many sudden impact disasters today has
become formalised in a range of activities symbolising national and sometimes international feelings of shock and empathy. The spirit of public
concern and outreach is expressed in the ritualised visits by public figures to
the scenes of tragedy, in increased religious and quasi-religious ritual
(Davie, 1993; Eyre, 1997; Pettersson, 1996), and in the enthusiasm to set up
and contribute to disaster funds. This range of responses suggests that,
although the impact of disasters often appears to be unremittingly negative,
there can also be some positive outcomes from tragedy. Taylor reinforces
this point:

'There is a tendency, for example, to assume that disaster outcomes are
necessarily bad or dysfunctional, whether at the individual, group community or societal level. Without being Malthusian, the possible positive
effects of certain catastrophic events should be traced.'

(Taylor, 1978: 258)

One explanation for the various social and psychological processes following disaster is that they contribute to the development of a 'therapeutic social system' (Barton, 1969: 207). In some ways this may help to compensate for feelings of sorrow and distress. For some relatives and survivors, meeting and engaging with others who have been involved in tragedy can help them come to terms with and recover from the disaster and associated losses. Here mutual support groups among survivors and relatives may have an important role to play as an opportunity to share common feelings, and to express anger and other difficult feelings in an environment of acknowledgement and trust that is free from rebuke or criticism.

Survivor groups may also become the focus for political activism in addressing circumstances which are seen as contributing to a particular tragedy. There have, for example, been a number of action groups initiated to campaign for improved safety on ferries, for better security measures in airports, for better standards of safety in sports stadia and for the outlaw of handguns and other lethal weapons. Becoming involved in focused campaigns such as these can be emotionally, as well as practically, important for survivors and relatives, though often the complexities, bureaucracy, legal delays and politics surrounding such efforts contribute to a continuing sense of setback, ongoing frustration and disappointment. As an example of lengthy process, it took ten years after the sinking of the *Herald of Free Enterprise* for measures addressing safety on ferries to be implemented. Meanwhile relatives of those killed over Lockerbie in 1988 are still campaigning for the alleged perpetrators of terrorism to be put on trial, while the families of Hillsborough victims continue to campaign for the reopening of inquests and further legal action in the wake of that disaster. The continuing psychological effects and ongoing distress and trauma of such unfinished business should not be underestimated and is a factor which should be acknowledged and addressed by those counselling and caring for victims of disaster many years after the initial impact.

Learning from survivors

One lesson that can be learned from the work of survivor groups and from other social responses to tragedy is that disasters bring about transformations in people, perceptions and social arrangements, some of which are positive, others negative. This is not to be confused with saying that disasters are a good thing; their very definition precludes such a narrow interpretation. But at the same time it must be recognised that a fuller understanding of the complex transition and change associated with the cycle of disasters acknowledges the range of its effects.

There is much to be learnt here from survivors and the long-term process of rehabilitation as coming to terms with a life-changing experience. In discussing survival, Hodgkinson & Stewart acknowledge that:

'Survival is not just the difference between living and dying – surviving is to do with quality of life. Survival involves progressing from the event and its aftermath, and transforming the experience.'

(Hodgkinson & Stewart, 1991: 2)

Survivors have spoken about the need to be listened to, to be understood and to be given the opportunity to contribute to society's understanding of the effects of disaster. Many, however, feel that more could be learned. This was the theme of a television programme produced by survivors in 1992. Headed *Disaster Never Ends* it stated that:

'From Aberfan to Zeebrugge the last twenty-five years have unfolded a horrifying catalogue of disaster and untold human misery, but as a society we seem to have learned nothing from past mistakes in dealing with the victims and our culture seems unable to recognise and accept long-term emotional pain.'

(BBC, 1992)

The programme's conclusion is an appropriate one for this chapter, namely that better understanding and response to disaster must include listening to those most centrally involved:

'The real experts on the effects of disaster are the victims themselves, but we are rarely consulted about anything. We are simply processed through systems set in place by non-victims. The media, the legal professions, the social services, the bureaucrats, the police, the fund trustees, the politicians, the churches ... any groups that come into contact with victims, direct or indirectly, should consult with us. Whether or not they actually do this really depends on whether they actually care.'

(BBC, 1992)

Teaching and learning focus on mass disaster

Rationale

The rationale is that by considering both objectively and sensitively the complex issues surrounding a mass disaster, participants will be better equipped to give useful help and support.

Activity 1: Brainstorming examples of mass disasters

Brainstorm examples of mass disasters with the whole group writing up contributions initially without comment or discussion on a flip chart sheet. A likely outcome of the brainstorm is a very selective, partial set of examples which are typically:

- Recent (rather than past)
- Local (rather than more distant)
- Localised (rather than more extended).

This can lead into a more extended discussion about the way we perceive and register disasters.

Activity 2: Classification of disasters

Using the examples generated in Activity 1, together with other examples emerging from the subsequent discussion, attempt various classifications of disasters:

- Natural v. man-made (technological)
- In terms of impact on victims and survivors – are they from the same community or different communities?

Likely issues to arise in subsequent discussion are those of blame, fault, responsibility, negligence, risk, reliability, etc.

Learning outcomes

The learning outcomes stimulated by the activities are for the course participants to:

- Understand the wide range and variety of mass disasters
- Appreciate the complex role of the helping professions in the aftermath
- Understand the influence of the media in the way we perceive and register disasters.

Chapter 12
Anger, Assertiveness and Aggression

Yvonne Anderson

The chapter explains the difference between anger, aggression and assertiveness. Each concept is explained and examples are given. These examples are intended to be helpful to both professional and lay helpers and the client/patient. Transactional analysis is used to enable all who work in this field to better understand communication, to enable others to communicate more effectively and to use anger appropriately.

The perspective from which this chapter is written is professional.

Introduction

'The poor cousin of fear is anger. It is the rage that rises in us when our children do not look both ways before running into busy streets, or take to heart the free advice we're always serving up to keep them from pitfalls and problems. It is the spanking or tongue lashing, the door slammed, the kicked dog, the clenched fist – the love, Godhelpus, that hurts: the grief. It is the war we wage against those facts of life over which we have no power, none at all.'

(Lynch, 1997: 61)

Anger is a common, if not a universal, reaction to loss (Shuchter & Zisook, 1986). There is some evidence that, even in cultures in which anger is not expressed in grief, it is nevertheless present, but suppressed by tradition and ritual (Rosenblatt *et al.*, 1976 and Chapter 14). The experiencing of anger at a time of loss can be unexpected and unwelcome. Sadness, despair and longing, these are anticipated, but anger can take the grieving person by surprise. In her seminal work on the stages of grief following catastrophic news, Kubler-Ross (1973) regards anger as a major stage through which people pass. In other words, according to the Kubler-Ross model, anger is a normal part of grieving and to be expected.

Whilst it is a common reaction to loss, anger in itself also creates a fresh set of losses. Someone who had formerly tended to be sanguine, easy-going, or placid, will be shocked and bewildered at this new, powerful emotion. The intensity of feeling associated with anger is, for some, frightening. It poses a challenge to the idea, the very ideal of self, and can lead to a loss, albeit temporary, of self-esteem and self-image. Laurie Lee (1975), in his moving story of the aftermath of Aberfan, told of this experience in a local bar:

> 'Dai, the proprietor, was a jumpy young man, rhetorical, wracked with nerves. On the night I arrived he'd just thrown out a party of tourists, and his dark eyes were damp with fury.'

> (Lee, 1975: 95)

Lee recounts that later the same night, after several drinks, Dai again leaned over the counter, telling, with his 'thick voice trembling', of the ways in which the tragedy had hit every one of the customers there that night, how they had all lost children or wives in the disaster. He continued:

> '... but I remember us crying in this bar, crying and clinging together. And some of my best friends up the road: young Glyn – kaput – his wife and his sister Doris ... What do they expect us to be then – idealists or what?'

> (Lee, 1975: 95)

According to Lee, no-one in the bar paid any attention as Dai's voice rose in emotion, except to complain when he put on a recording of Handel's Messiah. Dai said, 'I always play that when I'm angry. I haven't got time to read bloody books.'

Dai's is an example of the transformation which can occur within us, not just as a result of loss, but also because of the anger that is a response to the loss. Despite the fact that this emotion is part of the human condition, its expression is often frowned upon in our culture. We associate rage with children and lunatics. The phrase 'blind rage' implies the unthinking lack of control which is associated with the expression of anger. The incoherent rage of a football hooligan or vandal demonstrates the same lack of control, as does the tantrum of a young child, or the quick temper of a tired parent. The very inarticulate nature of such displays of anger permits the rest of us to look down upon them with disdain.

Interesting images and ideas are associated with anger. We speak of anger bubbling up inside and, sometimes, of its spilling out, when someone reaches boiling point. We talk of losing our temper, or we might say, 'I could not help it, I lost my cool'. Anger can be either ice cold or flaming hot. We often refer to flying into a rage. All these ideas and images convey speed, power and force. There is a popular image of anger as a pot with a lid on, the steam inside eventually forcing off the lid. It is reminiscent of the saying that someone 'blew his stack'. To avoid the force of anger, we refer to holding it in check, to keeping our temper. These words convey our desire to exert control over this gathering momentum inside us. Following an angry diatribe about her mother, Ann Frank wrote at the end of one day's entry, 'Don't condemn me, but think of me as a person who sometimes reaches bursting point!'

Shuchter & Zisook (1986) have described anger as an 'emotion seeking an outlet'. It is useful to distinguish between the anger, the emotion and the ways in which it manifests itself when seeking its outlet. Aggression may be seen as an inappropriate outlet for anger. Aggressive acts are threatening and sometimes overtly hostile and violent. How uncomfortable we feel when witnessing, first- or second-hand, acts of aggression. The discomfort is caused partly by ambivalence; we recognise the universality of the emotion, but find its uncontrolled expression unacceptable by the rules we have made for ourselves. Yet, is there not some vicarious satisfaction, at times, in seeing others vent that most powerful emotion?

Anger, then, is an emotion with which we are familiar from infancy. It is a common reaction in times of loss and change, but nevertheless it may be viewed as an inappropriate aspect of the process of adapting to change. Furthermore, the expression of anger through aggression is generally not viewed sympathetically in our culture. At times, though, we have a sneaking admiration for those who, when faced with the wall of their own fury, perhaps at some injustice or wrong deed, express it in the most hostile and violent ways. In the UK a few years ago, a spurned wife destroyed her estranged husband's entire wardrobe and gave away his cellar of wine; acts for which she received some public sympathy. How can this ambivalence be untangled? Despite a certain amount of sympathy with aggression which appears to have some justification (as opposed to so called mindless violence), aggressive acts remain anti-social. Arguably, disapproval of aggression and hostility is not simply an example of cultural norms of self-control for its own sake. As stated earlier, aggression always involves a degree of threat, sometimes the threat of violence, and as such is an unacceptable way to treat others in a civilised society. Sadly, many people never learn the skills required to express their anger in a more constructive and less damaging way.

At times anger can be a positive force in a period of loss and change. In her chapter in this book, Di Massimo in Chapter 8 describes the galvanising effects of anger in prompting people to find new work soon after redundancy. Accompanying the passively angry feelings of, 'Why me?' and 'It's not fair' are more powerful thoughts, such as, 'I'll show them', 'I am not on the scrap heap yet'. The strength of feeling which anger brings may also help us to assert ourselves, giving us courage where there was none before.

At other times anger becomes and remains a wholly negative experience. Some people feel angry at God and lose their faith. Others experience anger so intense that it turns into bitterness and never goes away. The family of Lesley Ann Downe, child victim of the Moors murderers, Ian Brady and Myra Hindley, continue to wage a bitter war against those who seek parole for Hindley. The venom with which the dead child's mother expresses her hatred of Hindley attracts considerable media attention each time the parole question is raised. Her bitterness must strike a chord in many people, for Hindley has, for many years, been denied the liberty that others in her position have been granted.

In the case of Lesley Ann Downe, there is no doubt as to where to attach blame for her untimely and tragic death. The blame lies squarely with the two people who took her life. Usually it is less easy to apportion blame for a loss. One way in which a bereaved person may express anger is by seeking to blame others for the death. The blame and, therefore, the anger, may be directed at the deceased person. Grieving children often blame the dead parent for leaving them alone and bereft. Widowed spouses may have a similar experience. Blaming the dead person will often lead to guilt and this, combined with anger and depression, may create a downward spiral of despair. Equally common is the tendency to blame oneself, 'Why wasn't I there?', 'I should have prevented this'. Self-recrimination, rarely deserved, is part of the complex relationship between anger, blame, guilt and regret, experienced in acute loss, including bereavement.

Anger turned inward becomes regret. In her portrayal of the death of her daughter, Elder, in Chapter 9, describes her own regret in the following brief statement:

'I kept thinking of the trivial decision I made that totally altered my life; that of asking Kate to stay on in London so my parents could have her bedroom. I thought of how we teach our children so many things; the importance of saying please and thank you, how to cross the road. We do not teach them how to step off a bus.' .

These words, in their very brevity, convey depths of regret and despair. There is no raging anger here, no righteous fury, but silent rage at the unspeakable bad luck and the quiet regret for having played her part in keeping her daughter in London, where the accident happened. Kate fell off a bus and died and nothing could have protected her against such an event. Sometimes we regret, not that we failed to act, but that there was no act which could have prevented the tragedy. Whether it is silent rage or seething fury, anger is a protest and by its very nature it is a protest against that over which we have no control.

This important feature is often overlooked. When very young infants cry in rage, we understand they are powerless, totally dependent and that they experience frustration when their needs are not met. The so-called mindless violence which seems to be practised by certain groups of young men may have similar roots. One way to understand pointless or unprovoked acts of aggression is to see the perpetrator as weak, with feelings of inadequacy. The rage which seems to us to be pointless is in fact a frustrated reaction to feelings of not having power. The protest takes the form of intimidating behaviour, which both allows the individual to let off steam and also to enjoy some transient control over others. This does not excuse hostile or violent behaviour towards others, but illustrates that aggression is an expression of anger.

Similarly, dying or bereaved people and their family members may seem to workers – nurses, therapists, doctors – to be expressing anger inappropriately. Those professionals or volunteers working with people who are mourning a loss are at the receiving end of expressions of anger. At best this means being subjected to excessive complaints, irrational accusations and verbal threats and at worst hostility, physical intimidation, or even violence. Those helping with the grieving process need to be aware of the reasons for anger and the context in which it has arisen. It may be asking too much of such helpers, but they have to learn not to take angry words and gestures personally. The least helpful response is the one which to many people comes most naturally. For many of us, the first, unthinking, response to the anger of another is to become angry ourselves. This can only cause the problem to escalate and will add nothing of value to the professional relationship.

Kubler-Ross (1973: 44) suggests that one reason why staff find it so difficult to deal with patients' anger is that it is, 'displaced in all directions and projected onto the environment at times almost at random'. In other words the complaining or aggressive behaviour of patients and others suffering loss seems to bear no relation to the event which has caused the anger. Instead, they may complain about the doctor, or their neighbours, or they may just become generally negative. Workers and helpers may find difficulty in empathising in these situations. As Kubler-Ross goes on to observe, 'The problem here is that few people place themselves in the patient's position and wonder where this anger might come from' (1973: 45) and later, on the same point:

> 'The tragedy is perhaps we do not think of the reasons for a patient's anger and take it personally, when it has originally nothing or little to do with the people who become the target of the anger.'
>
> (Kubler-Ross, 1973: 46)

From the above we can infer that empathy is all that is required for helpers to understand and cope with the anger of others. The argument needs to be taken further, however. Before considering how to deal with aggression we must first look to alternative ways of expressing anger. The next section discusses the role of assertiveness in dealing with anger.

Assertiveness

Perhaps inside us all are the children we were; susceptible to slights, injustices and perceived rejections and resistant to change. As children we scream, shout, sulk and sob, but as adults those actions will rarely be acceptable to others. Children react to anger in the way they do because they are powerless and their expressions of rage are a protest. Often as adults we still feel powerless and fail to communicate effectively as a result of that. Something we can learn to do is to assert ourselves in ways which give us more control over our emotions and their expression. Assertiveness has come to mean many things to many people. It also has an unfortunate connotation for some, in being associated with militant feminism. There is insufficient scope to do justice to such debates here; for the purposes of this chapter the meaning of assertiveness is taken as:

Saying what we mean and meaning what we say.

It may be easier to be clear about what does not count as assertiveness. Unassertive behaviour includes denying (to self and others) that there is an issue, being overly tactful and diplomatic, saying what the other person wants to hear and hiding strong feelings behind a façade. Saying what we mean is not always easy, as it can involve telling others what they do not wish to hear and risking their approbation. Being assertive need not, as it is often assumed, mean the same as being strident and forceful. Assertiveness can be quiet, but is always firm. Being assertive is always preferable to being aggressive, because it deals with the cause of the anger straight away, rather than leave it to grow out of proportion.

Nelson-Jones (1990) suggests a six-step framework for assertiveness. The steps are:

- Develop self-awareness
- Specify and clarify your goals
- Develop a plan to attain your goals
- Rehearse and practise
- Implement your assertiveness
- Evaluate.

Prevention is better than cure; if we can learn to incorporate assertiveness in our lives, we may be better able to avoid situations which cause us anger and hurt.

If the patients mentioned earlier by Kubler-Ross were able to assert themselves, they would not need to project their anger on to unsuitable targets. The first step is acknowledgement. If my close friend has died in an accident, I feel angry because I have had a pleasing relationship abruptly taken away from me. The assertive way for me to behave is to say to my family or friends, with honesty, 'I am angry that she has died. I miss her. I wish this had not happened'. In this way I am owning up to my feelings and expressing them clearly. If I tell nobody of my thoughts and feelings at this time, I will privately nurse them as they cause me increasing distress. Then, at some unconnected moment, another event will trigger my anger and I will express it inappropriately and in an aggressive manner. The unassertive way to communicate will be to say, 'Yes, I am coping very well thank you. I will get over it. These things happen'.

As well as acknowledging feelings, assertiveness is also about expressing our own wants and needs. This can be difficult, as many of us have grown up in a culture in which such expressions are seen as self-indulgent. However, it can mean the difference between a highly distressed person saying, 'I need some help, someone to talk to' and 'It's alright. I'll be okay on my own'.

The second statement is denial and is unassertive. The first is hardly self-indulgent.

Sometimes being assertive can mean having to say something about another person, to that person. This can never be easy. If the focus is on some negative aspect, then it is generally more helpful to criticise the act, rather than the person. For example, if my colleague has repeatedly parked in the bay marked with my name, any of the following would be assertive:

Thoughts:
I cannot allow this not to be remarked upon.
This is an infringement of my rights.
He must have the opportunity to explain himself, in case it was not deliberate.

Actions:
Make an early appointment to see the colleague.
Put my objections in writing.
Inform a line manager of the situation.
Involve an objective third party.

Comments to the colleague:
I cannot tolerate your parking in my allotted place.
I would like your assurance this will not happen again.
I am very unhappy about this.
Your actions have greatly inconvenienced me.

Alternatively, any of the following comments would be unassertive and some would be aggressive:

Thoughts:
Why me?
It's not fair.
He has done it on purpose to slight me.

Actions:
Glaring at the colleague.
Telling everyone except the offender how angry I am.
Taking time off work to recover.

Comments to the colleague:
You have no feeling for others.
I will do the same to you.
Why have you done this to me?
I'm sure you didn't mean it.

Analysing communication

This section will use the work of the psychoanalyst, Eric Berne, as a framework for coping with anger. Much of Berne's work, ground-breaking at the time, sounds to the contemporary reader like so much jargon, couched as it is in the psychotherapeutic language of its time. Furthermore, the immense popularity of books like *Games People Play* (1968) tended to give his work the appearance of being trivial, which it certainly was not. In his attempts to write in a simple language which could be readily understood by lay people, Berne adopted terms which seem to us now very dated. A therapist using Berne's transactional analysis (TA) has recently said of it:

'So if you go into it in depth it's actually very complex. However, Berne and the people who came after him, found ways of putting it in a very accessible way so that anybody can understand it. And one of the disadvantages is that people come across these quite simple terms: Parent, Adult, Child, games theory, script and so on and they sometimes think it's simplistic. I feel quite passionately that it isn't simplistic, in fact TA people have done themselves no favour by selling it as a sort of simple pop psychology, because actually it's a very serious useful tool.'

(Sills, 1996: 57)

It is not the view of this author that Berne's work is any less useful for being written in the language of a particular era. The importance of language, however, is such that the reader can just as readily be alienated as persuaded by it. The purpose of the following discussion is to offer an interpretation of Berne's work for use as a tool in the helping process. Berne was, after all, an advocate of simple language and it is hoped that in this reframing, the essence of meaning has not been corrupted or lost, but simply made more accessible to the new reader.

Berne (1961) argued that we function in three main psychological states. These states might be seen very simply as inner voices which manifest themselves in our interactions. They may be part instinct, part heredity and part learned. At any one time a person can be operating in any one of these states, according to the situation and how it relates to the person's history, self-esteem and current concerns. When we communicate with others we enter into a transaction, or exchange. During this exchange, each person responds according to the psychological state which is dominant at the time. Exchanges often fall into predicable patterns and these may become habit forming, so that in some of our encounters we behave in stereotypical or ritualised ways. Understanding which of the psychological states is dominant on each side of an exchange can help to unlock communications which are unsatisfactory for either person.

When angry exchanges happen, the experience is usually upsetting for one of the parties, often for both. What satisfaction there is to be gained by letting off steam is often short-lived and the feelings of triumph or vindication quickly replaced by shame and regret. The communication tool recommended here has many applications, but has been found by the author to be particularly useful in dealing with anger in helping relationships.

The three psychological states can be described as follows:

- *Emotion.* The inner voices of emotion motivate us to satisfy our needs and desires. These voices may be demanding or pleading, as reflected in the words we use and our non-verbal communication in this state. In a *demanding* emotional state, we use words like, I want, give me, shan't, shall, will, won't. In a *pleading* emotional state, we are more likely to be saying I wish, please may I, can't. Urges and wants which have been with us since childhood are behind our words and actions when the emotion state is dominant. The voice of someone in a demanding emotional state will be loud, even strident and gestures will be uninhibited and loose. When in a pleading emotional state, though, the voice is either placating or defiant and gestures such as pouting and a downcast face will be employed.

  This state corresponds with Freud's description of the id, the drives and instincts with which we are born, and which Berne called the Child.

- *Judgement.* As a counterpart to the self-centredness of the emotional state, judgement incorporates the taught elements we have acquired during our lives from authority. The inner voices of judgement are either critical or benevolent. In a *critical* judgemental state, we use words such as ought, should, must. Gestures include frowning, pointing and fist clenching and the tone of the voice is preaching and authoritarian. When in a *benevolent* judgemental state, we use words such as good, nice, never mind, said in a loving or concerned voice. Accompanying speech, gestures such as open arms, stroking and smiling are used.

  This state is close to the Freudian idea of a super-ego, the conscience, the moral and the rule-bound element of personality, and which Berne called the Parent.

- *Reason.* This state functions as an arbiter between emotion and judgement. Whilst the inner voices of emotional and judgemental states are not always heard consciously, the nature of reason is that we are thinking and using our intellect when functioning in this state. In reason we have a strong sense of reality and we make relatively objective decisions. Typically, someone operating in reasoning mode will talk in a neutral, even and measured voice, using words such as how, when, where. Gestures will be open and the person will appear alert and thoughtful, maintaining a steady gaze. Freud's concept of ego corresponds closely to this state, that which is concerned with our self-preservation and self-control, and which Berne called the Adult.

To analyse a transaction (hence transactional analysis), or exchange, it is helpful to map the lines of communication in some simple way. Figure 12.1 gives a template for mapping an exchange. The figure shows the three psychological states, subdivided where appropriate. To map an exchange, it is first necessary to identify the state in which each statement is made. To do so requires a consideration of the speech itself and any accompanying non-verbal responses, such as voice, expression, posture, body orientation, gesture and gaze.

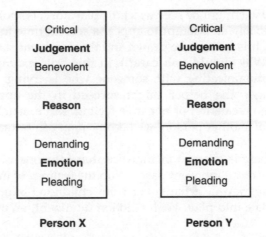

Fig. 12.1 Template for mapping lines of communication.

To illustrate the use of the template, the following example of an exchange will be mapped in Fig. 12.2, with a brief explanation.

First exchange between bereaved person Pat, and helper Chris:

C. So how have you been feeling since we last met? (1)
P. Huh. Fine. No thanks to you lot. (loud) (2)
C. Oh dear, that's not very good, is it? (neutral) (3)
P. No it's not! I am sick of the way I have been treated – someone in my condition. But why should you care?! (4)

The exchange starts with Chris's reason statement, appealing to Pat's reason also. Pat, however, responds in disgust, so is in a state of critical judgement and seems to be aiming at Chris's emotion. Chris's next state-

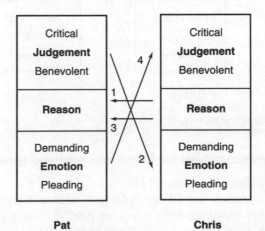

Fig. 12.2 Mapping of first exchange.

ment, whilst it might be seen as a little placatory, is spoken in a neutral voice and is probably an attempt to appeal a second time to Pat's reason. Unfortunately, Chris will not be drawn and the dominant state becomes pleading emotion (Why should you care?!). In this brief example we see an angry person communicating with someone who is trying to defuse the anger. Given longer, the helper might succeed in the appeal to reason, thus avoiding an escalation of negative feeling. More usually, when faced with the anger of another person, we become angry in return. What is the reason for this?

Often there is a sense of injustice that someone is venting anger inappropriately on an innocent party. With the feelings of injustice come feelings of being aggrieved, a hangover from childhood experience, bringing the emotion state into play. With emotion dominant, an angry retort is almost inevitable.

The lines of communication mapped on Fig. 12.2 show clearly the fixed psychological state of the helper, Chris, compared to the varying ones of the bereaved person, Pat. Simply observing the lines of communication in this way can reveal what was going on under the surface – there is consistency from Chris, contrasted with inconsistency from Pat. The next interaction shows what might occur if Chris, following on from Pat's last statement, responds in a way other than reason. The exchange is then mapped in Fig. 12.3.

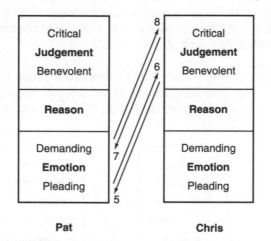

Fig. 12.3 Mapping of second exchange.

Second exchange between helper and bereaved person:

P. Why should you care?! (4)
C. Of course we care. I certainly care, I have demonstrated that. (5)
P. Oh yes, you care alright, you're paid to care. (6)
C. Look, I am trying to be patient here … (7)
P. Don't bother. I don't want your patience. (8)

The parallel lines clearly show that Pat and Chris have become locked into an unhelpful pattern of communicating. Pat is continuing to use pleading emotion and Chris responds every time in judgement. To begin with the judgement is benevolent, but finally it becomes critical.

Sometimes, communicating in these parallel lines is mutually agreeable for people. Even when it is satisfying, however, it should be viewed with caution. Once a pattern of communication is established as a habit, it can be very difficult to break. Perhaps one or both people would like to break out, but are constrained by the expectations of the other.

Berne was largely concerned with interactions in personal relationships, but here we are interested in professional dealings with others. In the act of helping another person to cope in a time of loss, we enter into a relationship which has different rules from those in our personal lives. It is not helpful to respond to a client's anger with more anger. Aside from occasions in which a client is encountered who is inherently hostile, anger for most people is temporary; a feeling which there is often an urgent need to express in some way. As helpers we do not wish to make people repress their anger, but alternatively, aggressive talk and actions need to be dealt with carefully.

Imagine, then, that instead of responding to Pat's emotion with judgement, Chris had continued to try to use reason. The next interaction, mapped in Fig. 12.4, shows Pat deliberately appealing to Chris's reason.

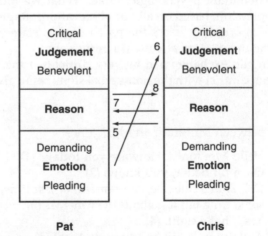

Pat   Chris

Fig. 12.4 Mapping of third exchange.

Third exchange – using reason:

P. Why should you care?! (4)
C. What makes you think that people don't care? (5)
P. Well you are just paid to do a job aren't you? (6)
C. That is true. But I do this job because I care and I try to do it well. (neutral) (7)
P. Oh, I'm sorry. I didn't mean to get at you. I have just been feeling so low, I want to blame it on something or someone. It's not your fault. (8)

As the arrows show, in this example Chris appeals to Pat's reason by asking an open-ended question. Pat resists by being critical. Chris continues the appeal to reason and Pat responds reasonably by finally apologising and offering an explanation. The anger is defused.

These examples show the potential of using analysis of communication as a tool in helping. By analysing and understanding small simulated case studies such as those here, the helper can start to develop an awareness of his or her own psychological states, as well as those of others. For the most part the analysis in helping has to be done internally and acted upon immediately. Mapping, in the way shown here, is useful after the event, as a way of learning and changing for the future.

Learning to recognise the dominant psychological state of the self and others requires practice and determined effort. We cannot hope always to be right in the analyses we make on the spot. In addition to the words being said, we have to pay attention to all the other non-verbal signs which give us the whole picture. Table 12.1 is a table which can be used as a checklist for each psychological state. If a helper had experienced a particularly difficult interaction with a client, notes taken immediately after parting could be used in conjunction with Table 12.1. This could assist in mapping the interaction, so that it can be analysed.

None of the factors listed in the table is sufficient on its own to inform us about the dominant psychological state. What we must do is arrive at an overall impression, based on all our observations. Rapid computations have to be done in order to assess the psychological state of people interacting. This is what many of us already do intuitively.

Analysing an exchange can be very difficult if the words the person is saying are in conflict with the non-verbal signs being given out. Consider the following:

Exchange between Mr Smith and Mrs Jones:

Mr S.   Hello Mrs Jones. How are you today? (1)
Mrs J.   Oh, a bit better, you know. (2)
Mr S.   OK. That's fine. Do you remember last time, we agreed to spend some time talking about the funeral? (3)
Mrs J.   Yes. That's right. (4)
Mr S.   And are you still happy to do that? (5)
Mrs J.   Yes. Yes, I am. (6)

Outwardly, the exchange looks straightforward. We would have no difficulty in mapping the lines of communication, from reason to reason. It is quite possible, nonetheless, for people apparently to be functioning in one state, whilst their inner voices are giving conflicting messages. When Mr Smith makes the first statement, which looks as if it is coming from reason, the dominant state may in fact be benevolent judgement. Inwardly he could be feeling sympathetic towards Mrs Jones and anticipating that she will be needing a lot of care and support during this meeting. This underlying

Table 12.1 Checklist for identifying psychological states. Adapted from Berne (1961).

	Judgement		Reason	Emotion	
	Critical	Benevolent		Demanding	Pleading
Words	ought, should, must, always, never, I say so, you had better, I am telling you, bad, how dare you	good, nice, well done, I love you, I will look after you, let me help you	how, when, what, where, open-ended questions, OK, alright, fine	I want, give me, let me, now, I can't wait, brilliant! great!	can't, why should I, please may I, I am not loved
Voice	critical, preaching, disgusted, bombastic, strident	loving, tender, comforting, concerned, soft	even, measured, calm, medium pitch	loud, insistent, shrill	whining, aggrieved, defiant
Gesture	pointing, frowning	stroking, smiling, nodding, open armed, reaching out	loose, open movements, hands still, gestures held – not changed rapidly	energetic movements, lack of inhibition	folded arms, shrugging, crying, downcast face
Gaze	glaring, long eye contact, staring, eyeballing	eye to eye, long, attentive	eye to eye – but not held	penetrating, but not maintained	avoidance of eye contact
Posture	standing, sitting tall, hands on hips	leaning forward, head to one side	still and controlled, may mirror the other person	changeable, knee hubbing, cupping face in hands	curled up, slumped, head on hand
Overall impression	moralistic, authoritarian, dictatorial, paternalistic	understanding, caring, giving, approving, maternalistic	objective, controlled, rational, realistic	excitable, changeable, demanding	ashamed, needy, procrastinating

benevolence will reveal itself through non-verbal signs that Mr Smith will unwittingly emit. His voice, for instance, will be warm and soft and he will adopt the position of leaning forward and inclining the body fully towards Mrs Jones, perhaps employing touch as well.

This offers just one example of the confusion which can arise when someone is deliberately speaking in the manner of a particular psychological state, whilst being betrayed by the true dominant state through non-verbal clues. It is highly disconcerting to try to understand the other person in an interaction when the messages are mixed in this way. Elsewhere this disturbed way of communicating has been called the 'double bind', because neither party can really gain from it (Bateson, 1956).

There are other possibilities for confusion in the above exchange. We have considered one scenario, in which the helper is in inner conflict. For the client, too, a similar conflict can occur. When asked if she is happy to talk about the funeral, Mrs Jones says yes, quite reasonably. If it were the case that internally she has some doubts about that, she also could be giving out mixed messages. Perhaps since the last meeting she has become angry about aspects of the funeral – words said or not said by the minister, behaviour of family members and so on. Her anger will be expressed non-verbally through emotion, so her voice might be whining or choked and her posture huddled and turned away from the helper.

With access to all the above information, we might assume that the inner state, that which is manifesting itself unconsciously, is the state in which the communication is really happening. Clearly this would change the pattern produced by mapping, considerably.

Conclusion

Encouraging yourself and your clients to be courageous and assertive may help to deflect anger in its early stages so it is not expressed as aggression. Analysing communication using this adaptation of Berne's work, is a useful way to identify and deal with your own anger and that of the people you are helping.

If you wish to work in an equal, mutually respectful relationship with clients, then it can be most beneficial to explain the communication mapping and analysis with them, rather than keeping it to yourself as a tool of the trade. Instead of manipulating interactions by rendering the client passive, sharing the tool with the client permits a whole new way of working. From time to time, when one or the other of you is uneasy about the way an interaction has developed, the subsequent mapping of the interaction will be that much more dynamic and challenging if performed together than if you were to do it privately. Not all clients are capable or even interested in such a degree of self-awareness and reflexivity, but a surprising number are and will respond so much more rapidly to the help they are receiving if some of it is within their own control.

Teaching and learning focus on anger

Rationale

When we have run courses on anger and aggression, we have often ended a session with this maxim:

Remember, the anger you are dealing with may be your own.

The rationale for the teaching and learning focus is to to promote greater self-awareness of our own anger. In this context you can benefit from doing the exercise yourself, but you can also use it with the groups you teach or counsel.

Activity: Understanding our own anger

Take a sheet of paper and a pen, pencil, or some coloured pens. Think about times when you feel really angry. Focus in on the memory of your anger and, when you are ready, draw yourself when angry and label the drawing. You do not need any artistic ability for this exercise to be successful.

When the drawing is complete, have a few minutes break, then return to it and consider it carefully. What does your drawing tell you about yourself? How would others respond to you when you are angry? Are the signs of your anger very obvious, or more subtle? Do you attempt to contain yourself, or do you just explode? How do you feel about your angry image? Do you want to change anything about the ways in which you manage anger?

If using this exercise with groups which you are facilitating, invite them to share their images, either in pairs or in the main group. For your own purposes, you might benefit from discussing this activity with someone who knows you well.

Learning outcomes

The learning outcomes stimulated by the activities are for the course participants to:

- Reflect on their own experience of anger
- Have some understanding of the way they appear to others when angry
- Think about ways of dealing with their anger.

Chapter 13
Preparing Children for Loss and Bereavement

Jenny McWhirter, Noreen Wetton and Anna-Michelle Hantler

This chapter explains the importance of including change, loss and grief theories within the school curriculum. It is based on international research carried out with primary and secondary age children and by the authors themselves. It supports Goleman's (1996) theories about the necessity of paying attention to emotional intelligence not only in the curriculum but within the ethos of the school and its wider networks and partnerships. The main argument the authors put forward is that we need to help children to develop the vocabulary, skills and confidence to explain, explore and talk about their feelings. The teaching focus gives students an opportunity to explore case studies, which are based on true accounts. They concern children who, having been denied such an opportunity to explore and explain their pain and grief, subsequently required special help and therapy.

The perspectives from which this chapter is written are: professional and empirical.

Introduction

The aim of this chapter is to set out a rationale for the inclusion of 'loss' in the curriculum for pupils of all ages. We hope to demonstrate the importance of such a curriculum and offer some practical ways to deliver it. This chapter is not a detailed description of the impact of loss and bereavement in childhood and adolescence, which are well covered elsewhere (Epstein, 1993; Hemmings, 1995; Balk, 1996; Raphael, 1996; Rowling, 1995) but seeks to illuminate the current philosophy about how children perceive and deal with loss and change and the implications for schools. It draws on research by the authors and others about children's ways of dealing with loss of many kinds.

The literature on loss, related to children and grief after death of a parent or loved one, is growing. We can learn too from the literature which focuses on the experiences of adults including the link between loss and physical illness (Irwin & Pike, 1993), the importance of social support networks (Averill & Nunley, 1993) and the value of 'normal routines' within a caring context which help to restore equilibrium. For adults, grief is sometimes portrayed both as an illness to be treated in a medical setting, using medical approaches, and also as a social role which is played out in a series of stages and settings as individuals come to terms with their loss and the changed environment (Averill & Nunley, 1993). Children are not a separate race, distinct from the rest of the human population. For them, too, grief has similar physical and emotional consequences to that of adults such as shock, protest, despair and reorganisation. There is a growing consensus that children need to be helped to explore change and loss issues and the appropriate coping strategies (Rowling, 1995), facilitated by a developmental curriculum. To achieve this there is a need to understand loss related to the cognitive, emotional and social development of children. A developmental curriculum on change and loss should be planned in such a way as to enhance the developmental processes of childhood and adolescence to provide young people with opportunities to rehearse and prepare for change and future loss. Such a curriculum would need to take account of the fact that such change work may trigger memories of past situations. These may well be conscious or unconscious and facilitators need to be prepared for such eventualities.

Research relating to children's reaction to grief

There is some research which illustrates how children react to the death of a parent. This is seen as a series of events rather than one (Worden, 1982, 1991; Silverman & Worden, 1993; Raphael, 1996). The works of Schonfeld (1993) and Smilansky (1987) show how children's understanding of death develops. Structured interviews were used to explore ways in which children can be helped to learn, in a school setting, about death and illness.

The absence of comprehensive and relevant research about children and their perceptions of change and loss is a problem for those developing a curriculum. This is, methodologically, an area fraught with difficulty, not least because of the lack of researchers with training in dealing with sensitive issues as well as appropriate methods to carry out such research. A good example of a study of children's experience of loss due to death is the study by Silverman & Worden (1993) who followed up children who had experienced the death of a parent, and compared their responses and behaviour with a control group. Silverman & Worden's study focuses on the impact of the bereavement on the children's mental and emotional health as well as their coping strategies (Rowling, 1995).

When the loss is what adults would describe as significant and irreversible, involving, for example family break-up, divorce, death of a grandparent, parent or sibling, moving house, or the loss of a much loved pet, the adult response may be to try to exclude the child, as much as possible, from the experience. This may be because, in the adult view, the emotion is seen as too great for the child to comprehend or to cope with. Alternatively it may be that the adult fears being unable to cope with the strength of the child's emotions, when overwhelmed with their own emotions, and the practical tasks which must be got through (Chapter 1).

Raphael (1996) speaks of the failure of adults to talk about or even tell children about the death of a parent as having many origins. For example, surviving parents may think the child is unable to comprehend what has happened or may be so distraught as to be unable or unwilling themselves to put into words what has happened. In the same chapter Raphael describes how children as young as 2 years can mourn, but that this must be enabled by supportive adults if the trauma is to be resolved; see the early work of Bowlby (1969) on separation which is corroborated by Winnicott (1958). Even where parents have prepared their children for the expected death of a close family member, there seems to be little recognition that the child is mourning a different person – their father, not their mother's husband, or their grandmother, not their mother's or father's mother. Developmental psychologists have shown that the ability to see an event from another person's perspective develops slowly. This is particularly relevant when dealing with emotions. Giddens (1991) describes the importance of the 'developing self' in relation to early ontological security and trust (Chapter 1).

Following a death, children may be sent away or told not to talk about the event. This could be because adults fear being upset themselves or upsetting other people. In the case of terminal illness, adults may deny that a loved one is dying and talk to children about the future as if everything will go on unchanged. This may be an attempt to protect the child from worry or fear. In the case of family break-up, adults may share too little information with their children, in a mistaken desire to protect the child. Alternatively they may share too much emotion, treating the child as a confidante yet the child and the adult are each dealing simultaneously with their own feelings which may result in cognitive dissonance. These adult responses, though understandable, fail to recognise the reality of the child's relationship to the dead or divorced parent, their conflicting feelings, confusion, hurt or pain and their ability and need to grieve for their loss.

Death, however, is not the only event which provokes feelings of loss and bereavement, as other authors in this book illustrate. There seems to be little research which explores children's perception of bereavement. It is sad to think that no aspect of bereavement is being explored with children, other than death. The *Collins Concise English Dictionary* defines bereavement through a transitive verb: to bereave, that is to deprive someone of something or someone valued, especially through death. To illustrate this we would like to describe research that has explored children's perceptions of change and managing change.

In this chapter we focus particularly on children during their lives in school and on loss in its widest sense. Young children live their lives in the present, their past experience is limited yet it is used developmentally to understand the world and the context in which they live. Other research shows how children make sense of their world by reference to this limited experience (see Piaget, 1950, 1972; Kelly, 1963; Bowlby, 1969; Kohlberg, 1969;

Erikson, 1980; and Chapter 1 of this book). They are only just beginning to comprehend the long future which stretches ahead and because of this the losses they experience are immediate and all the more acute, not ameliorated by the understanding that time can heal, or that they will feel joy again in contrast to sadness. The grief which results from the loss of a toy, of a close friendship or of the freedom to go in the playground without the fear of being bullied, can often be dismissed by adults as trivial, as the child making a fuss, as easily overcome. Adults may perceive these acute losses as insignificant, as passing worries. They may dismiss the child's attempts to talk about such loss as telling tales or dismiss them as childish, rather than acknowledge that it is in fact child-like and therefore valid.

In proposing a curriculum which prepares children for loss we therefore focus not only on death or divorce, but emphasise the importance of understanding the range of losses which children may experience and therefore the validity of their subsequent emotional response. We take a positive and holistic approach to the subject of loss which is only one of the many forms of change that children experience. Growing up, puberty, moving house, changing schools, making and losing friends, are normal life events that need to be addressed in the present but that nearly always involve feelings related to other 'loss' situations in the past. We propose that there needs to be a continuous strand within the Personal, Social and Health Education (PSHE) programme which prepares children for loss and bereavement, and that this should be for all ages using appropriate language and activity. At secondary and tertiary level this could become an important component of cross curricular studies such as literature, geography, history as well as parenting programmes. As Giddens (1991) suggests the world is mobile, uncertain, fragmented and complex for adults as well as children. Any skills we can give children to help them understand and negotiate this must be worthwhile.

We believe that such an approach will be effective in helping children and young people learn to cope with and celebrate some of the many changes they will experience. Through a well-planned curriculum, children can be helped to acquire the skills needed to recognise and manage the impact of change of all kinds. Using these same skills and with appropriate help and support from families, schools and other agencies, children can anticipate and rehearse loss, cope with its impact and emerge as well-balanced people, able to live and learn, able to talk with confidence about their feelings and relationships, and to empathise with the loss experienced by others. Above all we believe in the value of a whole school approach which recognises the importance of the mental and emotional health of the children in its care, and demonstrates this both in the curriculum and in the ethos of the school.

School as a context for education about loss and change

School provides an important social context for children and is a critical place to prepare for and deal with loss of all kinds. The study by Silverman &

Worden (1993) showed that, following the death of a parent, children who received support at home and in school displayed fewer behavioural or emotional problems than those who did not have similar support networks. How much more then could schools do to enable children to work through loss of all kinds to express and share grief, and demonstrate their understanding of that need in others?

Following a death in the family, many children are sent back to school as soon as possible with the hope that re-establishing the normal routine will ease the pain they feel. Research has shown the wisdom of this (Silverman & Worden, 1993), demonstrating that when children's routines are disrupted after a bereavement they suffer more physical health problems than when a supportive routine is maintained. It is interesting to note, however, that only 50% of the teachers of children in Silverman & Worden's study had told the class about the death of their classmate's parent. Where the class had been prepared, grieving children took comfort from the expressions of condolence they received from their classmates. Raphael (1996), however, reminds us that the return to school brings additional stress for some children, who may attempt to hide the fact of death or family break-down from the teacher to avoid being seen as different. Raphael suggests that this stigma of being different is most acute for 5 to 8-year-olds, but our own research and experience in the classroom does not support this view. Being different becomes an increasingly sensitive issue as children move into the stage where peer approval is paramount. It may be that older children are more able to hide their fear of being different, but without doubt it is there. They are more able to use defensive behaviours perhaps or may not be aware of their fears and feelings and unable to articulate them (Chapters 1 and 3). Primary and secondary teachers with whom we have carried out in-service training identify 'being different' in any way as the most sensitive issue for their pupils.

School programmes which address loss and change, allowing children the opportunity to rehearse skills, language and coping strategies would provide a strong framework which is supportive for children who are experiencing bereavement and may help to reduce the feeling of being 'different'; see the Afterword for explanations of valuing 'difference' by challenging society norms and expectations and also Usher & Edwards (1994).

Many teachers feel unable to tackle this sensitive issue and therefore we need to help and support them by illuminating, as Goleman (1996) has, the importance of this in their curriculum. Teachers need to develop facilitation skills and be able to use appropriate language. With these skills and a developmental curriculum the grieving child, classmates and teachers would have a framework for acknowledging and moving through the stages of shock, protest, despair and reorganisation, helping to create a new world in which the person who has died is no longer present but retains a place in the child's life. As Walter (1996a) says:

'The purpose of grief is not to move on without those who have died but to find a secure place for them ... bereavement is part of the process of auto biography ... - the need to make sense of self and others in a continuing narrative. [This] is the motor that drives bereavement behaviour.'

(Walter, 1996a: 20)

The value to families and communities is immeasurable as Giddens suggests. He is in agreement with Walter, that negotiating such complex feelings and behaviours is part of the 'developing self'. There could, however, be conflict between the parent's view of an appropriate way for their child to cope with death and the way the school is offering support. A health-promoting school which integrates sensitive issues within their ethos and curriculum will also have positive partnerships with parents and home. This would enable a positive curriculum and classroom work.

This school–home partnership is in contrast to specific interventions in the curriculum which focus on teaching the facts about death in isolation from experience or context. For example Schonfeld (1993) asserts that there is no necessity for education about death to take a strict curricular form:

'... but can utilize teachable moments, such as when the fish in the classroom dies or when the class finds a dead bug out on the playground.'

(Schonfeld, 1993: 2)

We disagree but accept that teachers are well versed in using such 'teachable moments' to make sense of impromptu experiences for pupils but a planned programme related to mental and emotional health cannot be determined by chance events only.

Other authors recognise this dilemma. Too often we leave the emotional education of our children to chance. Goleman (1996) emphasises the importance of social and emotional skills in the development of a well-balanced individual, able to cope with a wide range of life events. He also speaks of an expanded mission for schools which have specific programmes for what he describes as emotional literacy and which:

'... begin early, are age appropriate, run throughout the school years and intertwine efforts at school, at home, and in the community.'

(Goleman, 1996: 280)

He demonstrates the positive impact of such programmes on the behaviour of pupils and teachers.

A curriculum for loss and change

We propose that a curriculum which prepares children to cope developmentally with their own and other people's experiences of loss will have two major themes:

- A visible planned set of competencies related to emotional skills for dealing with loss, grief and change
- A planned programme for developing a language of feelings to both use and to enable the child/adolescent to share the variety of ways in which people express their feelings.

To be successful these themes should be introduced in non-threatening contexts such as story and poetry, religion, education, history, literature, geography, science, and developed through the sharing of real-life experiences. These approaches should not shrink from using specific language about death, a language which children themselves may be more able to use than many adults.

The language of feelings is a critical tool in enabling discussion of sensitive issues in the classroom and at home. Silverman & Worden (1993) identify that one of the early tasks of bereavement is the development of a language which gives children the tools to talk about death. Many of the children in their study did not appear to have the words to express what they were experiencing. While acknowledging the importance of this observation we would argue that it is far too late to wait for a child to be bereaved to begin to develop an adequate language of feelings. Children cannot suddenly, especially when experiencing a traumatic loss such as a death or divorce, develop a language with which to articulate their confused range of feelings. Indeed Raphael and others have observed how children's behaviour may regress in the stress of the crisis and revert to egocentric or magical thinking. Those children who appear to be coping may actually be demonstrating withdrawal, denial, or extreme stress. Previously articulate children may not wish to test reality by putting their worst fears into words.

Hemmings (1995) has reported that children can be more discreet in their expression of grief. The result of this may be that children's needs may be underestimated by adults, who are also grieving. Children in the 8- to 12-year-old age range with a recently consolidated understanding of the irreversibility of death, face the reality of their own mortality, and may develop phobias and hypochondria. Thus recently bereaved children or children facing emotional stresses need a language with which they are comfortable and familiar – and access to supportive adults who have time to listen and can cope with their grief and sadness.

Action research on a way of understanding children's needs

A draw and write strategy (Wetton & McWhirter, 1997) revealed that while the children aged 7–8 years experienced, and could begin to empathise with, a wide range of emotions including delight, excitement, anger, frustration, despair, remorse, guilt and relief, they did not have an adequate vocabulary to express their feelings. The data, which was quantified, demonstrated the pervasive poverty of the children's language. The emotions were largely expressed through the words 'mad', 'bad', 'sad', 'glad' and 'silly'. When interviewed the children revealed that 'silly' covered any emotion stronger than 'sad' and could mean being overwhelmed by regret, remorse, guilt or embarrassment. This poverty of language may contribute to adults being unable to comprehend the strength of feelings which children experience, the impact of these feelings on children and the frustration wrought through an inability to express oneself. Giddens would suggest that a lack of such skills may mean that the development of self-narrative is hindered. This suggests that it is necessary to explain experiences and feelings and come to both a cognitive and emotional understanding of self. We have based our learning on the development and use of a research strategy known as 'draw and write'. We have, over the years, systematically developed this technique further both qualitatively and quantitatively (see Wetton & McWhirter, 1998). Many health-related issues, some of them very sensitive, have been explored using this technique. The value of this approach is that it has its roots in everyday classroom practice. Drawing and writing are activities in which all children are expected to take part. Those children who have not yet learned to write for themselves can use the teacher or other adult as a scribe able to put the child's own dictated thoughts onto paper. Those who are beginning to see themselves as writers can proceed with only a little help using the teacher as a reference point or walking dictionary. Those confident to write for themselves can do so, using their own creative spelling at times.

It is this activity which has been reworked to become the draw and write research strategy, a strategy which in our experience helps children to feel comfortable. It enables the research to be carried out with a whole class simultaneously, rather than through laborious face-to-face interviewing, a situation with which children may be unfamiliar or find uncomfortable. Large quantities of data may be gathered in this way, using teachers as researchers and without the necessity for transcription of tape-recorded interviews. Furthermore a draw and write approach can enable a researcher to obtain answers to questions which one would never consider asking directly, such as:

Do you know that smoking causes cancer and that people die from cancer?

From such direct, but unaskable, questions the researcher then devises a series of invitations to draw and write which focus increasingly on the children's own perceptions or beliefs, revealing not only their knowledge and attitudes, but also their misconceptions.

One of the most useful structures to emerge from the data is a spiral of children's perceptions as they change with age and developmental stage (see Piaget, 1950, 1972; Kelly, 1963; Kohlberg, 1969).

Figure 13.1 shows a spiral of children's perceptions of what makes them sad, which emerged from an investigation into children's changing per-ceptions of relationships (Williams *et al.*, 1989). It became clear that children are acutely aware of their own sad feelings and the causes of their sadness. They also showed that they increasingly understand some of the ways in which they contribute to such feelings in others. They know from an early

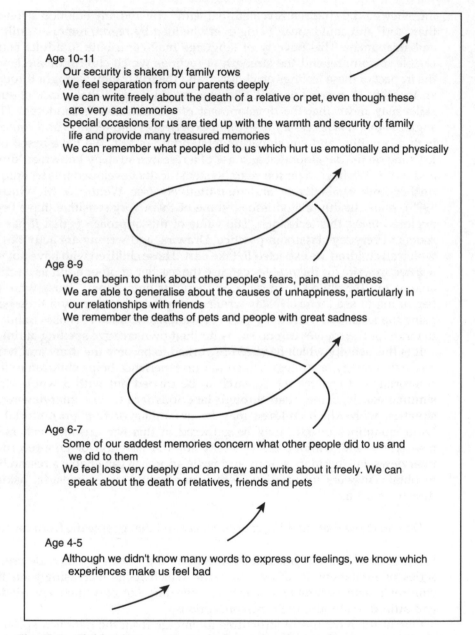

Fig. 13.1 Children's perceptions of what makes them sad.

age the behaviours which make others cross or unhappy and also demonstrate an understanding of other people's pain, injury or unhappiness. This, however, falls short of real empathy which only emerges when we begin to see events from the perspective of others. The research showed that from the age of 4 years children used specific language to refer to death. For example a 7-year-old wrote:

'My cat died last year and my great grandma died I was crying.'

It is interesting to note that in repeated studies using this technique no child in the primary school age range used a euphemism to refer to death or dying. Children do not speak of 'losing someone' except in terms of getting separated from parent or carer. When they speak of a 'lost' toy that is exactly what they mean – a toy mislaid or dropped, hopefully to be found again soon. Similarly children do not speak of someone 'passing on'. 'Passing on' is much more likely to be used to refer to the rules of a game played with a ball or a parcel to be unwrapped. These phrases are used in the adult world to avoid having to use the words dead, died, death.

The data we have gathered also reveals the range of losses which children experience, and shows that their perceptions of loss are constantly changing as they develop physically, cognitively and emotionally. In one draw and write study we sought to uncover pupils' perceptions of how their bodies were changing at puberty and how they felt about these changes. Their responses provided us with a powerful insight into the loss of childhood which this change can entail (McWhirter, 1993). An 11-year-old girl summed up the mixed feelings of many when she wrote that she was looking forward to the changes that puberty would bring

'...but sad to be leaving my childhood behind.'

In a recent replication of this study in Essex schools, a 9-year-old girl wrote:

'I feel that I want to grow up but at the same time because once you have grown up you can never have childhood back again. You can't play games. When your grown up you have responsibilytys (sic) like bills, rent, and children. But children have fun always.'

These children recognise loss as an important part of growth and change and have a language to express their feelings about it. They appear to have been offered the opportunity to develop emotionally at home and in school.

One teacher who took part in this action research was struck by the desire of the children in her class to go on talking about the topic of growing and changing. She turned this into an opportunity for the pupils to write poetry about these themes. An analysis of the 24 poems reveals that eight have the theme of loss, either of childhood or a specific role in the family and three of these specifically deal with death. Two children have expressed a recognition of the link between growing up, growing older and dying, and one poem is about the death of a sibling (see Chapter 9). Seven poems are almost entirely positive with a focus on the opportunities ahead and two more incorporate both loss and opportunity. The remaining poems are life cycles or other narrative accounts, see Giddens (1991), Usher & Edwards (1994), Walter (1996b) and Weston (1997b) on narrative. Some of the poems are very moving (see Fig. 13.2) and the exercise revealed how important it was to the

Growing up

I'm growing up,
I'm growing up,
I don't want to grow up
When you grow up you leave home,
get a job
get married.
I don't want to leave home.
I'm growing up,
I'm growing up,
I want to be with my family,
I want to be with my friends
When you grow old you die.
I don't want to die.
I'm growing up
I'm growing up
I'm growing up.

By Stacey Dawson
Age 10

Fig. 13.2   Poem.

children to capture their feelings and express them in a permanent record. This is an excellent example of a way in which the curriculum can provide a means by which children can share their experiences and begin the process of 'reflexivity', the ongoing narrative about self.

Bubble dialogue

More recently we have been using an alternative research technique which is useful for older children who are able to write with more ease, but who may need encouragement to draw. This technique is known as bubble dialogue in which young people are asked to write about an imaginary person close to them in age, describing how this person would feel when faced with some common life experiences. We have developed the projective version of this technique (Cohen & Mannion, 1994) by going on to ask the young people to consider how they themselves would feel if they were in a similar situation. Respondents can then be asked to propose what strategies they would use to overcome the problems they themselves have identified.

In research using this technique (unpublished observations) with pupils aged 12–13 years in schools in England and in Hungary, we asked the young people to think about a person called Chris (Kris in Hungary) who could be male or female. We told them that something had happened to disturb the balance of Chris's life at school. The pupils were asked to write down what might have happened to cause this imbalance (cognitive dissonance) and to underline the one which would be the most disturbing. They were then asked to say how they would have felt if this happened to them, and what they could do to find a new balance (dissonance). These questions were then repeated in the context of home, relationships with girls and boys, and health. The responses were similar in both countries, although the Hungarian pupils used fewer words to express their strong feelings.

At school the loss of friendship seemed to invade every aspect of the pupils' lives, as it did in their relationships with same and opposite sex friends. The language of feelings was powerfully used to express their anger, their sense of betrayal and rejection. In Chris's life at home, family rows of all kinds were perceived as disturbing, and divorce was identified as more disturbing than the death of a family member. Strategies for dealing with death were much more positive – 'think of the good times', 'help each other' – than strategies for dealing with divorce. Many children expressed despair; their solutions were either naïve – 'try to get them back together' – or simply they wrote 'there is nothing anyone can do'. It would appear that this balance is more difficult for children to achieve after a divorce than after death. Once again the Hungarian children offered fewer suggestions than their English counterparts. Other authors, e.g. Rowling (1995), have explored 'death and grief' as a topic in its own right.

One of the strategies for achieving balance, the one most frequently offered by the children to all four scenarios, was to find someone to talk to, to get help. The pupils seem to assume not only that there are people able to listen and advise, but also that they themselves would have the language, the skill and the confidence to ask for the help they need. There are many implications here for the curriculum and for school policy. How can we ensure that pupils acquire the skills, language and confidence to deal with these powerful life events? How can we make certain that schools and the wider community provide approachable adults who recognise the needs of young people and make provision for those needs in ways which are accessible and acceptable?

Some authors (see Schonfeld, 1993 and Aspinall, 1996) have proposed specific death education programmes, and it would be possible to envisage 'divorce education programmes'. Our experience, however, leads us to suggest a more holistic approach to bereavement, loss and change – of which death and divorce are examples.

As Clarkson (1993) said during the workshop:

'Life is too hard, confusing painful mystifying and beautiful without added difficulty of having nowhere to talk about these feelings, to someone who will really listen.'

The studies using open-ended illuminative research techniques, such as draw and write and bubble dialogue, start where children are, (compare other narrators in this book who also value such experience and autobiographical research) and have provided us and others with a window through which we can view the world as perceived by a child. Something about the view we see is familiar, and corresponds to what is known about child development, see theorists listed earlier. Some is unfamiliar, surprising, full of unsuspected depths of emotion. Every study has revealed how much the children know and feel, are prepared to share, and the language they use to do so. Whatever we have learned it has always been more than we, as researchers, anticipated. Classroom materials developed as a result of this kind of action research is more likely to be relevant to the needs of the children because they start from their own experience as Kelly (1955) suggests, that is, how they view the world and use such experience to negotiate the here and now as well as the future (see also Chapters 1, 3 and 9).

Above all what becomes clear from this kind of research is that children are extremely good at making sense of what they see, hear, mis-hear, what is told to them and what others attempt to hide from them. Sometimes, however, the sense they make of this is non-sense in adult terms, but it is never nonsense.

The literature is full of examples of the non-sense children make of death. This sense is in their terms entirely logical. If grandma can go on holiday and come back then she can also go to heaven and come back. If heaven is in the sky then you can take a plane to go and visit her there (Raphael, 1996). If Jesus chooses good children to be angels, then he might not be so keen to take children who behave badly in church (Schonfeld, 1993).

The role of the curriculum

To ensure success, each subject in the statutory curriculum is planned and taught as part of a spiral where information, language and activity are chosen for the developmental age and stage of the learner. This enables the teacher to plan experiences for the pupils which will build on their prior learning, helping them to revisit and reconstruct their understanding. It is our view that this same structured and coherent approach should apply to preparing children for the experiences of change and loss. We need to offer pupils skills and competencies which they can make use of and adapt in whatever circumstances they find themselves.

Once again we find ourselves in agreement with Goleman (1996) who reinforces the importance of an holistic, spiral approach:

'As children change and grow the preoccupation of the hour changes accordingly. To be most effective, emotional lessons must be pegged to the development of the child, and repeated at different ages in ways that fit a child's changing understanding and challenges.'

(Goleman, 1996: 273)

The danger of not planning to offer practice in appropriate skills and competencies is that children who encounter loss for which they have no coping skills may be harmed, resulting in behaviours which 'mask' the confusion, distortion and disturbance within. These behaviours may ultimately alert us to the child's inner turmoil, but in the meantime may have developed into habitual patterns which are more difficult to resolve. If instead we were to help children to build up the language to share their feelings, and permission and planned opportunities to do so, we might be able to remove the need for children to express themselves through disturbed or disruptive behaviour. We should provide ways and means for children to ask the questions to which they fear they know the answer. This would give adults the much needed opportunity to recognise the strength of the child's needs and to respond appropriately.

In extreme cases some children may be so badly damaged by their experience of loss and express themselves through such disturbed behaviour that they need one-to-one help from specially trained adults. A psychotherapist may be asked by a parent or school to 'make a child better', to stop the child stealing, to help develop assertiveness, rather than be asked to help the child deal with their feeling of loss.

It is our experience that many of the activities through which the therapist helps children express their emotions and come to terms with loss can be equally at home in the classroom and the consulting room. Many of the skills children develop in therapy could be laid down through good practice in the classroom. This is not to say that the roles of teacher and therapist should be confused, rather that each can learn from the other.

Both teachers and therapists commonly use the same strategies to help children to develop cognitively, socially and emotionally although the teacher may be focusing more on cognitive and social elements while the therapist focuses more on social and emotional elements. These strategies include:

- *Children's literature.* Stories which describe common experiences of loss or change with which children can identify, and in which the character in the story resolves or comes to terms with the situation, without calling on supernatural powers to bring about a happy ending, provide a valuable tool for developing emotional literacy. The choice of story will always be a personal matter, however there are some questions a teacher will want to ask before using it to raise issues of loss and grief. These will include questions about the quality of the language, strength of the storyline and its power to draw the children into the situations and feelings of the characters, about opportunities for moving the discussion from the storyline itself to the children's own experiences.

  Children quickly respond to a story which draws them into situations both known and unknown and makes them feel they are part of what is happening. Powerful though this is, there is always the reassurance that, however real it seems, it is only happening in a story, the book will eventually be closed. But the child who has been there, in that story, will have moved on in terms of emotional development and literacy. The teacher can draw out and extend the children's vocabulary of feelings and help them to gain new depths of understanding of their own and each others responses.

- *Creative play.* One route into creative play can be through stories. The storyline can be rerun, revised and rewritten according to the way the children think the situation could be resolved, starting from a critical moment in the narrative. While literature provides a safe environment for exploring strong emotions with a finite ending, creative play provides a safe context and the freedom to exit at any time. Any criticism that the play has been abandoned will be met with the response 'But we are only playing'. This signifies that the children have given themselves permission to pass, either because the emotion is too strong or because the situation has been resolved satisfactorily. Although there may be ground rules about behaviour during play, play itself has no rules; there is no proper way to play.
- *'Circles of feeling'.* 'Circles of feeling' provide a useful strategy for collecting up and displaying the vocabulary of feelings children may have heard or used in stories or creative play. Children are asked to contribute words and phrases to express how a character felt, or how they themselves would have felt. The words are recorded around by the teacher as a circle, so that no feelings are given greater prominence than any other. The words can be grouped by the teacher to demonstrate the range of vocabulary around one emotion, Fig. 13 3. Circles of feeling can be used to start a day, to round off a lesson, to prepare for a long anticipated event, or to share an unexpected happening (such as the death of a classroom pet).
- *Dance and drama.* These activities provide another rich, safe context for self-expression and help the development of emotional understanding

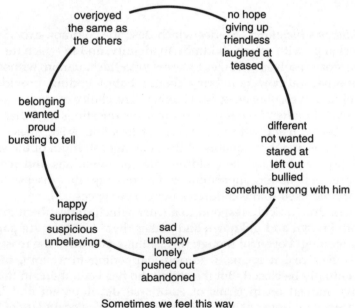

Fig. 13.3   Circles of feelings.

and competence. Children can be encouraged to express their strong emotions physically, and then be offered a vocabulary which carries the same meaning in words. Through such experiences children can be helped to internalise the language of their feelings and recognise the emotions expressed through the body language of others. Dance and drama are unique in being able to express movement, feelings and language and there are many opportunities to use this strategy in religious/moral education and the humanities.

- *Creative arts.* The creative arts provide other opportunities to express and understand the world of emotions. Children can, with encouragement, become totally involved in painting pictures or constructing collages through which they capture in colour, shape and pattern the feelings which they and others have experienced. Naming the feelings expressed in such a range of ways, perhaps as part of the collage, makes the vital link with language development.

- *Music and art therapy.* Sharing these activities as a group or a class helps children to recognise where their emotional experiences are similar to or different from their peers, encouraging the development of empathy. If these strategies are to be successful there will need to be a positive, trusting atmosphere in the classroom. A truly safe classroom climate is essential where the children and their teacher work together to build respect for self and others, confidentiality and trust. Once the classroom ethos has been established all of these strategies can be introduced, reviewed and reworked in increasingly demanding ways.

Planning to include loss and change in the curriculum

The strategies outlined above require coherent planning, monitoring and reviewing. Children may not make the links between the feelings they shared with a character in a story, the drama lesson where they explored the heights and depths of feelings or the picture they painted to capture some of those feelings. They will need help at first in recognising those links, in recognising how those feelings colour their lives and influence their behaviour and the behaviour of others. They will come to realise that being able to talk about their feelings with an adequate language and with confidence is a skill for life.

There needs to be, therefore, within and across the whole curriculum, a set of coherent strands which put the development of emotional skills as a priority into plans for productive teaching and learning outcomes. These strands need to be part of a coherent whole-school policy which is translated in to day-to-day practice.

Such a policy could be founded on the following themes, which have been described or illustrated in this chapter:

- *Start where the children are.* Use an illuminative research strategy to assess the children's needs by discovering what they see as loss, grief and bereavement; how they perceive, explain and describe their own feelings and those of others. From these insights it will be possible to shape an appropriate programme which responds to those needs, to the logic which underpins their explanations and the language they use to share this.

- *Plan a spiralling approach.*   Ensure that the development of emotional skills and competencies and the language of feelings begins with the youngest children in school. Provide experiences in the safe environment of the classroom where they can reflect on life situations (real and possible) – situations of loss, grief and bereavement. Revisit and rework this as children move through the school, with increasingly challenging activity and more specific language. This should reflect the realities of children's lives in today's society, and the possible conflict between how emotions are handled at home and at school.
- *Plan across the curriculum, taking a positive approach.*   Celebrate human feelings and emotions rather than view them as something to be coped with, kept down, denied or modified. Use the full potential of the curriculum to provide children with the opportunity to explore their emotions, to reflect, record and celebrate their growing emotional competencies.
- *Work towards a whole-school commitment.*   Whether a class teacher, lunchtime supervisor, school nurse, school counsellor or educational psychologist, all can have an impact on the emotional development of the children. For real success the contribution of all these individuals and of the curriculum must be part of a whole-school philosophy which includes a trusting relationship with parents and carers. This philosophy may be articulated through a school mission statement or discernible in the school ethos, and in a shared methodology, explicit to all those who work in the school, whether full time or visiting professionals.

And finally...

What we propose is not a prescription for dealing with loss. Just as each person's experience of loss and change is unique, so is each person's way of making sense of it. We do not suggest that children should be offered a particular language of feelings or a particular way to behave, but that they should be prepared for loss and change in a way which validates their response, utilising and developing their own emotional intelligence.

Teaching and learning focus on preparing children for loss and bereavement

Rationale

The rationale is that preventative interventions can significantly affect the way that children deal with grief.

Activity

Read the following case histories of two boys who were profoundly affected by loss while they were at primary school.

Mark's story

Mark is a 10-year-old boy whose mother died when he was 5 years old. He lives with his grandmother and until recently his older brother. Mark has a reading age of 5e, but is a competent artist. He is a quiet child, who makes few demands on his teachers. He never speaks about his mother. Through a discussion with Mark's grandmother about his learning difficulties it emerges that when his mother died, Mark was told she had gone on holiday. Mark himself was sent away for a short time and when he returned the house was full of flowers carrying cards, which he could read, but which he didn't understand. When he asked for an explanation he was simply told his mother wasn't coming back. Mark's brother has only recently told him that his mother is in fact dead. The teacher believes that some of Mark's learning problems may relate to the death of his mother and the way it was handled by the family.

Tom's story

Tom is an 8-year-old boy, the only son of a family with high expectations. He is a sensitive, articulate child, of above average ability. At school Tom is persistently teased and bullied for being different. He has told his parents about this and they have encouraged him to 'hit back' but Tom does not feel able to do this. He believes his parents are disappointed in him. As he puts it, he is 'too frightened to holler, too scared to hit – not exactly the kind of son my parents were hoping for'.

Tom's wit, intelligence and sensitivity are the very characteristics which make him vulnerable to the bullies' taunts. He is quite aware of being different, but breaks down easily under pressure, rewarding the bullies, who seem to gain further strength from Tom's apparent weakness. Tom's loss of self-esteem is profound.

In discussing these two cases you should:

- Consider how as an adult with a professional responsibility towards the child you would help the children to find a new balance in their lives
- Propose how a school, through its curriculum and policies could have reduced the impact of the events on the lives of the two boys.

Learning outcomes

The learning outcomes stimulated by the activities are for the course participants to:

- Understand appropriate interventions for children dealing with loss
- Appreciate the range of loss situations which can trigger grief reactions in children.

Chapter 14
Community Rites and the Process of Grieving

David Durston

This chapter sets out to explore the ways in which individuals and communities grieve, make public their grieving and feel safe to grieve. It emphasises the perspective of the community. It is largely based on the practices of the white communities of the UK which look to Christianity as their main religion, and form the majority of the population. Other cultures, for example Hindu or Muslim, which have retained close ties with the culture of the Indian sub-continent, frequently show much more active participation in community rites of mourning. The chapter explores the problems of suppressed grief. It makes a plea for greater freedom in the public expression of grief, arguing that this will lead to a more sensitive culture which recognises the pain of those who are grieving.

The perspective from which this chapter is written is professional.

Introduction

In the autumn of 1996 Matthew Harding, Vice-Chairman of Chelsea Football Club, was killed in a helicopter crash on his way back from an away game. A multi-millionaire, he had invested heavily in the club, enabling it to buy new players and build a new stand, but he had never lost the common touch and was immensely popular with the fans.

The following Saturday at Chelsea's home game they expressed their grief at his death. On a wire fence, just inside the entrance, were draped flowers and bouquets, Chelsea scarves and hats, messages and mementoes. Wreaths were placed in the centre circle, together with a pint of Guinness, his favourite tipple. The whole crowd stood for a minute's silence. For many of those present it was a profoundly moving and appropriate occasion.

From one point of view this event can be seen as an example of the way in which communities evolve rites to give expression to their grief. Widely used expressions of mourning, such as the giving of flowers and bouquets, and the keeping of silence, were combined with ordinary objects which gained a symbolic significance: Chelsea scarves and hats and a glass of Guinness. A shared emotion found fitting ritual expression.

A month earlier Daniel Pettiward had died. He was an actor, a poet, and for many years a contributor to *Punch* of both cartoons and articles. He had a wide circle of friends in the worlds of theatre and the arts. A bachelor in his eighties, he had outlived his immediate family, and when he died his friends planned his funeral.

The coffin was brought in to 'O Danny Boy' played by a solo flute. After the opening hymn and reading from the New Testament, a poem of his was read by a well-known television actress. A second poem, written in his honour, was read by a young woman who had known him well. A tribute was given by a friend. 'O Danny Boy' was sung as a solo and, after a second hymn, 'In Paradisum' from Faure's Requiem. A group of young people, Dan's Band, played the music as the coffin was carried out. The whole took place within the funeral liturgy of the Church of England, and in the historic medieval cathedral of Salisbury. Afterwards many people expressed their appreciation of the service.

This also can be seen as an example of the way in which a community can evolve rites to express its grief at the death of one of its members. But in this case these were placed within a setting that had been inherited from the past, both the physical setting of an ancient cathedral and also the words and music of the liturgy. The event gave expression to the individuality of the person who had died, but its setting was one in which many other people have been mourned over the centuries. Both individual personality and communal experience were given expression in the service.

Community rites: the public expression of grief

Both the events just described brought together a wide range of people who shared in the public expression of grief. It is the public nature of this expression of grief that is the focus of this chapter.

As a generic term such events may be called 'community rites of mourning'. They are rites in that objects and actions are given symbolic meaning, and are combined with words, music and silence into a ritual form.

The use of the word 'community' brings out the fact that the majority of those who take part already share a sense of common identity and belonging to one another. This may be based on residence, the community of a village or town. It may have an ethnic or religious basis, e.g. the Polish Community, the Jewish Community. In some cases it may be based on an institution with a strong sense of identity, for example a regiment or a school.

Two criteria can be identified as defining community rites in the sense used here. First they are public events (or patterns of behaviour) in which any member of the community may take part. They are open and visible in the public arena. Second they are very widely understood and accepted. People in the community or within a particular religious or cultural group find them an appropriate way of mourning, and expressing the grief they feel.

The thesis of this chapter

The thesis of this chapter is that public expression of grief in community rites assists the process of grieving, and provides support to those who have suffered a painful bereavement. This section and the next one give examples of this. As members of a community we are not only helped ourselves by participation in such events, but we also help one another.

Historical evidence suggests that in contemporary society many people are bewildered by death, and embarrassed and very uncertain in relating to those who have recently been bereaved. As a result the public expression of grief is now often inhibited when a 100 years ago it would have been expressed. Those who have been bereaved do not receive the help and support in their grief that could be available to them. This applies to other cultures that are a part of our multi-cultural community in the UK. Our ethnocentricity may well block their grieving as many of us have very little knowledge about grieving processes or other religions. Dickenson & Johnson (1993) refer to this in their text and Victim Support have published a text which outlines other religious practices and their funeral rites. The second half of the chapter sets out evidence for this from the UK Christian perspective.

The repercussions of a death

The death of a person may elicit a wide range of different repercussions, depending on the nature of the person and the circumstances of the death. A very elderly person who has been widowed and has outlived most of her own generation, and who has spent a long period in a nursing home, has to a large extent withdrawn from the community before dying. Jones (1994) refers to this as 'social death'. Death has been expected, perhaps awaited as a release. There are likely to be few who mourn the death, and for most of them their grief is likely to have anticipated the death. However, this does not mean that for relatives and friends it might not be painful.

By contrast, if a man dies of a heart attack in his fifties, for those who are closest to him the process of grieving is likely to be acutely painful. Studies such as those by Parkes (1996a) have depicted the intensity of the anguish and distress they experience. There may also be many other people who are affected by grief, other members of the family, close friends, neighbours and colleagues at work. For them the grief may be less intense and less long-lasting than for his immediate family but they may be deeply shaken by his sudden death and experience a profound sense of sadness. Beyond them, those who knew him less well may share this sense of sadness but less deeply.

At the extreme end of the range of repercussions is the sudden and tragic death of a number of people in an event that assumes national significance because it is given prominence in the mass media, especially television. A profound sense of shock and grief may be experienced by thousands of people across the country who look for ways of expressing that grief.

This chapter is concerned to explore those ways in which grief is given public expression, and the ways in which this public expression assists the process of grieving.

National rites of mourning

The extreme end of the range, the sudden and tragic death of a number of people which receives national publicity, provides a starting point for exploring community rites. The shooting of 16 children and their teacher in the primary school at Dunblane in March 1996 is a tragic recent example.

The national organs of communication, press, radio, and television, presented the picture of a nation in mourning. There were descriptions of the children and their families. Television news bulletins included pictures of the churches in Dunblane, of people walking through the churchyards to the churches and attending services within them. The prominence given to these pictures reflects the assessment of the public mood by those selecting items for the news. Through the medium of television a very large number of people from right across the country were able to share in the mourning of the people of Dunblane.

In the days after the deaths we received a number of requests in Salisbury Cathedral from people asking to sign a book of condolences. Anecdotal evidence indicates this happened at other churches and cathedrals. A book was provided, and during the next few weeks messages of sympathy and comfort and prayers were written in the book, which was signed by dozens of people. Some when writing in the book lit candles and offered prayers for those who had been bereaved. After the period of mourning the book was sent to Dunblane Cathedral. It was clear that many people felt that writing in a book in a church was an appropriate way of expressing their grief and sympathy for those who had been bereaved.

Another, rather different example, of a national rite of mourning is Remembrance Sunday, the Sunday nearest to 11 November, which has been widely observed across the country for many years. The national service at the Cenotaph in Whitehall is usually attended by the Queen and members of the royal family. The Prime Minister and leaders of the other political parties lay wreaths. The service is very widely screened in television news bulletins later in the day. In many towns and villages services are held at war memorials. The Act of Remembrance with its 2 minutes' silence is observed in nearly all churches at the service in the middle of the morning.

The focus of the event is on remembering those who died in the First and Second World Wars and the other conflicts of this century. From interviews and conversations it is clear that for many people who lost colleagues or members of their family Remembrance Sunday is what its name implies. It is a time of remembering the dead, a time of mourning again long after the main grief work has been done.

In 1996 there was a call for the observance of 2 minutes' silence on 11 November itself which fell on a Monday. The aim was to keep the original observance of Armistice Day, started after the First World War of 2 minutes' silence at the eleventh hour of the eleventh day of the eleventh month. This call was widely observed in shops, offices and factories. It was clear there was a great deal of popular support for it. The reasons for this increase in observance are not yet clear. It may have been linked with the tragic loss of life in Dunblane. It may be that as we approach the end of a century where there has been greater loss of life through war than in any other century, many people feel it is appropriate to remember solemnly those who have died.

The funeral: a facilitating environment for mourning

To complement those public events in which a very large number of people right across the nation join in mourning, it is worth considering those public rites by which the death of each person is customarily marked.

Central among these community rites is the funeral. For nearly every person who dies there is a funeral in a church or cemetery or crematorium chapel or some other appropriate place. It is the principal event in which the dead person is mourned and there is public expression of grief. Any other events are complementary or additional to the funeral.

A key element in understanding the funeral is the recognition that it gives expression to an emotion that is widely shared, but at very different levels of intensity by different people. These emotions provide the context in which the funeral takes place.

Interestingly, and perhaps unexpectedly in an increasingly secular society, a very great majority of funerals are still religious. Whereas religious rituals at birth are now probably only practised by a minority, at death they are still very much the norm. Forty years ago this would have meant Church of England or Roman Catholic, Methodist or some other Christian denomination. Today this needs to be extended to include Muslim, Hindu, Sikh and other religions.

While religious funerals continue there is considerable uncertainty in our society about their purpose and value. Perhaps that is not surprising. A society in which many people are bewildered by death is likely to be very uncertain in its relationship to the rituals around the disposal of the body of the dead person.

It often seems that the ritual that people regard as ideal is one in which nobody gets upset and the whole event is got through as quickly and efficiently as possible. The result of this attitude gives the effect of a service on a production line. While this protects people against the embarrassment of the intrusion of powerful emotions, it also frequently leaves them dissatisfied.

This dissatisfaction is reflected in for example Tony Walter's book *Funerals and How to Improve Them* (1990) and in the formation of the National Funerals' College in 1994 with the Reverend Dr Peter Jupp as its first Director. In 1996 the College launched *The Dead Citizen's Charter* which set out to describe what people are entitled to at a funeral.

This dissatisfaction can be seen as a reflection of the expectations that people have that the funeral will be a significant event. Over against it are the many expressions of appreciation that mourners make about funerals in which they have been able to express their grief and find consolation and this section sets out to explore the potential that funerals have to assist the process of grieving.

At its best the funeral provides what is, to use Winnicott's (1965) apt phrase, a 'facilitating environment'. This environment depends on the physical setting for the funeral and music and language that are evocative of meaning. It also depends on the quality of attention and understanding conveyed by those who lead the funeral.

Helping mourners to 'take it in'

The funeral usually takes place at an early stage in the process of grieving, most commonly within seven to ten days of the death. If the death has been sudden it may well be a time when the mourners are struggling to take in the reality of the death against those factors that resist and reject the idea that the loved person is dead. 'I can't take it in', 'I still can't believe it', are phrases that are often used at this stage. Or as one young man said to me three times after his father died suddenly of a heart attack, 'It's unbelievable ... it's unbelievable ... it's unbelievable.' These may be seen as examples of what is often called the phase of denial, the first phase of the grief process.

A significant part of the function of the funeral is to help people 'take it in' by providing a public ritual at the point at which the body of the dead person is disposed of.

'Making sense' of the death

One of the findings of the research that Parkes (1996a) did into the experience of widows was the importance for the bereaved person of 'making sense' of the death.

'There is a conscious need to "get it right" and getting it right is not just a matter of recalling the traumatic event correctly; it includes the need to "make sense" of what has happened, to explain it, to classify it along with other comparable events, to make it fit into one's expectations of the world.

It seems then that several components go to make up the process of grief work:

(1)   There is preoccupation with thoughts of the lost person...
(2)   There is painful repetitious recollection of the loss experience...
(3)   And there is the attempt to make sense of the loss, to fit it into one's assumptions about the world...

These are not three different explanations of the same phenomenon but three interdependent components of a larger picture. Attempts to make sense of what has happened would seem to be one way of restoring what is lost by fitting its absence into some superordinate pattern.'

(Parkes, 1996a: 76–78)

Part of the process of 'working through the grief' is the acceptance of the death as something 'that makes sense', that it is part of an ordered, meaningful world and not a world that is chaotic or absurd. Part of the attraction of a religious service at a funeral is the contribution that it can make to this process of 'making sense'.

An act of worship creates a mood and puts people in touch with belief. They may or may not share these beliefs. Quite frequently they hold them in a very attenuated form, in most circumstances giving very little thought to them. The religious service, however, affirms the beliefs and the fact that some people believe them. It conveys the sense that this is God's world, that God is in control of it, and that this death is in some mysterious way part of his plan.

At a time when the mourners' personal world has changed dramatically, and where everything feels that it is in turmoil, the use of prayers and hymns that they have known from childhood conveys a sense of stability and permanence. The Lord's Prayer and 'The Lord is My Shepherd', familiar to many people in this country, and the belief they express in the loving care of a powerful Father, put the death in a wider context. The act of worship can give mourners the sense that in some way the death does 'make sense', even though they cannot articulate it in words.

A safe place to mourn

The process of 'working through' grief requires that the pain has to be experienced and borne and this implies a losing or relaxing of control. Bereaved people are often afraid of breaking down in the presence of others, and so tend to build defences to make sure they are not overwhelmed by their feelings.

They are only able to relax this control in a context in which they are confident that someone or something else can 'hold them together'. If they can depend on another person or situation in this way, then they can engage in what has been described as 'regression to childhood dependence'. They can let go because they feel they are in a safe place where another will hold them.

The word 'regression' is not used here in a pejorative sense, implying that it is a bad thing. Rather it describes a going back to a pattern of behaviour that is characteristic of the childhood phase of life. For example children often hurt themselves while playing. They run to father or mother and collapse in a flood of tears in their parent's arms. They are hugged and held; in a few moments they are quickly better and rush off to play again.

Regression to childhood dependence on the part of the adult may be a way of giving up and opting out, but it may also be a means of *reculer pour mieux sauter*, a constructive response to stress, pain or anxiety. It can enable the person who felt 'shattered' to re-gather themselves and feel whole again, to face a situation which previously felt overwhelming and to find it manageable. The concept of 'regression to dependence' in adults is elaborated and discussed in Reed (1978).

To some people the symbols of God in the place of worship make it a safe place which allows them to lose control and grieve. Consider for example this account of a mourner at the funeral of her mother. She lived within a hundred yards of the church and had lived there all her life.

'Half an hour before the funeral she was in her house quite composed being the good hostess, introducing people to one another, making sure all the arrangements for the meal afterwards were in hand.

At the start of the funeral, when the family reached the gate at the entrance to the churchyard, she was in tears, half collapsed, leaning heavily on her brother. She cried a lot in the church service and subsequently at the crematorium.

Back at the house, ten minutes after leaving the crematorium, she was again the composed hostess, passing around the cups of tea and making sure everyone had a sandwich.'

It would seem that for her the church was a safe place where she could mourn and entrust herself to the process of grieving. The church symbolised for her the presence of God, and this allowed her to relax control and weep and grieve.

The responding leader

For many people who have little experience of worship, coming into a place of worship often makes them freeze up rather than relax control. In these circumstances the capacity of the person who is leading the funeral is of critical importance.

Consider this account of the funeral of a young man killed in a road accident, written by a theological student on placement in the parish.

'Many of the mourners were young, drinking and footballing friends of the man who had been killed. They came into the service grimly, their faces set...

During his talk the Vicar's voice wavered. This clearly surprised most people. I observed many people looking up and craning their necks to see. After the initial surprise on the part of the congregation an infectious reaction seemed to set in. Many others expressed their grief openly for the first time, e.g. sniffing and taking out handkerchiefs. It was at this point that a lump came into my throat and I shed a tear or two.'

The vicar gives this account of the funeral:

'As a result of their bereavement I got to know the family well. During the course of the funeral I became caught up in their grief. Tears were running down my face, and I began to choke and found it difficult to go on speaking.'

The most likely explanation would seem to be that the vicar's own mourning, and the open expression of the grief that he felt, gave the people in the congregation a sense that it was 'safe' to mourn and released them to express their grief. His leadership in mourning openly would seem to have been the critical factor in this case in allowing them to mourn.

The potential of the funeral

It is not easy to assess the capacity of the funeral for assisting people in the process of grieving, which will in any case vary from one person to another, but its potential may be indicated by this account of a funeral of a 7-month-old baby.

The parents had been married for seven years before the baby, their first child, was born, and for much of this time they had been longing for a child. The new baby was a great delight to them. She was healthy, and continued healthy until at about the age of 7 months she was taken ill. Her condition deteriorated rapidly, and within a few days she died.

The family, her parents, and grandparents, were heartbroken. In the days before the funeral they sat together for long periods in silence with the curtains drawn.

At the funeral they grieved freely. The vicar spoke on the words:

All flesh is grass, and all its beauty is like the flower of the field.
The grass withers, the flower fades;
But the word of our God will stand forever.

(Isaiah 40: 6,8)

He made the comparison between the child and the flower, both beautiful, but vulnerable and short lived. The family seemed to find this helpful, and asked if he could write out the words of the Bible for them, although they did not regard themselves as churchgoers.

Three or four days after the funeral the vicar visited the young couple in their council flat, and found that since the funeral they had redecorated the bedroom in which the baby used to sleep. It seemed to symbolise a new found capacity to envisage a future without their child.

Other community rites

In addition to the funeral there are a number of other rituals in contemporary British society, as there are in other societies, by which people give expression to their grief and from which many people find comfort.

Flowers play an important role in communal expressions of grief. Wreaths and flowers are sent to be placed on the coffin at the funeral, and they are usually displayed after the funeral so that the mourners are able to look at them. In other cultures the symbols may be different.

Many families place flowers on the grave where the body or the ashes of the one who has died are buried. This is very often done on anniversaries of the birth or death of the deceased and on festivals such as Christmas and Easter.

When people have died in particularly tragic circumstances, flowers become the way in which large numbers of people are able to express their grief. Following the Hillsborough disaster part of the Liverpool football ground became a shrine where hundreds of fans placed flowers, scarves, and other objects as a mark of respect to those who had lost their lives in the tragic events of that match.

Flowers are also used to mark the site of a tragic death. After a road accident in North Staffordshire in which a young couple lost their lives, fresh flowers were placed by the side of the road at the site of the accident for several months. Reports suggest this is becoming an increasingly common practice.

The beauty and vulnerability of flowers and their short life span makes them a fitting expression of the beauty and vulnerability and brevity of human life.

War memorials with the names of those who lost their lives in the two World Wars of this century are a familiar feature of most towns and villages. They often play a central role in ceremonies on Remembrance Sunday early in November each year. To some of them have been added the names of those who have died in subsequent conflicts such as the Falklands campaign. For their colleagues who survived, and for members of their families, these memorials and the annual ceremonies held by them are an important way of expressing the significance of their death, and the grief that it caused.

Less widespread, but still frequent are other memorials. On the bank of the River Thames just south of Osney Lock in Oxford there is a small obelisk with the inscription

In memory of Edgar George Wilson who after rescuing two boys from drowning lost his life June 15 1889 aged 21 years.

The inscription goes on to say that it was erected by public subscription. It is not hard to imagine the sense of anguish and distress that would have been felt by many people at this tragic loss of a young life.

Characteristically memorials are erected when death is seen as the sacrifice of life for the benefit of others, whether in war or in carrying out a rescue.

Increasingly common in recent years have been gifts made in memory of those who died. They are usually designed to be of items that will be widely used and appreciated by the public. Seats in public places are a common choice.

For people who have held positions of leadership, the funeral service is often complemented by a memorial service. The leadership may have been institutional, the headmaster or headmistress or the company chairman, political, intellectual or cultural. Because of their leadership position they are likely to have influenced the lives of many people. The memorial service is a way of giving public expression to the sense of the significance of this life which has now ended.

The loss of the communal understanding of grief: a historical perspective

Public mourning

In his seminal book, Gorer (1965) reflected on the changes that he had seen in patterns of mourning in this country during his lifetime. The trigger that caused him to write the book was the experience of his sister-in-law when her husband died. It made him aware that profound changes had taken place in society, and as a result of these many widows and widowers were being left alone and unsupported at the time when they most need help and comfort.

The books starts with an autobiographical introduction:

'There were no deaths in my family of which I was conscious during my childhood; but I was certainly conscious of the fact of death. The parade of funerals – horse-drawn, of course, with black plumes and all the trimmings – was a constant feature of street life; and we children had to keep an eye out for them and take off our hats or caps for the whole time that the funeral procession passed us; it was very rude not to, and showed a lack of respect for people in their great trouble and when people were dressed in mourning – they might be visitors or shop assistants – we had to be quiet, and not fidget or make a noise. As small children we learned that mourners were in a special situation or state of mind and had to be treated differently from others, with more consideration and more respect; and I think our education on this subject was typical of that period.

(Gorer, 1965: 1–2)

Gorer's father died in the sinking of the *Lusitania* in May 1915 when he was just 10 years old.

'I was treated with great kindness, but like an invalid; no demands were made on me, I was indulged, conversation was hushed in my presence...'

'I was given black ties and had bands of crepe sewn on to the sleeves of my suit; but I remember the first days I wore these insignia of woe feeling, despite my unhappiness, somehow distinguished, in nearly every sense of the word. I was set apart; and this was somehow fitting and comforting.'

(Gorer, 1965: 3)

These descriptions portray a world which has now passed. To some it may seem quaint or even bizarre. Some may regard it as morbid in its attitudes because it gave so much attention to death. On the other hand it is worth analysing what these conventions were able to provide to that society.

Firstly, they provided a ceremonial which demonstrated a public recognition of the significance of death, and of grief and mourning as a natural response to it. Death was acknowledged, and not hidden or swept under the carpet.

Secondly, they provided a means of identifying those who had been bereaved as people who needed to be treated with particular consideration. Someone who has a leg in plaster and is on crutches is clearly identified as someone who needs particular consideration when shopping or in the street or on public transport. Those who have been bereaved carry no visible sign of their condition by which they can be identified unless social convention provides them with one.

Thirdly, they provided a pattern of educating children to understand the condition of grief, and to show sympathy to the feelings of the bereaved. Would it be fair to say that the average 7-year-old in 1912 had a better understanding of grief than the average 7-year-old in 1998? Sweeping generalisations like this are impossible to substantiate but the description that Gorer gives makes this seem very likely.

A fairly common reaction to descriptions like these is to wish to have the same kind of consideration of the bereaved that was shown at that time, but without the ritual and ceremonial that accompanied it. The historical evidence is that as the ritual and ceremonial were gradually abandoned over the next two generations, the consideration for the bereaved that it symbolised was also lost. Accounts of what happened suggest that society needs visible signs and actions to embody and make visible attitudes towards those who have been bereaved.

The suppression of mourning

Gorer described his own experience at the sudden death of his brother in 1961:

'I was able to mourn freely, to indulge in passionate bouts of weeping without self-reproach. I lost about twenty pounds in weight over the following three months, and my sleep tended to be disturbed. . . . I did all the routine work necessary, but felt disinclined for anything that demanded prolonged concentration. I wore a black tie for about three months. I had great pleasure in seeing real friends, but was unwilling to meet strangers. A couple of times I refused invitations to cocktail parties, explaining that I was mourning; the people who invited me responded to this statement with shocked embarrassment, as if I had voiced some appalling obscenity... Educated and sophisticated though they were (they) mumbled and hurried away. They clearly no longer had any guidance from ritual as to the way to treat a self confessed mourner...'

'This would certainly seem to be the explanation of the way in which Elizabeth was avoided by her and Peter's friends; they treated her, she said, as though she were a leper. Only if she acted as though nothing of consequence had happened was she again socially acceptable... At the period when she most needed help and comfort from society she was left alone.'

(Gorer, 1965: 14–15)

The same word 'leper' was used by another author writing at this time. In his classic account of bereavement C.S. Lewis also describes the feelings of being an embarrassment and the need to be isolated.

Uncertainty and embarrassment are the dominant features in people's response to someone who has been bereaved in the account Jill Tweedie gives of the response of friends following the death of her first child at 5 months old.

'After the first formal visits, letters and flowers, friends stayed away for a long while, clutching their own children, angry with me for introducing to their circle such a vulgar fellow as death. When, finally, they began to see me again, it was on condition that I behaved myself. Occasionally, forgetting, I would join in a conversation and say oh yes, I remember, he didn't like stewed prunes either. Cheeks burned, faces turned away, silence fell sharp and disagreeable. My child died then, because they would not let me remember.'

(Tweedie, 1970)

In his magisterial study of attitudes to death in Western society over the past 1000 years, Aries comments:

'The suppression of mourning is not due to the frivolity of survivors but to a merciless coercion applied by society. Society refuses to participate in the emotion of the bereaved.'

(Aries, 1981: 579–80)

The phrase 'merciless coercion' is a cutting description but probably a justified one. There is an unwitting cruelty on the part of people, bewildered and embarrassed by death, who refuse to allow those who are bereaved to mention the dead person whom they are mourning.

The past 40 years has seen a growing awareness of the lack of support given to those who have been bereaved in our society, and growing efforts to provide it. CRUSE (now known as Cruse Bereavement Care), was formed in 1959 by Mrs Margaret Torrie, as a national organisation for the widowed and their children. It is now the largest agency in this country providing support for those who have been bereaved. It is interesting that its formation is very close in time to the period in which as C.S. Lewis and Geoffrey Gorer were writing their books, in the early 1960s.

Since then a number of other organisations have been formed, to link together and to care for those who have been bereaved in particular circumstances. There has been an increasing flow of publications at all levels, scholarly, for practitioners, and for popular reading. Taken together the developments of the past 40 years can be legitimately called a movement.

On the other hand for much of this period, while an increasing number of individuals have been concerned with the support and care of those who have been bereaved, there has been little evidence that social attitudes to death and bereavement prevalent in society have been changing. The sense of uncertainty and embarrassment in meeting bereaved people, and the consequent tendency to wish to avoid them (and so to treat them like lepers) has continued. So has the resistance to allowing bereaved people to speak about their bereavement in ordinary conversation.

Only in the last few years have there been indications that the movement of support and care for the bereaved is actually beginning to dent entrenched social attitudes.

The significance of the public expression of grief

Aries contrasts attitudes through history up to the start of this century with those in Western society today.

'The death of each person was a public event that moved, literally and figuratively, society as a whole. It was not only an individual who was disappearing but society itself that had been wounded and that had to be healed... Death has always been a social and public fact... In the course of the twentieth century an absolutely new type of dying has made an appearance in some of the most industrialised, urbanised, and technologically advanced areas of the western world... Society has banished death.'

(Aries, 1981: 559–60)

It is in the light of this assessment of the phenomenon described in the last section that we assess the significance of the public expression of grief.

First those who are suffering most acutely from the death are made aware of being part of a larger community which shares their grief and supports them in it. This can often be seen at a funeral. Large numbers of people attending a funeral is experienced as supportive and comforting by members of the immediate family. They feel themselves surrounded by a body of people who acknowledge, and to some extent share, the pain they are experiencing at their loss.

Second the public expression of grief is a public recognition of the significance of the death of this person. The person who has died is acknowledged and honoured by those who share in the mourning. Death is not denied nor banished.

It is an issue for every human being how or whether they come to terms with their own mortality. Through the centuries different societies have offered different resources to their members, and different guidelines to enable them to live at ease with the prospect of their own death. Indications are that many sections of contemporary Western society offer very limited resources to their members.

'The suppression of mourning (in public) ... is a way of denying the presence of death in practice, even if one accepts its reality in principle.'

(Aries, 1981: 579–80)

By contrast the public expression of mourning acknowledges the significance of death and so assists people in coming to terms with their own.

Third the expression of shared grief tends to strengthen the bonds that hold a community together. After several decades which have seen the weakening of these bonds and the development of an increasingly individualistic society, with all the loneliness and lack of social support that implies, this may be judged a significant factor.

The consequences of the suppression of mourning

Research over the past 30 years has made us aware of the consequences for individuals whose process of mourning is stifled or never adequately completed. The suppression of mourning in contemporary society described in this chapter raises the questions of its influence on society as a whole when the processes of grieving and mourning are blocked by social pressures.

One possible consequence for individuals is the development of a protective shell, a carapace, which acts as a defence against ever again having to endure so much pain. The obverse of this defence against pain is frequently a lack of sensitivity to the pain of others. Another possible consequence is a continuing bitterness or resentment. It may take the form of an unresolved anger which finds disguised expression in an attitude which is quick to be critical of others. It may take the form of a kind of disgust which expresses itself in a chronic contemptuous attitude towards other people or institutions.

If we live in a society which suppresses mourning and blocks the expression of grief in the ways described we need to consider how this is affecting attitudes and behaviour in society as a whole. Such a consideration is inevitably speculative because it is based on assessments of society about which there are many different opinions.

Many commentators, however, consider that we live in a society which is on the whole hard-hearted towards those who are homeless or suffering from poverty. Occasional appeals may break through this hard-hearted attitude and produce sudden unexpected generosity, but there is no consistent readiness to respond to the suffering of the deprived and marginalised. It has been suggested that this lack of sensitivity to the suffering of others results from defences built up as a result of unresolved grief.

Many would also judge that we are a society that is quick to blame and to condemn. There is powerful resentment towards 'scroungers', and often little concern to distinguish between those who are genuinely deprived and those who are taking advantage of the provisions of the welfare state. There is a widespread punitive attitude which leads to demands for more and more severe penalties for offenders. It is a question how far these attitudes are a reflection of a widespread bitterness or resentment springing from suppressed mourning.

Another characteristic of our society is the widespread use of magazines and videos which depict brutal acts causing injury and death in a sadistic way. It was Gorer who first coined the phrase 'the pornography of death'. There are grounds for supposing that the suppression of the public acknowledgement of death has made it appear illicit and, therefore, has given it a particular distorted attraction. This finds a perverted expression in such things as the so-called 'video nasties'.

The consequences of public attitudes which seek to suppress any public display of grief and to banish death may be much wider than has previously been recognised.

Postscript

In the early hours of Sunday 31 August 1997 (some weeks after this chapter was completed) Diana, Princess of Wales, was killed in a car crash in a Paris subway, together with her companion Dodi Fayed, and their driver Henri Paul. Her death resulted in a great public expression of grief and mourning without parallel in this country in living memory. The only comparable public expression of grief was in Liverpool following the Hillsborough disaster of 1989 in which 95 football supporters were killed, but that was confined to a single city, and a city with a highly distinctive community character.

A number of features could be identified in this public mourning. It arose out of the spontaneous response of large numbers of people. Television, radio and the press gave publicity to their actions, and encouraged many more people to join them. The spontaneity of the response was a key feature of the public mourning.

One of the most common forms that this mourning took was the laying of flowers in appropriate places, Kensington Palace, Diana's home, Althorp, her family home, but also in many other local places all over the country. They piled up into huge banks of thousands of flowers. Both of these features were similar to the mourning after the Hillsborough tragedy.

Even more widespread was the writing of messages. Many of these were attached to the flowers. More were written in Books of Remembrance, or Books of Condolence as they were often called, in cathedrals, churches, town halls and other public buildings. (This followed a pattern that became widespread following the shooting of 16 schoolchildren and their teacher at Dunblane in March 1996.)

Vast numbers of people queued for hours outside St James' Palace, where Diana's body was lying, to write in these books. At one stage people were queuing for between 7 and 8 hours for their turn to write, and it was very publicly announced that the number of books would be increased to 43. One of the features of these messages was that they allowed people to express their own feelings in a distinctive, personal way.

Special services were held in churches, and the details of the services to be held in cathedrals were published in the national press. Large numbers of people visited churches to lay a wreath of flowers, to write a message, to light a candle, to pray or to take part in a service. A significant number of them were people who had very rarely, if ever, been in church before.

On the day of the funeral in Westminster Abbey huge crowds lined the route that the cortege followed. Many of them had spent the night there in order to secure a place. Another huge crowd gathered in Hyde Park to watch the funeral on large screens. Special train and other arrangements were made to bring people from other parts of the country to London for the funeral. Estimates of the crowds range between one and two million. Several million more people watched the funeral on television.

A characteristic feature of the mourning was the way in which people simply wanted to 'be there'. Large crowds gathered outside the royal palaces, not simply to lay flowers or to queue to write in the books, but simply to be present with others in an appropriate place. The desire to be part of a gathering, of a temporary community united by the shared experience of grief, to be part of a gathering, was strong for many people. One person who was among the crowds near one of the royal palaces commented that as he walked around he realised that people were talking in soft voices, as if they were in church.

People's behaviour suggested that many of the norms which usually govern behaviour were dissolved. At times it seemed that the whole nation was in a state that can best be described by Turner's concept of 'communitas'. It is a condition in which the usual structures of society that differentiate people from one another are temporarily dissolved, thus recognising and affirming an essential underlying human bond without which there could be no society (Turner, 1969: 82–3).

During the week there were numerous indications in conversations with people in the crowds that this public expression of grief had for many people released private grief that had previously been inhibited. It seems as though people who had not been 'allowed' to grieve earlier deaths were now 'permitted' to experience and express that grief. For example, Tom Wright, the Dean of Lichfield, commented in a sermon later published in the *Church Times*.

'Our society is no good at grief. Funerals and cremations are often perfunctory, impersonal. Mourners often suppress the natural, God-given emotion of grief. As a result, many carry around their grief which they do not know what to do with. Diana gave us a chance to express it. Ironically, it was all right to grieve in public for Diana, in a way that it would not have been in our heartless world, for a parent, spouse or child. Many of the thousands who came to Lichfield Cathedral last week spoke of the private grief that had now come to the surface. Diana's last gift was to unlock the floodgates of grief.'

(Wright, 1997: 6–7)

As one man said to a priest in the crowd

'My mother died eight years ago and it did not mean anything to me, but this has broken me up.'

The release of grief previously inhibited is likely to have had a significant contribution to the strength of feeling expressed during the days that followed Diana's death.

What are the implications of this public outpouring of grief for the thesis of this chapter? Does it indicate a decisive shift to a new culture in which the open expression of grief in public has again become acceptable? Or is a new pattern emerging in which most of the time death continues to be hidden and the public expression of grief discouraged, but in which on rare occasions, following particular tragedies, whole communities join a public mourning? Or was it simply a 'one-off', a never to be repeated phenomenon? Only time will allow us to answer these questions.

Teaching and learning focus on community rites and the process of grieving

Rationale

The rationale is to enable course participants to become familiar with the process of the communal expression of emotion and to appreciate the task of devising appropriate rites for such expression.

Activity: Devising a community rite for a public expression of celebration or thanksgiving

As an alternative to a focus on grief but to retain the focus on community rites, invite the group working in twos or threes to devise a community rite for a public expression of celebration or thanksgiving for either a colleague retiring or an institutional anniversary.

They will need to address the following issues:

- Who or what is the community?
- How are they to be involved in both the planning of the rite and participating in it?
- What emotions are people likely to experience on the occasion?
- What opportunities will there be to give these feelings appropriate expression?

Learning outcomes

The learning outcomes stimulated by the activities are for the course participants to:

- Understand that planned rituals can complement spontaneous expressions of grief
- Consider the careful planning required to ensure that rituals help rather than hinder the grieving process.

Afterword

Ros Weston

The afterword draws together the themes of:

- *Diversity in grieving and mourning; the 'voices' of those who grieve*
- *Theory and practice of bereavement support and care; the professional 'voices'*
- *Reflexivity through discourse analysis and autobiographical research.*

Introduction

Accepted ways of thinking about and acting upon our experience and knowledge of change, loss, grief and bereavement, may block our ability to understand the many different meanings and interpretations inherent in various models, theories and practices (Walter, 1996a). In this book we have illustrated how diverse meanings and interpretations may be even though we ground our work in similar and familiar theory and practice. Different individuals and organisations all have a different story to tell. No matter which models, approaches or discourses we prefer in helping and supporting individuals, or in educating and training professionals in this complex field, there are many other ways in which we might understand the perceptions and contexts in which people change or grieve. We have illustrated the many ways in which all who are involved in the helping process might use their current knowledge, research and experience creatively to further develop such processes, the caring services and subsequent policy development (Department of Health, 1992). This includes the teaching and learning focuses at the end of each chapter which are intended to give trainers and educators an opportunity to develop their work, professional skills and critical thinking.

The need for critical appraisal and thinking

Firstly, and most important of all, we as practitioners and theoreticians, possibly also as victims and survivors, need to periodically review the way we have chosen to work and the reasons why we have done so. This is referred to by Murdoch (1970); Giddens (1991), Schon (1991) and Usher & Edwards (1994) as:

- *Reflective practice* – the need to concentrate and reflect upon all the work we do in order to understand what it is we do and learn to do it more effectively
- *Reflexivity* – the ongoing process of deep concentration which Murdoch likens to prayer and the art of meditation.

Secondly, in addition to reviewing our knowledge and experience, reflexivity reveals that we are inextricably embedded in the social context of the world in which we live and have our being and do our work. Giddens (1991) refers to this as embeddedness and Usher & Edwards (1994) refers to it as intertextuality.

Such a process can engender insight about why we do what we do, and how we do it. Reflexivity is more than the autobiographical project which seeks to understand self and others, but also seeks to understand the social world with which we interact. It is the placing of ourselves as practitioners, theorists or researchers in the texts we ourselves create that enables us to review, analyse, learn and reconstruct in order to clarify our theory and practice. However, this is with the acknowledgement that we too create texts and speak within a particular discourse. This analysis can enhance our practice by illuminating how far theory can often be divorced from practice to the detriment of clients, students, teachers and facilitators. It thereby detracts from the goal of supporting those in the process of changing or grieving and their subsequent development and growth. Tillich (1967) refers to this as the chance 'to become'.

Thirdly, reflexivity is the ability to develop an ongoing narrative about 'self' in an effort to better understand our lives, and to use the skills learned to enable us to negotiate the present and the future in the complex world of high modernity. Such a narrative helps us to make sense of who we are and our relationships with those with whom we interact. This is our discourse about 'self' and the social world we inhabit and is crucial to our sense of self. By coming to such an understanding we may be helped in our efforts to reduce the practice–theory gap and to acknowledge practice as informal theory. We can learn as much directly from practice as indirectly from theory. This is the double hermeneutic, that is, the ongoing dynamic between theory and practice and can be crucial in working more effectively with clients.

Theories have two important functions in this text:

- The analytical skills they offer professionals and lay people to better understand the work they do as well as themselves
- The recognition that change and grief work is about helping individuals to develop a reflexive ongoing narrative of self using past as well as current knowledge and experience; a constructive process of helping them in their quest for personal growth and development.

Understanding the many paradigms we can choose can help us to understand why we practice, research or theorise the way we do. We can understand better why, as professionals, we prefer certain ways of working and how our original training has encouraged us in particular directions. Our preferred choice can be reviewed by reading research, critiquing such research and reflective and reflexive practice.

The most powerful 'stories', or ways of thinking and practising, are those which have purchase with our concerns and therefore resonate within us. We recognise what they are saying and mean to us and feel that they can be useful in our work. However, we may need to consider the way these 'stories' and our acceptance of them may be distorted by rhetoric, persuasion by researchers or others who 'know', and by ideology, the power that sustains them.

As editors and authors we have developed ways of teaching and learning about change and loss which combines the evidence (empirical perspective), the humanist model (phenomenological perspective), autobiography and experiential learning. This constructivist approach can encourage individuals to work realistically with their own experience, to review and reconstruct meanings for themselves and offers them the chance to change and grow. It has allowed us to work from the client's perspective to enable them to become powerful in their own healing or survival, and in their physical, mental or emotional health. We have benefited from theories and new ways of working which:

- Promote a sensitive health-promoting environment with appropriate supporting policies and strategies which are becoming the responsibility of local, regional and national governments as well as the individual; this is important as it helps to avoid a victim-blaming culture
- Use the increasing evidence from quantitative and qualitative research, which supports theory and practice. However, the quality of the design of the studies should be taken into account when assessments about practical use are made; see Weston (1997b) on evidence-led health promotion
- Develop our skills as practitioners to use and apply evidence in our work and yet use appropriate strategies tailored to particular situations or individuals
- Ensure that our work is led by client need and at the pace clients/patients choose
- Help practitioners to recognise the ability in everyone to grow and develop; the professional is a facilitator for such a process
- Recognise that every situation has its complexities and there are no simple answers
- Avoid victim blaming by over interpreting the models and approaches as ultimate 'truth' or necessary processes which all who grieve must go through before they can be seen by professionals or others as 'over' the grief event or through the grief process.

By doing this, individuals and communities can determine how they wish to change, the pace of such change and how they wish to implement change.

This inevitably means a different role for the professional where their authority is not required in the same way as before. The facilitation role demands a different philosophy and working practice, that of enabling individuals to determine what is appropriate for them.

The use of discourse analysis in reflective practice

This is a post-modern approach and questions positivist assumptions about the nature of knowledge and power, the acceptance of reality, the objectivity of observation and the transparency of language (Usher & Edwards, 1994). The post-modernist world is seen as fragmented. Different groups in society all have their own understandings of the world, construct both their reality and meaning, and reconstruct too as they negotiate life and living. Reality is not fixed and language does not just reflect a given reality but constructs it too. Hence models and approaches do not only reflect reality but also construct how it should be for those who grieve.

Discourse analysis is increasingly seen as a method for studying social change as well as the cultural and ideological content of the text. It draws on several disciplines such as linguistics and social political theories. It differs from linguistics in two main ways in that it is concerned with:

- Texts which are not just verbal
- Cultural as well as linguistic meaning and is therefore not accountable methodologically in the same ways as empirical social science.

As McQuail (1987: 189) suggests it refutes these as unknowable since social reality consists of discrete 'universes of meaning'. There are problems with this approach since if there is no definitive 'truth' how can constructivists argue for their version of 'truth'? (Hammersley, 1995). We are not arguing that we have yet another answer, neither do we reject the knowledge and experience outlined by other theorists. We are suggesting that those of us involved in this work can review all theories and practice with the aim of improving what we do. We are seeking to understand the various meanings which appear natural and incontestable merely because we have grown up with them or because they are constantly expressed in the literature and research.

As Eco says:

'This is such a natural inclination (the taking for granted) I have no reason to consult the truth tables; rather I decide to suspend my disbelief and take that discourse as a fictional one. I do this because it is the only way to assign a form of existence in whatever world to the entity posited by the statement. Once posited by the discourse – it exists, and since researchers are supposed to tell the truth about the actual world, people believe it. This would not matter if this was only the empirical author. But now the text exists, obedient readers follow the instructions. What is the ontology of such possible worlds and their inhabitants and what is the position of the model reader?'

(Eco, 1995: 100–108)

Models and perspectives are all products of discourse and yet they are often presented as objective accounts and taken as given. The role of discourse analysis is to make visible that which is taken for granted. Different worlds are brought into being through knowledge and language (Usher & Edwards, 1994) and can be questioned. One way of carrying out such an analysis is to count the times concepts and themes are repeated in any text. This would also give some quantitative data on the content analysis. Content analysis according to Cohen & Manion (1994: 55) is about:

'...collecting, classifying, ordering, synthesising, evaluating and inter-preting of symbolic material.'

Other ways of deconstructing relate to language and its system of signs. These signs are connotative, that is they can signify other additional implied meanings. Codes of connotation depend on prior social knowledge on the part of the reader. Readers may choose to reject meaning at a connotative level but it may require skills and practice not often encouraged in our society. Eco suggests texts can be closed, they become accepted truths, meanings appear static and taken for granted. Without such deconstruction skills people can be subject to and colonised by dominant ideologies. We need mastery over a secondary discourse of critical analysis which has to be learned and practised, as opposed to primary discourses learned and absorbed through the process of socialisation.

The danger with this approach is that it seeks to create another discourse with its own inherent power and knowledge. In other words it could seek to promote or privilege yet another discourse. This, however is not our intention.

We make sense of our lives by developing a narrative which changes through time and is dependent upon the context in which we live our lives. As Eco says:

'The story, that is the real story of a fictional construction has many morals. In the first place it shows that we are continually tempted to give shape to life through narrative schemes. Second, it demonstrates the force of existential pre-suppositions. In every statement involving proper names or definite descriptions, the reader or listener is supposed to take for granted the existence of the entity about which something is pre-dicated.'

(Eco, 1995: 99)

The need to give some kind of coherence to our life stories is well docu-mented, as is the need to understand meaning (Lather, 1991; Hammersley,

1995; Swindells, 1995). The texts in this book are part of changing and continuing narratives as we attempt to make sense of our own experience and that of others. We use the metaphor of 'stories' and 'voices' to illustrate throughout this text the many meanings inherent in any one account. These change according to the context and location of the organisation or individual with respect to time and place. Historical, cultural, physical, biological, geographical, developmental, maturational, financial and social factors are all relevant to the level of support.

Authors are telling their 'stories', both professional and personal, in which inhere many possible meanings and interpretations. They have something to say not only about the particular, in change and loss work, but also the general. Moreover they challenge any sense of the universal truth. They celebrate difference and fragmentation and yet at the same time illustrate how we can use this in our work to enhance the knowledge we already have and work more effectively with people who are in any change process.

The use of critical autobiography

Critical autobiography and biography is an innovative research method that has quickly gained authority as a means of establishing veracity in personal experience. This provides the opportunity of introducing the 'voice' in the context of a 'story' exemplified in this book. Critical auto/biography is a way of allowing the 'voices' and 'stories' to be told. This allows authors to integrate themselves into their work. It is impossible to be objective about issues where there is so much subjective experience, and autobiographical approaches acknowledge this. The approach raises questions as to its validity as a research method and what can be discussed in academic settings or in public consultation. Some researchers and authors have argued for such inclusion: Horchschild (1975); Oakley (1981); Rockhill (1987); Jackson (1990); Zola (1991). Yet even today emotions are seldom recorded because of the fear that such subjectivity will render the account meaningless. Such an approach does not, as Church (1995) suggests:

> '... wipe out the 'public', 'theoretical' and 'rational', rather it suggests that what we experience and present of ourselves as subjective or personal is simultaneously objective and public...'

> (Church, 1995: 1)

This is supported by Haug (1992), Jackson (1990) and Weedon (1987).

We can learn in the caring professions from the experience of other fields and disciplines. There is much evidence of a growing body of auto/biographical literature expressive of feminist and post-modern ideas though in fields of sociology and anthropology. For example, Britzman (1989), Cully & Portuges (1982), Nelson (1986) and Jackson (1990) trace the development of autobiographies from traditional male forms to life history work (e.g.

feminist, gay, anti-sexist men's movement) to collective forms other writers in the field are Silverstein (1977), Steinberg (1977), Oakley (1981), Fraser (1984), Walkerdine (1985), Mairs (1986, 1989), Steedmen (1986), Grieg (1987) and Heibrum (1988). DiGiacomo (1988) argues that autobiographical work encourages the author to 'stay within' as opposed to being 'author evacuated'. All these writers give intellectual legitimacy to personal narrative and experiential knowledge. Post-structuralism according to Church (1995), quoting Strives, adds another dimension by asserting:

'There is no such thing as removing the observer from the knowledge acquisition process, since to do so would be like trying to see without eyes.'

(Church, 1995: 331)

The issues raised in these chapters are significant beyond the authors' testimony for the theory and practice in transition, change, loss and grief. Such an approach reflects the changes which are happening in our understanding of knowledge and constitute an alternative way to write social science Church (1995). Contributors were selected in some instances where they represented a particular relevant discipline or organisation and hence other 'voices' are heard.

These testimonies need to be set in the context of current knowledge and beliefs and their relationship with health promotion and education, and be equally open to scrutiny, criticism and analysis. This is reflected in the intersections of the professional, public and private; also illustrated are the different stages of development and transition of the various authors, which may be described as their own hermeneutic journeys. The *world view* of the authors is reflected in the different paradigms in which each is situated.

Church argues that in the phenomenological participatory paradigm there is a process which she describes as *breaking through*. By this it is meant that for participants' 'voices' to be genuinely heard and have some role in changing policy, then the liberal-social maxim needs to be challenged. This is justified by arguing that the model adopted by Friere (1976) is inappropriate, as it only represents and interprets others' voices; they do not speak for themselves. Church further suggests that only when the objective self comes face to face with the subjective self at the intersection, the mask is revealed. Only then, she claims, is it possible to move into the participatory mode. In her case this meant that such a process challenged and caused a break down which she referred to as 'falling off the fence'.

'There has been a major shift in my participation in the community mental health field over the last five years. I understand this as, variously, becoming a translator between two world views, becoming fluent in two discourses, having my professionalism punctured, and falling off the fence.

(Church, 1995: 51)

and

> 'I had to "unlearn" many of the ways I had been taught to relate to people
> as a professional and about initiating a new set of relationships ...'

> (Church, 1995: 52)

Church proceeds to explain that her subjective exploration has drawn her to
the theories of post-structuralism and their rejection of 'totalising, uni-
versalising, meta-narratives and autonomous and fully conscious selves'
(Lather, 1991: 5 cited in Church, 1995).

This author does not believe a breakdown is necessary but that there may
be a need for such a personal confrontation which acknowledges the tensions between our personal and professional selves and our subjective
experience. This can give us the freedom to be involved in the 'stories' rather
than remaining outside them as a professional interpreter or representative.
As one of the professionals with whom Church (1995) was working says:

> 'We were yelled at. I remember someone shouting from the back of the
> room: "We are going to make you people hear us, Don't ever forget it.
> Damn it. You know? And when I went to bed that night I was very upset. I
> couldn't sleep in the hotel. Because I said I did not come on these things to
> be yelled at ... What I finally said to myself is 'You have got to listen to
> these horror "stories" in order to know where these people are coming
> from'. And that sort of is the bottom line. And what these people are
> looking for are those four things that I mentioned to you which is no
> different to what I am looking for a roof over my head, a job to go to,
> income and respect. They are not any different from me. That has been a
> two year process. So now I am an advocate on their side."'

> (Church, 1995: 92)

This challenges some of the dominant paradigms, their power and
knowledge, in the field of mental health. Such interactions are crucial to
furthering our knowledge and are examples of what has been termed *arche-
health* (Fox, 1993). People are rarely passive and if constrained by normative
or other pressures will act to change things. In this text such different world
views may be seen as a challenge to each other as well as to accepted theory
and practice. The presentation of the material throughout the book, will it is
hoped, provide us with the opportunity to explore further our research and
practice for the benefit of those whom we seek to help or support.

The ethics of transition, change and loss

The ethical parameters for our work are partly determined by the choice of
approach we use in our work, our personal beliefs and values, our professional training, our professional bodies and ethical theory. We have

professional guidelines for our work and follow these. However, working with change theory does raise some important questions which relate to the improvement of practice and also to the rights of the client or individual.

In our work on change we need to be sure that we do good (beneficence), do not harm (non-maleficence) and therefore the approach to clients needs to be well thought out. We need to know that what we see as good actually is good in that the client gains without undue stress, (autonomy and justice). As Murdoch (1970) suggests often what we see as good is good for us not the client. It enhances our professional aura rather than brings a gain to the client.

For this reason we have a duty to ground whatever we do in up-to-date research and to keep up with such research in order that we know when we need to review our practice. Research in transition, loss and change is growing rapidly and some things which appeared written in tablets of stone are now shown to be inappropriate. Others have stood the test of time and gathered credence because of recent research. We have a duty to review our practice through reading professional journals, training and education and reflective practice.

In the teaching and professional training arena it is important that we give choice to our students in order that they may determine how they wish to learn and to review their theoretical practice As teaching about transitions and change is deeply personal and touches on personal experience and pain it is very important that no-one is forced into a position where they feel they need to expose personal stories or experiences, and that they have space for reflection. The primary purposes are educational not therapeutic, although there is a need for exploration and there may be cathartic experiences. The boundary between education and therapy is a thin one but it is one to be respected. However, there is no wish to deny the psychodynamic element of experiential group work (Heron, 1990). With a mixture of teaching methods and caring and empathetic facilitators this balance should be possible without in any way diminishing the dynamic, indeed it has been shown to enhance it.

References and Bibliography

Abel, B.J. & Haslip, B. (1986) Locus of control and attitudes toward work and retirement. *The Journal of Psychology*, **120**(5), 479–88.

Adams, J.D., Hayes, J. & Hopson, B. (1976) *Transition: Understanding and Managing Personal Change*. Martin Robertson, London.

Adler, Z. (1987) *Rape on Trial*. Routledge & Kegan Paul, London.

Aguilera, D.C. (1990) Cited in Coupe, D.J. (1991) *A study of relatives', nurses' and doctors' perceptions of the support and information given to the families of potential organ donors*, p. 23. M Phil Thesis, University of Wales, College of Cardiff.

Azjen, I. & Fishbein, M. (1980) *Understanding Attitudes and Predicting Behaviour*. Prentice-Hall, Englewood Cliffs, NJ.

Alexander, S. (1984) Women, class and sexual differences in the 1830s & 1840s: some reflections on the writing of a feminist history. *History Workshop Journal*, **17**, 125.

Allan, D. (1988) The ethics of brain death. *The Professional Nurse*, May, 295–8.

Alspach, J.G. (1990) Should baccalaureate programs include critical care nursing? A readership survey. *Critical Care Nurse*, **10**(2), 12.

American Psychiatric Association (1980) Diagnostic and Statistical Manual of Mental Disorders, 3rd edn. American Psychiatric Association, Washington, DC.

American Psychiatric Association (1987) *Dianostic and Statistical Manual of Mental Disorders*, 3rd edn, revised. American Psychiatric Association, Washington, DC.

American Psychiatric Association (1994) *Diagnostic and Statistical Manual of Mental Disorders*, 4th edn. American Psychiatric Association, Washington, DC.

Anderson, R.R. (1990) *Cognitive Psychology and Its Implications*, 3rd edn. W.H. Freeman, New York.

Angell, R.C. (1965) *The Family Encounters The Depression*. Peter Smith, Gloucester, MA.

Arber, S. & Ginn, J. (1991) *Gender and Later Life: A Sociological Analysis of Resources and Constraints*. Sage, London.

Archer, J. & Rhodes, V. (1987) Bereavement and reactions to job loss: a comparative review. *British Journal of Psychology*, **26**, 211–24.

Archer, J. & Rhodes, V. (1993) The grief process and job loss: a cross-sectional study. *British Journal of Psychology*, **84**, 395–410.

Aries, P. (1981) *The Hour of Our Death*. Oxford University Press, Oxford.

Aspinall, S.Y. (1996) Educating children to cope – a preventive model. *Psychology in the Schools*, **33**(4), 341–9.

Averill, J.R. & Nunley, E.P. (1993) Grief as an emotion and as a disease: a social constructionist perspective. In *Handbook of Bereavement: Theory, Research, and Intervention* (M.S. Stroebe, W. Streobe & R.O. Hansson, eds), pp. 77–90. Cambridge University Press, Cambridge.

Aziz, A. (1990) Women in UK universities: the road to casualisation? In *Storming the Tower: Women in the Academic World* (S. Stiver Lie & V.E. O'Leary, eds). Kogan Page, London.

Bakke, E.W. (1940) *Citizens Without Work*. Yale University Press, New Haven, CT.

Balk, D.E. (1996) Models for understanding adolescent coping with bereavement. *Death Studies*, **20**(4), 367–87.

Bannister, D. & Fransella, F. (1986) *Inquiring Man: The Psychology of Personal Constructs*, 3rd edn. Routledge, London.

Barton, A. (1969) *Communities in Disaster: A Sociological Analysis of Collective Stress Situations*. Ward Lock Education, Columbia.

Bartucci, M.R. (1987) Organ donation: a study of the donor family perspective. *Journal of Neuroscience Nursing*, **19**(6), 305–309.

Bateson, G., Jackson, D.D., Haley, J. & Weakland, J.H. (1956) Toward a theory of schizophrenia. *Behavioural Science*, **1**, 251–64.

Bauby, J.D. (1997) *The Diving Belle and The Butterfly*. Fourth Estate, London.

BBC (1992) *Open Space – Disaster Never Ends*. British Broadcasting Corporation, London.

Becker, E. (1973) *The Denial of Death*. The Free Press, New York.

Beechey, V. (1983) *The Changing Experience of Women*. Open University Coure, U221, Unit 7. Open University Press, Milton Keynes.

Bennet, N., Martin C.L., Bies, R.J. & Brockner, J. (1995) Coping with a layoff: a longitudinal study of victims. *Journal of Management*, **21**(6), 1025–40.

Berger, P. & Luckmann, T. (1967) *The Social Construction of Reality: A Treatise in the Sociology of Knowledge*. Allen Lane, London.

Berne, E. (1961) *Transcactional Analysis*. Souvenir Press (Educational & Academic), Montreal.

Berne, E. (1968) *Games People Play*. Penguin, Harmondsworth.

Bertman, S. (1991) *Facing Death: Images, Insights, and Interventions: A Handbook for Educators, Healthcare Professionals, and Counsellors*. Taylor & Francis, London.

Bettelheim, B. (1960) *The Informed Heart*. The Free Press of Glencoe, Il and Thames and Hudson, London.

Bidigare, S.A. & Oermann, M.H. (1991) Attitudes and knowledge of nurses regarding organ procurement. *Heart and Lung*, **20**(1), 20–24.

Bisnaire, D., Burden, J. & Monik, L. (1988) Brain stem death: managing the family in crisis. *The Canadian Nurse*, **84**(1), 28–30.

Borozny, M. (1988) Brain death and critical care nurses. *The Canadian Nurse*, **84**(1), 24–7.

Boronzy, M. (1990) The experience of intensive care unit nurses providing care to the brain dead patient. Codman Award Paper. *AXON*, **12**(1), 18–22.

Boud, D., Cohen, R. & Walker, D. (1993) *Using Experience for Learning*. Society for Research into Higher Education/Open University Press, Milton Keynes.

Boud, D. & Griffin, V. (eds) (1987) *Appreciating Adults Learning: From the Learner's Perspective*. Open University Press/Kogan Page, London.

Bowker, J. (1991) *The Meanings of Death*. Cambridge University Press, Cambridge.

Bowlby, J. (1969) *Attachment and Loss. Vol. 1: Attachment*. Hogarth, London/Basic Books, New York.

Bowlby, J. (1973) *Attachment and Loss. Vol. 2: Separation: Anxiety and Anger*. Hogarth, London/Basic Books, New York.

Bowlby, J. (1980) *Attachment and Loss. Vol. 3: Loss, Sadness and Depression*. Hogarth, London/Basic Books, New York/Penguin Books, Harmondsworth.

Bowlby, J. & Parkes, C.M. (1970) Separation and loss within the family. In *The Child in his Family* (E.J. Anthony & C.M. Koupernil, eds), John Wiley & Sons, New York.

Bridges, G.S. & Weis, J.G. (1989) Measuring violent behaviour: effects of study design on reported correlates of violence. In *Violent Crime, Violent Criminals* (N.A. Weiner & M.E. Wolfgang, eds), pp. 14–34. Sage, London.

Britzman, D. (1989) The terrible problems of 'knowing thyself': toward a post-structural account of teacher identity. Cited in *Forbidden Narratives: Critical Autobiography as Science* (K. Church, 1995), p. 4.

Brown, G.W. & Harris, T.O. (1978) *Social Origins of Depression: A Study of Psychiatric Disorder in Women.* Tavistock, London.

Buckley, P.E. (1989) The delicate question of the donor family. *Transplantation Proceedings*, **21**(1), 1411–12.

Burgess, A.W. & Holmstrom, L.L. (1979) *Rape-Crisis and Recovery.* R.J. Brady, Maryland.

Burr, V. (1995) *An Introduction to Social Constructionism.* Routledge, London.

Camus, A. (1983) *The Outsider.* Penguin, London.

Caplan, G. (1961) *An Approach to Community Health.* Tavistock, London.

Carr, W. (1993) What is an education practice? In *Educational Research: Current Issues* (M. Hammersley, ed.), Paul Chapman, London.

Cavan, R.S. & Ranck, K.H. (1938) *The Family and The Depression.* The University of Chicago Press, Chicago, Il.

Central Statistical Office (1995–96) *Key Data 95, Monthly Digest.* HMSO, London.

Cheng, N. (1995) *Life and Death in Shanghai.* Flamingo, Glasgow.

Chomksy, N. (1979) Language and responsibility. In *Men of Ideas* (B. McGee, ed.), pp. 170–93. Oxford University Press, Oxford.

Church, J. (ed.) (1997) *Social Trends 27 (1997).* Office of National Statistics, HMSO, London.

Church, K. (1995) *Forbidden Narratives. Critical Autobiography as Science.* Gordon and Breach Publishers, Toronto.

Clark, D. (ed.) (1993) *The Sociology of Death: Theory, Culture, Practice.* Blackwell, Oxford.

Clarkson, P. (1993) *Creativity and Destruction.* Workshop Series. The Institute of Arts and Therapy and Education, London.

Cockburn, C. (1983) *Brothers: Male Dominance & Technological Change.* Pluto Press, London.

Cohen, L. & Manion, L. (1994) *Research Methods in Education*, 4th edn. Routledge, London.

Coleman, P.G., Ivani-Chalian, C. & Robinson, M. (1993) Self-esteem and its sources: stability and change in later life. *Ageing and Society*, **13**, 171–92.

Collins, J. & Mayblin, B. (1996) *Derrida for Beginners.* ICON, Oxford.

Collinson, D.L. & Hearn, J. (1996) *Men as Managers, Managers as Men.* Sage, London.

Conference of Medical Royal Colleges and their Faculties (1979) Diagnosis of death. *British Medical Journal*, **i**, 332.

Conference of Royal Colleges and Faculties (1976) Summary of diagnosis of brain death. *British Medical Journal*, **ii**, 1187.

Coulter, M.A. (1989) The needs of family members in intensive care units. *Intensive Care Nursing*, **5**, 4–10.

Coyle, A. (1984) *Redundant Women.* The Women's Press, London.

Crombie, I.K. (1989) Trends in suicide and unemployment in Scotland 1976–1986. *British Medical Journal*, **298**, 1180.

Cully, M. & Portuges, C. (eds) (1985) *The Dynamics of Feminist Teaching.* Routledge & Kegan Paul, Boston, MA.

Dahl, R. (1984) *Boy.* Penguin, London.

Davie, G. (1993) You'll Never Walk Alone – Liverpool's 23rd Psalm. In *Pilgrimage in Popular Culture* (I. Reader & T. Walter, eds), pp. 201–219. Macmillan, London.

Davies, K.M. & Lemke, D.M. (1987) Brain death – nursing roles and responsibilities. *Journal of Neuroscience Nursing*, **19**(1), 36–9.

Davis, I. & Wall, M. (eds) (1992) *Christian Perspectives on Disaster Management*. Inter-church Relief and Development Association/Tear Fund, Middlesex.

Deleuze, G. & Guttari, F. (1984) *Anti-Oedipus: Capitalism and Schizophrenia*. Athlone, London.

Dennett, D. (1991) *Consciousness Explained*. Little, Brown and Co., Boston, MA.

Dennett, D. (1996) *Kinds of Minds: Towards an Understanding of Consciousness*. Weidenfeld & Nicolson, London.

Department of Health (1992) *Mental Health Handbook: The Health of the Nation*. HMSO, London.

Department of Health (1993) *Key Area Handbook: Mental Illness*. HMSO, London.

Department of Health (1995) *Report of a Two-year Study into the Reasons for Relatives Refusal of Organ Donation*. HMSO, London.

Department of Health and Social Security (1983) *Cadaveric Organs for Transplantation: A Code of Practice Including the Diagnosis of Brain Stem Death*. HMSO, London.

Dewey, J. (1925) Experience and nature. In *John Dewey, The Later Works, 1925–53* (J.A. Boydson, ed), 1981, pp. 244. Southern Illinois University Press, Carbondale, IL.

Dex, S. (1985) *The Sexual Division of Work*. Wheatsheaf Books, Brighton.

Dickenson, D. & Johnson, M. (eds) (1993) *Death Dying and Bereavement*. Sage in association with the Open University, London.

DiGiacomo, S. (1988) Metaphor as illness: post-modern dilemmas in the representation of body, mind and disorder. *Medical Anthropology*, **14**, 109–37.

Di Massimo, C.A. (1997) *Pre-retirement education*. Dissertation in part fulfilment of the degree of MA(Ed), Southampton University.

Drucker, P. (1996) cited in Pritchett, p. (1996) *New Work Habits for a Radically Changing World*. Pritchett and Associates, Washington, Tyne and Wear.

Durkheim, E. (1987) *Suicide: A Study in Sociology*. IL Free Press, New York.

Durkheim, E. (1947) *The Division of Labour in Society*. The Free Press, New York.

Dyregrov, A. (1989) Caring for helpers in disaster situations: psychological debriefing. *Disaster Management* **2**.

Eco, U. (1995) *Six Walks in the Fictional Woods*. Harvard University Press, Harvard/London.

Edwards, D. & Potter, J. (1992) *Discursive Psychology*. Sage, London.

Egan, G. (1990) *The Skilled Helper*. Brooks/Cole, Belmont, CA.

Egan, G. (1994) *The Skilled Helper: A Problem-Management Approach to Helping*, 5th edn. Brooks/Cole, Pacific Grove, CA.

Eisenberg, P. & Lazerfeld, P. (1938) The psychological effects of unemployment. *Psychological Bulletin*, **35**, 358–90.

Elias, N. (1985) *The Loneliness of the Dying*. Blackwell, Oxford.

Elshtain, J.B. (1981) *Public Man, Private Woman*. Princeton University Press, Princeton, NJ.

Epstein, S. (1993) Bereavement from the perspective of cognitive-experiential self-theory. In *Handbook of Bereavement: Theory, Research, and Intervention* (M.S. Stroebe, W. Stroebe & R.O. Hansson, eds), pp. 112–28., Cambridge University Press, Cambridge.

Erikson, E. (1980) *Identity and the Life-cycle*. Boston, New York.

Erikson, E.H. (1963) *Childhood and Society*, 2nd edn. W.W. Norton, New York.

Eyre, A. (1991) You'll Never Walk Alone?: The continuing tragedy of the Hillsborough Disaster. *Hillsborough Interlink*, Issue 8, April 1991.

Eyre, A. (1992) The loneliness of the long distance supporter. *Hillsborough Interlink*, Issue 9, April 1992.

Eyre, A. (1997) *After Hillsborough: Implications for the Sociology of Disaster* (unpublished).

Fairbairn, G.J. (1995) *Contemplating Suicide, The Language and Ethics of Self Harm.* Routledge, London.

Fairclough, N. (1995) *Discourse and Social Change.* Polity Press, Cornwall.

Festinger, L. (1977) Cited in Pfeiffer, J.W. (ed.) (1991) *Theories and Models in Applied Behavioural Science*, Vol. 1, pp. 119–23. Pfeiffer & Co., San Diego, CA.

Firestone, R.W. (1994) Psychological defenses against death anxiety. In *Death Anxiety Handbook* (R. Neimer, ed.), pp. 217–41. Taylor and Francis, Washington, DC.

Flax, J. (1990) *Thinking Fragments, Psychoanalysis, Feminism & Postmodernism in the Contemporary West.* University of California, Berkeley, CA.

Foucault, M. (1967) *Madness and Civilization.* Tavistock, London.

Foucault, M. (1969) *L'archéologie du savoir.* Gallimard, Paris.

Foucault, M. (1975) *Surveiller et punir.* Gallimard, Paris.

Foucault, M. (1980) The history of sexuality: an interview. Trans. G. Bennington. *Oxford Literary Review*, 4(2), 13.

Foucault, M. (1986) *The History of Sexuality. The Care of The Self.* Penguin, Harmondsworth.

Fox, N. (1993) *Post-Modernism, Sociology and Health.* Open University Press, Milton Keynes.

Fraser, R. (1984) *In Search of a Past.* Verso, London.

Freud, A. (1936) *The Ego and Mechanisms of Defence.* Chatto & Windus, London.

Freud, C. (1976) *The Psychology of Everyday Life.* Pelican Freud Library, Penguin, Harmondsworth.

Freud, S. (1917a) *Mourning and Melancholia. SE, Vol. XIV.* W.W. Norton, New York.

Freud, S. (1917b) *On Mourning and Melancholia* reprinted in *On Metapsychiatry, The Theory of Psychoanalysis.* Pelican Books, first published 1984, reprinted 1987, London.

Friedman, M. (1981) *Family Nursing.* Appleton Century Crofts, New York.

Friere, P. (1976) *The Politics of Education.* Bergin and Garvey, South Hadley.

Fritz, C. (1961) Disaster. In *Contemporary Social Problems* (R. Merton & R. Nisbet, eds), pp. 684–9. Harcourt, New York.

Gaarder, J. (1995) *Sophie's World.* Phoenix, London.

Gergen, K. (1991) *The Saturated Self: Dilemmas of Identity in Contemporary Life.* Basic Books, London.

Gerrard, N. (1997) Facing the final taboo. *Waterstones Magazine*, 9, 2–11.

Gersie, A. (1992) *Storymaking in Bereavement: Dragons Fight In the Meadow.* Kingsley, London.

Giddens, A. (1991) *Modernity and Self-Identity.* Polity Press in association with Blackwell Publishers, Cambridge.

Gitlin, A. Siegel, M. And Bom, K. (1993) The politics of method: from leftist ethnography to educative research. In *Educational Research: Current Issues* (M. Hammersley, ed.). Paul Chapman, London.

Glover, J. (1988) *I: The Philosophy and Psychology of Personal Identity.* Penguin, London.

Goffman, E. (1968) *Asylums.* Penguin, Harmondsworth.

Goffman, E. (1971) *The Presentation of Self in Everyday Life.* Penguin, Harmondsworth.

Goleman, D. (1996) *Emotional Intelligence.* Bloomsbury, London.

Gorer, G. (1965) *Death, Grief and Mourning in Contemporary Society.* Cresset, London.

Greenfield, S. (1995) *Journey to the Centres of the Mind: Toward a Science of Consciousness.* W.H. Freeman, New York.

Grieg, N. (1987) Codes of conduct. In *Heterosexuality* (G. Hanscrombe & M. Humphries, eds) GMP Publishers, London.

Gross, R.D. (1993) *Psychology. The Science of Mind and Behaviour*, 2nd edn. Hodder & Stoughton, London.

Grosz, E. (1990) Philosophy. In *Feminist Knowledge: Critique* (S. Gunew, ed.) pp. 147–70. Routledge, London.

Hall, C. (1992) *White, Male and Middle Class: Explorations in Feminism and History*. Polity Press, Oxford.

Hall, C.S. & Lindzey, G. (eds) (1985) *Introduction to Theories of Personality*. John Wiley & Sons, Chichester.

Hamacheck, D. (1978) *Encounters with the Self*, 2nd edn. Holt, Rinehart and Winston, New York.

Hammersley, M. (1995) *What's The Use of Ethnography*. Open University Press, Milton Keynes.

Hammersley, M. & Atkinson, P. (1995) *Ethnography: Principles and Practice*, 2nd edn. Routledge, London.

Hampe, S.O. (1975) Needs of grieving spouse in a hospital setting. *Nurse Research*, **24**(2), 113–20.

Hancock, E. (1989) *The Girl Within, A Radical New Approach to Female Identity*. Pandora, London.

Handy, C. (1990) *Inside Organizations: 21 Ideas for Managers*. BBC Books, London.

Haralambos, M. & Holborn, M. (1991) *Sociology Themes and Perspectives*. Collins Educational, London.

Harre, R. and Gillett, G. (1994) *The Discursive Mind*. Sage, Thousand Oaks, CA.

Haug, F. (1992) *Beyond Female Masochism: Memory, Work and Politics*. Verso, London.

Hawton, K. & Rose, N. (1986) Unemployment and attempted suicide among men in Oxford. Health Trends **18**. Cited in Townsend, P. & Davidson, N. (eds) *Inequalities in Health: The Black Report: The Health Divide*, pp. 239–40. Penguin Books, London.

Heilbrum, C. (1988) *Writing a Woman's Life*. W.W. Norton, New York.

Hekman, S.J. (1990) *Gender and Knowledge: Elements of Postmodern Feminism*. Blackwell, Oxford.

Hemmings, P. (1995) Social work intervention with bereaved children. *Journal of Social Practice*, **9**(2), 109–130.

Hepworth, S.J. (1980) Moderating factors of the psychological impact of unemployment. *Journal of Occupational Psychology*, **53**, 139–45.

Herbert, G. (1989) A whole school approach to bullying. In *Bullying in Schools* (D. Tattum & D. Lane, eds), pp. 73–80. Trentham Books, Stoke-on-Trent.

Heron, A. (1961) *Preparation for Retirement: Solving New Problems*. National Council for Constitutional Studies, London.

Heron, J. (1989) *The Facilitators' Handbook*. Kogan Page, London.

Heron, J. (1990) *Helping the Client*. Sage, London.

Heron, J. (1992) *Feeling and Personhood*. Sage, London.

Hickey, M. & Lewandowski, L. (1988) Critical care nurses' role with families: a descriptive study. *Heart and Lung*, **17** (6, part 1), 670–76.

Hill, S. (1974) *In the Sprintime of the Year*. Penguin, London.

Hobbs, M., Mayou, R. & Harrison, B. (1996), A randomised controlled trial of psychological debriefing for victims of road traffic accidents. *British Medical Journal*, **313**, 1438–9.

Hochschild, A. (1975) The sociology of feeling and emotion: selected possibilities. In *Another Voice* (M. Millman & R. Kaplan, eds). Anchor Books, New York.

Hodgkinson, P. & Stewart, M. (1991) *Coping with Catastrophe: A Handbook of Disaster Management*. Routledge, London.

Holland, W.M. (1959/60) Medical Records. Ministry of Defence: British Legion, Newcastle upon Tyne.

Holland, Henry Scott (1910) All is well. In *Funerals: A Guide, Prayers, Hymns and*

Readings (J. Bentley, A. Best 7 J. Hunt, eds), p. 231, 1994. Hodder & Stoughton, London. *Death is Nothing at All*.

Holmes, J. (1993) *John Bowlby and Attachment Theory*. Routledge, London.

Holmes, T. & Rahe, R. (1967) The social readjustment rating scale. *Journal of Psychosomatic Research*, **11**, 213–18.

Home Office (1995) Home Office Criminal Statistics England and Wales 1995. HMSO, London.

Hopson, B., Scally, M. & Stafford, K. (1984) *Build Your Own Rainbow: A Workbook for Career and Life Management*. Mercury Books, Leeds.

Hopson, B., Scally, M. & Stafford, K. (1998) *Transitions: The Challenge of Change* (1988, 1992) Mercury Books, Didcot.

Horowitz, M. (1976) *Stress Response Syndromes*. Aronson, Northvale, NJ.

Horton, R. (1997) Mind and body: why society should take the plunge and put and end to ... (suicide, that is). *Observer*, 24 August 1997, London.

Humphrey, G. and Zimpfer, D. (1996) *Counselling for Grief and Bereavement*. Sage, London.

IFRCRCS (International Federation of Red Cross & Red Crescent Societies) (1996) *World Disasters Report*. Oxford University Press, Oxford.

IFRCRCS (International Federation of Red Cross & Red Crescent Societies) (1997) *World Disasters Report*. Oxford University Press, Oxford.

Illich, I. (1977) *Limits to Medicine*. Pelican Books, London.

Institute of Personnel and Development (1997) *IPD Key Facts: Redundancy*. Institute of Personnel and Development, London.

IRS (1996) Employment Trends 615, 618, 621. Industrial Relation Services.

Irwin, M. & Pike, J. (1993) Bereavement, depressive symptoms, and immune function. In *Handbook of Bereavement: Theory, Research, and Intervention* (M.S. Stroebe, W. Stroebe & R.O. Hansson, eds), pp. 160–71. Cambridge University Press, Cambridge.

Jackson, D. (1990) *Unmasking Masculinity: A Critical Autobiography*. Unwin Hyman, London.

Jahoda, M. (1979) The impact of unemployment in the 1930s and 1970s. *Bulletin of the British Psychological Society*, **32**, 309–14.

Johnson, D. & Johnson, F. (1987) *Joining Together: Group Theory and Group Skills*, 3rd edn. Prentice-Hall, Englewood Cliffs, NJ.

Jones, L. (1994) *The Social Context of Health*. Macmillan, London.

Jones, W.H. (1979) Grief and involuntary career change: its implications for counselling. *Vocational Guidance Quarterly*, **31**, 196–200.

Jung, C.G. (1954) *The Practice of Psychotherapy*. Routledge & Kegan Paul, London.

Jung, C.G. (1963) *Memories, Dreams and Reflections*. Collins/Routledge & Kegan Paul, London.

Jung, C.G. (1964) *Man and His Symbols*. Aldens Jupiter Books, London.

Jung, C.G. (1993) *The Practice of Psychotherapy*. Routledge & Kegan Paul, London.

Kalisch, B. (1971) Strategies for developing nurse empathy. *Nursing Outlook*, **19**(11), 714–18.

Karmen, A. (1990) *Crime Victims. An Introduction to Victimology*. Thompson Information Publishing Group, Brookes/Cole, New York.

Katz, J.H. (1984) *The Healing Process After Rape*. R&E Publishers, Saratoga, WY.

Keenan, B. (1992) *An Evil Cradling*, Vintage Edition. Arrow, London.

Kelly, G.A. (1955) *The Psychology of Personal Constructs*, Vols I and II. W.W. Norton, New York.

Kelly, G.A. (1963) *A Theory of Personality. The Psychology of Personal Constructs*. W.W. Norton, New York.

Kennedy Bergen, R. (1996) *Wife Rape.* Sage, London.

Kennedy, H., QC (1993) *Violence, Women and the Law.* James Smart Memorial Lecture. Strathclyde Police, Glasgow.

Kesey, K. (1973) *One Flew Over the Cuckoo's Nest.* Pan Books, London.

Kim, K. & Jacobs, S. (1993) Neuroendocrine changes following bereavement. In *Handbook of Bereavement: Theory, Research, and Intervention* (M.S. Stroebe, W. Stroebe & R.O. Hansson, eds), pp. 143–59. Cambridge University Press, Cambridge.

Kinchin, D. (1994) *Post Traumatic Stress Disorder.* Thorsons, London.

Kirst, H.H. (1964) *Officers Factory.* Penguin, Middlesex.

Klein, M. (1959) Our adult world and its roots in infancy. *Human Relations,* **12**, 291–303.

Knight, S. (1995) *NLP at Work.* Nicholas Brearly Publishing, London.

Kohlberg, L. (1969) Stage and sequence: the cognitive developmental approach to socialisation. In *The Handbook of Socialisation Theory and Research* (D.A. Goslin, ed.), pp. 347–480. Rand McNally, Chicago, IL.

Kolb, D. (1984) *Experiential Learning: Turning Experience into Theory.* Prentice-Hall, Englewood Cliffs, NJ.

Kootstra, G. (1988) Will there still be an organ shortage in the year 2000? *Transplantation Proceedings,* **20**(5), 809–11.

Kreitman, N. & Platt, S. (1984) Suicide, unemployment and domestic gas detoxification in Great Britain. *Journal of Epidemiology and Community Health,* **38**, 1–6.

Kubler-Ross, E. (1969) *On Death and Dying.* Springer, New York.

Kubler-Ross, E. (1973) *On Death and Dying.* Social Science Paperback.

Kuhn, M.H. & McPartland, T.S. (1954) An empirical investigation of self attitudes. *American Sociological Review,* **19**, 68–76.

Lasch, C. (1980) *The Culture of Narcissism.* Abacus, London.

Latack, J.C. (1984) Career transitions within organisations: an exploratory study of work, nonwork, and coping strategies. *Organizational Behavior and Human Performance,* **34**, 296–322.

Latack, J.C. & Dozier, J.B. (1986) After the axe falls: job loss as a career transition. *Academy of Management Review,* **11**(2), 375–92.

Lather, P. (1991) *Getting Smart: Feminist Research and Pegagogy with/in the Post-Modern.* Routledge, London.

Leana, C.R. & Feldman, D.C. (1990) Individual responses to job loss: empirical findings from two field studies. *Human Relations,* **43**, 1155–81.

Leana, C.R. & Feldman, D.C. (1992) *Coping with Job Loss: How Individuals, Organizations and Communities Respond to Layoffs.* Lexington, New York.

Ledray, L.E. (1986) *Recovering from Rape.* Henry Holt, New York.

Lee, L. (1975). *I Can't Stay Long.* Penguin, Harmondsworth.

Lees, S. (1996) *Carnal Knowledge.* Hamish Hamilton, London.

Lendrum, S. & Syme, G. (1992) *The Gift of Tears: A Practical Approach to Loss and Bereavement Counselling.* Routledge, London.

Leske, J.S. (1986) Needs of relatives of critically ill patients: a follow up. *Heart and Lung,* **15**(2), 189–93.

Leventman, P.G. (1981) *Professionals Out of Work.* The Free Press, York.

Levi, P. (1989) *The Drowned and the Saved.* Sphere Books, London.

Lewin, K. (1943) *A Dynamic Theory of Personality.* McGraw Hill, New York.

Lewin, K. (1944) Dynamics of group action. *Educational Leadership,* **1**, 95–200.

Lewis, C.S. (1961) *A Grief Observed.* Faber & Faber, London.

Liddle, K. (1988) Reaching out to meet the needs of relatives in intensive care units. *Intensive Care Nursing,* **4**, 146–59.

Lifton, R.J. (1983) Responses of survivors to man-made catastrophes. *Bereavement Care*, **2**, 2–6.

Locke, J. (1967) Cited in *Two Treatises of Government* (P Laslett, ed.) 2nd edn. Cambridge University Press, Cambridge.

Luft, J. (1970) *Group Processes*. Mayfield, Palo Alto, CA.

Lynch, T. (1997) *The Undertaking. Life Studies from the Dismal Trade*. Jonathan Cape, London.

MacFarlane, C.M. (1995) *Bullying*. Unpublished dissertation for MSc, University of Southampton.

McGinn, C. (1997) *Ethics, Evil and Fiction*. Clarendon Press, Oxford.

McLauchlan, C.A.J. (1990) Handling distressed relatives and breaking bad news. *British Medical Journal*, **301**, 1145–49.

McLellan, J. (1985) The effect of unemployment on the family. *Health Visitor*, **58**, 157–61.

McLeod, J. (1993) An Introduction to Counselling. Open University Press, Buckingham.

McCullagh, P. (1993) *Brain Dead, Brain Absent, Brain Donors, Human Subjects or Human Objects*. John Wiley & Sons, Chichester.

McQuail, D. (1987) *Mass Communication Theory – An Introduction*. Sage, London.

McWhirter, J. (1993) A teenager's view of puberty. *Health Education* (6), May, 9–11.

Mairs, N. (1986) *Plaintext: Deciphering a Woman's Life*. University of Arizona Press, Tuscon, AZ.

Mairs, N. (1989) *Plaintext: Deciphering a Woman's Life*. University of Arizona Press, Tuscon, AZ.

Malecki, M.S. & Hoffman, M.C. (1987) Getting to yes: how nurses attitudes affect their success in obtaining consent for organ and tissue donations. *Dialysis and Transplantation*, **16**, 276–8.

Mandela, N. (1994) *Long Walk to Freedom*. Little, Brown and Co., London.

Marris, P. (1986) *Loss and Change*, 2nd edn. Routledge & Kegan Paul, London.

Marsh, L.C. (1938) *Health and Unemployment: Some Studies of their Relationship*. Oxford University Press, Toronto.

Martin, J. & Roberts, C. (1984) *Women and Employment: A Lifetime Perspective*. HMSO, London.

Martin, V. (1997) *Out of My Head*. Book Guild, Lewes.

Masson, J. (1992) *Against Therapy*. Fontana, London.

Matten, M.R., Sliepcevich, E.M., Sarvela, P.D. *et al.* (1991) Nurses' knowledge, attitudes and beliefs regarding organ and tissue donation and transplantation. *Public Health Reports (USA)*, **106**(2), 155–66.

Mellor, P. & Shilling, C. (1993) Modernity, self-identity and the sequestration of experience. *Sociology*, **27**(3), 411–32.

Menzies Lyth, I. (1960) A case-study in the functioning of social systems in defence against anxiety. *Human Relations*, **13**, 95–121.

Menzies Lyth, I. (1988) *Containing Anxiety in Institutions: Selected Essays, Vol. 1*. Free Association, London.

Miles, I. (1983) Adaptation to unemployment? *SPRU Occasional Paper No. 20*. Science Policy Research Unit, University of Sussex.

Mill, John Stuart (1971) *On Liberty, Representative Government, The Subjection of Women*. Oxford University Press, London.

Miller, A. (1984) *For Your Own Good. The Roots of Violence in Child Rearing*. Virago Press, London.

Miller, J. (1974) *Aberfan: A Disaster and Its Aftermath*. Constable, London.

Miller, J.R. (1980) *Come Ye Apart*. Marshall Morgan & Scott, London.

Mollaret, P. & Goulon, M. (1959) Le coma depasse. *Revue Neurologique*, **101**, 3–15.

Molter, N. (1979) Needs of relatives of critically ill patients: a descriptive study. *Heart and Lung*, **8**(2), 332–9.

Moran, M. (1986) Acting out faith through organ donation. Cited in Horton, R.L. & Horton, P.J. (1990) Knowledge regarding organ donation: identifying and overcoming barriers to organ donation. *Social Science Medicine*, **31**(7), 798.

Murdoch, I. (1970) *The Sovereignty of Good*. Penguin, Middlesex.

Myers Briggs Type Indicator (1987) Oxford Psychologists Press, Oxford.

National Funerals College (1996) *The Dead Citizen's Charter*. National Funerals College, Stamford, Lincs.

Neimer, R. (ed.) (1994) *Death Anxiety Handbook*. Taylor & Francis, Washington DC.

Nelson, G. (1986) *Theory in the Classroom*. University of Illinois Press, Chicago, IL.

Nelson-Jones, R. (1990) *Human Relationship Skills*. Cassell Educational, London.

Neruda, P. (1992) *The Captain's Verses*. A New Directions Paperback.

Newburn, T. (ed.) (1993) *Working with Disaster: Social Welfare Interventions During and After Tragedy*. Longman, Harlow.

Nias, J. (1993) Grieving times, changing identities: grieving for a lost self. In *Educational Research and Evaluation for Policy and Practice?* (R. Burgess, ed.), pp. 139–56. Falmer Press, London.

Nicholson, P. (1996) *Gender, Power & Organization: A Psychological Perspective*. Routledge, London.

Noonan, H. (1989) *Personality Identity*. Routledge, London.

Norris, C. (1987) *Derrida*. Fontana Modern Masters, London.

Norton, D.J. (1992) Clinical applications of brain death protocols. *Journal of Neuroscience Nursing*, **24**(6), 354–8.

NVSS (1996) *Supporting Victims of Crime*. National Victim Support Service, London.

Oakley, A. (1981) Interviewing women: a contradiction in terms. In *Doing Feminist Research* (H. Roberts, ed.), Routledge & Kegan Paul, London.

O'Connor, J. & McDermott, I. (1996) *Principles of NLP*. Thorsons, London.

Olweus, D. (1987) Bully/victim problems among school children in Scandinavia. In *Psykolog Profesjonen mot ar 2000* (J.P. Myklebust & R. Ommundsen, eds). Unversitetsforlaget, Norway.

O'Neill Norris, L. & Grove, S.K. (1986) Investigation of selected psychosocial needs of family members of critically ill adult patients. *Heart and Lung*, **15**(2), 194–9.

Open University, The (1985) *E206 Personality, Development and Learning. Unit 16: The Self-concept*. Open University, Milton Keynes.

Open University, The (1992a) *K260 Death and Dying. Workbook 1: Life and Death*. Open University Press, Milton Keynes.

Open University, The (1992b) *K260 Death and Dying. Workbook 4: Bereavement: Private Grief and Collective Responsibility*. Open University Press, Milton Keynes.

Owen, K. & Watson, N. (1995) Unemployment and mental health. *Journal of Psychiatric and Mental Health Nursing*, **2**, 63–71.

Pallis, C. (1983) *ABC of Brain Stem Death. Articles from the* British Medical Journal. British Medical Journal, London.

Pallis, C. (1987) Brain stem death – the evolution of a concept. *Medical Legal Journal*, **55**(2), 84–107.

Parkes, C.M. (1971) Psychosocial transitions: a field for study. *Social Science and Medicine*, **15**, 101–15.

Parkes, C.M. (1985) Bereavement: a review. *British Journal of Psychology*, **146**, 11–17.

Parkes, C.M. (1993) Bereavement as a psychosocial transition: processes of adaptation to change. In *Handbook of Bereavement: Theory, Research, and Intervention*, (M.S. Stroebe, W. Stroebe & R.O. Hansson, eds), pp. 91–101. Cambridge University Press, Cambridge.

Parkes, C.M. (1996a) *Bereavement: Studies of Grief in Adult Life*, 3rd edn. Routledge, London.

Parkes, C.M. (1996b) *Counselling in Terminal Care and Bereavement*. British Psychological Society, Leicester.

Parkes, C.M. & Sills, C. (1994) Psychotherapy with the dying and the bereaved. In *The Handbook of Psychotherapy* (P. Clarkson & M. Pokorny, eds), pp. 494–514. Routledge, London.

Parkinson, F. (1993) *Post Trauma Stress*. Sheldon, London.

Parry, C. (1995) *An Ordinary Boy*. Coronet Books, London.

Partridge, F. (1996) *A Pacifist's War*. Phoenix, London.

Pearlin, L.I., Lieberman, M.A., Menaghan, E.G. & Mullan, J.T. (1981) The stress process. *Journal of Health and Social Behavior*, **22**, 337–56.

Pearlin, L.I. & Schooler, C. (1978) The structure of coping. *Journal of Health and Social Behavior*, **22**, 2–21.

Peck, M. (1993) *Further Long the Road Less Travelled*. Simon & Schuster, London.

Pelletier, M. (1992) The organ donor family members' perception of stressful situations during the organ donor experience. *Journal of Advanced Nursing*, **17**, 90–97.

Peplau, H.E. (1969) Professional closeness. *Nursing Forum*, **8**(4), 343–59.

Perez-San-Gregorio, M.A., Blanco-Picabia, A., Murillo-Cabezas, F., Dominguez-Roldan, J.M. & Nunez-Roldan, A. (1992) Psychological profile of families of severely traumatised patients – relationships to organ donation for transplantation. *Transplantation Proceedings*, **24**(1), 27–8.

Pettersson, P. (1996) *Implicit religion turned explicit: a case study of the* Estonia *disaster*. Unpublished paper presented at the XIV Denton Conference on Implicit Religion, May 1996, Denton, Yorkshire. Network for the Study of Implicit Religion, Winterbourne, Bristol.

Piaget, J. (1950) *The Psychology of Intelligence*. Routledge & Kegan Paul, London.

Piaget, J. (1951) *Play, Dreams and Imitation in Children*. Routledge & Kegan Paul, London.

Piaget, J. (1972) Intellectual evolution from adolescence to adulthood. *Human Development*, **15**, 1–21.

Piaget, J. (1973) *The Child's Conception of The World*. Palladin, London.

Platt, S. (1984) Unemployment and suicidal behaviour: a review of the literature. *Social Science and Medicine*, **19**, 93–115.

Platt, S., Micciolo, R. & Tansella, M. (1992) Suicide and unemployment in Italy. *Social Science and Medicine*, **34**, 1191–201.

Porter, R. (1997) *Rewriting the Self*. Routledge, London.

Pritchard, C. (1995) *Suicide the Ultimate Rejection? A Psycho-social Study*. Open University Press, Buckingham.

Pritchett, P. (1996) *New Work Habits for a Radically Changing World*. Pritchett and Associates, Washington, Tyne and Wear.

Prosser, J. (1998) *Image Based Research: A Source Book for Qualitative Researchers*. Falmer Press, Brighton.

Quarantelli, F. (ed.) (1978) *Disasters: Theory and Research*. Sage, Beverley Hills, CA.

Rahe, R.H. (1979) Life-change measurement as a predictor of illness. *Proceedings of the Royal Society of Medicine*, **61**, 1124–6.

Raphael, B. (1996) *Anatomy of Bereavement*. Routledge, London.

Reed, B. (1978) *The Dynamics of Religion.* Darton, Longman and Todd, London.

Reed, B. (1985) Stress – the individual and the system. *Educational Management and Administration,* **13**, 82–9.

Renvoize, E. & Clyden, D. (1989) Suicide and unemployment. *British Medical Journal,* **298**, 1180.

Rockhill, K. (1987) The chaos of subjectivity in the ordered life of academe. *Canadian Women's Studies,* **8**(4), 12–17.

Rogers, C.R. (1961) *On Becoming a Person.* Houghton Mifflin, London.

Rogers, C.R. and Stevens, B. (1967) *Person to Person: The Problem of Being Human.* Real People Press, Lafayette, CA.

Roland, E. (1989) Bullying: the Scandinavian research tradition. In *Bullying in Schools.* (D. Tattum & D. Lane, eds), pp. 21–32. Trentham Books, Stoke-on-Trent.

Rorty, R. (1979) *Philosophy and the Mirror of Nature.* Princeton University Press, Princeton, NJ.

Rosenblatt, P.C. (1983–93) *Bitter, Bitter Tears. Nineteenth Century Diarists and Twentieth Century Grief Theories.* University of Minnesota Press, Minneapolis, MN.

Rosenblatt, P.C., Wash, R.P. & Jackson, D.A. (1976) *Grief and Mourning in Cross-cultural Perspective.* Human Relations Area Files Press, New Haven, CT.

Rotter, J.B. (1966) Generalized expectancies for internal versus external control of reinforcement. *Psychological Monographs,* **80**(1), 290–301.

Rowe, D. (1988) *Choosing not Losing.* Fontana, London.

Rowe, D. (1991) *The Courage to Live.* Fontana, London.

Rowe, D. (1993) *The Successful Self.* Fontana, London.

Rowling, L. (1995) *Children and Grief.* Unpublished PhD, University of Southampton.

Russell, D. (1997) *The History of The Maudsely and Bethlem Hospitals.* Scutari and The Royal College of Nurses, London.

Sacks, O. (1984) *A Leg to Stand On.* Duckworth, London.

Sacks, O. (1985) *The Man Who Mistook His Wife For a Hat.* Duckworth, London.

Sacks, O. (1990) *Awakenings,* 5th edn. Duckworth, London.

Samaritans, The (1996a) *Challenging the Taboo.* The Samaritan Organisation, London, UK.

Samaritans, The (1996b) *The Cost of Stress.* The Samaritan Organisation, London, UK.

Samaritans, The (1997a) *Information Resource Pack, 15 April 1997.* Attempted suicide (8 April 1997). The Samaritan Organisation, London.

Samaritans, The (1997b) *Information Resource Pack, 15 April 1997.* Suicide statistics 1995 (3 April 1997). The Samaritan Organisation, London.

Samaritans, The (1997c) *Information Resource Pack, 15 April 1997.* Understanding Suicide Data (7 April 1997). The Samaritan Organisation, London.

Samaritans, The (1997d) *Information Resource Pack, 15 April 1997.* Young People and Suicide (4 April 1997). The Samaritan Organisation, London.

Sassoon, S. (1968) *Selected Poems.* Cited in Wilkinson, A. (1996) *The Church of England and The First World War.* SCM Press, London.

Savin, H.B. (1973) Professors and psychological researchers, conflicting values in conflicting roles. In *Dialogues and Debates in Social Psychology* (J. Murphy, M. John & H. Brown, eds), pp. 176–8. Lawrence Erlbaum, London.

Saward, J. (1990) *RAPE My Story.* Bloomsbury Publishing, London.

Schenck, C. (1988) *Critical Autobiography.* Cited in Swindells, J. (1995) *The Uses of Autobiography.* Taylor & Francis, Portsmouth.

Schlossberg, N.K. (1981) A model for analyzing human adaptation to transition. *The Counselling Psychologist,* **9**, 2–18.

Schon, D.A. (1991) *The Reflective Practitioner.* Jossey Bass, San Francisco, CA.

Schonfeld, D.J. (1993) Talking with children about death. *Health Care*, **7**, 269–74.

Scott, D. (1989) *Coping with Suicide*. Sheldon Press, London.

Scott, J. (1988) Deconstructing equality – versus – difference: or the uses of deconstructionist theory for feminism. *Feminist Studies*, **14**(1), 33–50.

Scraton, P., Jemphrey, A. & Coleman, S. (1995) *No Last Rights: The Denial of Justice and the Promotion of Myth in the Aftermath of the Hillsborough Disaster*. Liverpool City Council, Liverpool.

Selye, H. (1956) *The Stress of Life*. McGraw-Hill, New York.

Sheehy, G. (1981) *Pathfinders*. Morrow, New York.

Shuchter, S.R. & Zisook, S. (1986) Multidimensional approach to widowhood. *Psychiatric Annals*, **16**, 295–308.

Sills, C. (1996) Transactional analysis. In *Therapists on Therapy* (B. Mullan, ed.), pp. 56–76. Free Association Books, London.

Silverman, P.R. & Worden, J.W. (1993) Children's reactions to the death of a parent. In *Handbook of Bereavement: Theory, Research, and Intervention* (M.S. Stroebe, W. Stroebe & R.O. Hansson, eds), pp. 300–316. Cambridge University Press, Cambridge.

Silverstein, M. (1977) The history of a short, unsuccessful, academic career (with postscript update). In *A Book of Readings: For Men Against Sexism* (J. Snodgrass, ed.). Times Change Press, New York.

Silvey, S. (1990) Bereavement support. *Nursing Times*, **86**(7), 58.

Simon, R.J. & Baxter, S. (1989) Gender and violent crime. In *Violent Crime, Violent Criminals* (N.A. Weiner & M.E. Wolfgang, eds), pp. 171–97. Sage, London.

Sinfield, A. (1981) *What Unemployment Means*. Martin Robertson, Oxford.

Singer, P. (1994) *Rethinking Life & Death: The Collapse of Our Traditional Ethics*. Oxford University Press, Oxford.

Skynner, R. (1989) *Institutes and How to Survive Them: Mental Health Training and Consultation/Selected papers by Robin Skynner*. Edited by J.R. Schlapobersky (1990). Routledge, London.

Smilansky, S. (1987) *On Death: Helping Children Understand and Cope*. Peter Lang Publishing, New York.

Smith, R. (1987) *Unemployment and Health*. Oxford University Press, Oxford.

Spier, M.S. (1973) Kurt Lewin's 'Force-field Analysis'. In *The 1973 Annual Handbook for Group Facilitators* (J.W. Pfeiffer & J.E. Jones, eds), University Associates, San Diego, CA.

Sque, M. & Payne, S.A. (1996) Dissonant loss: the experiences of donor relatives. *Social Science Medicine*, **43**(9), 1359–70.

Stake, R. (1995) *The Art of Case Study Research*. Sage, Thousand Oaks, CA.

Steedmen, C. (1986) *Landscape for a Good Woman: A Story of Two Lives*. Virago, London.

Stein, H.F. (1996) *Death Imagery and the Experience of Organizational Downsizing: Or Is Your Name on Schindler's List?* Unpublished paper available on the World Wide Web at ISPSO archive at URL: http://www.sba.oakland.edu/ispso/html/stein.html

Steinberg, D. (1977) *Father Journal: Five Years of Awakening to Fatherhood*. Times Change Press, New York.

Stephenson, P. & Smith, D. (1989) Bullying in the Junior School. In *Bullying in Schools* (D. Tattum & D. Lane, eds), Trentham Books, Stoke-on-Trent.

Stern, D. (1985) *The Intrepersonal World of the Infant: A View from Psychoanalysis and Developmental Psychology*. Basic Books, New York.

Stevens, R. (1983) *Erik Erikson – An Introduction*. Open University Press, Milton Keynes.

Stevens, R. (ed.) (1996) *Understanding the Self*. Sage Publications in association with the Open University, London.

Stockdale, M. (ed.) (1996) *Sexual Harassment in the Workplace: Perspectives, Frontiers and Response Strategies*. Sage, London.

Stoeckle, M.L. (1990) Attitudes of critical care nurses towards organ donation. *Dimensions of Critical Care Nursing*, 9(6), 354–61.

Stroebe, M.S., Schut, H. & Van Den Bout, J. (1994) The dual process model of bereavement. Paper read at the *Fourth International Conference on Grief and Bereavement in Contemporary Society*, Stockholm, 12–16 June 1994.

Stroebe, M.S. & Stroebe, W. (1987) *Bereavement and Health: The Psychological and Physical Consequences of Partner Loss*. Cambridge University Press, Cambridge.

Stroebe, M.S., Stroebe, W. and Hansson, R.O. (1993) *Handbook of Bereavement: Theory, Research, and Intervention*. Cambridge University Press, Cambridge.

Stybel, L.J. (1981) *Implications of logotherapy in working with dismissed executives*. Paper presented at the annual meeting of the National Academy of Management, San Diego, August 1981.

Styron, W. (1992) *Sophie's Choice*. Pan, London.

Suls, J. & McMullen, B. (1981) Life events, perceived control, and illness: the role of uncertainty. *Journal of Human Stress*, 4, 30–34.

Swindells, J. (1995) *The Uses of Autobiography*. Taylor & Francis, Portsmouth.

Tatelbaum, J. (1980) *The Courage to Grieve*. Redwood Barn Ltd, Trowbridge.

Tattum, D. & Lane, D. (eds) (1989) *Bullying in Schools*. Trentham Books, Stoke-on-Trent.

Taylor, R., Ward, A. & Newburn, T. (1995) *The Day of the Hillsborough Disaster*. Liverpool University Press, Liverpool.

Taylor, V. (1978) Future directions for study. In *Disasters: Theory and Research* (E. Quarantelli, ed.), pp. 251–80. Sage, Beverley Hills, CA.

Teilhard, P. (1965). *The Phenomenon of Man*. Collins/Fontana, London, UK.

Tillich, P. (1967) *The Courage to Be*. Fontana, London.

Tillich, P. (1973) *The Boundary of Our Being*. Fontana, London.

Toole, J.F. (1971) The neurologist and the concept of brain death. Cited in McCullagh, P. (1993) *Brain Dead, Brain Absent, Brain Donors, Human Subjects or Human Objects?*, p. 9. John Wiley & Sons, Chichester.

Townsend, P. (ed.) (1970) *The Concept of Poverty*. Heinemann, London.

Townsend, P. & Davidson, N. (eds) (1988) *Inequalities in Health: The Black Report: The Health Divide*. Penguin Books, London.

Tschudin, V. (1989) *Beginning with Empathy: A Learners' Handbook*. Churchill Livingstone, Edinburgh.

Tschudin, V. (1997) *Counselling for Loss and Bereavement*. Baillière Tindall, London.

Turner, B. (1978) *Man Made Disasters*. Wykeham, London.

Turner, V. (1969) *The Ritual Process*. Penguin, London.

Tweedie, J. (1970) Article in the Women's Guardian Page. *The Guardian*, 12 October, London.

UKTCA & BACCN (1995) *Report of a Two-year Study into the Reasons for Relatives' Refusal of Organ Donation*. United Kingdom Transplant Co-ordination Association and British Association of Critical Care Nurses, Department of Health, London.

UKTSSA (1997) *Transplant Update: End of Year 1996*. United Kingdom Transplant Support Services Authority, Bristol.

Usher, R.S. (1993) Experiential learning or learning from experience: does it make a difference? In *Using Experience for Learning* (D. Boud, R. Cohen & D. Walker, eds). Society for Research into Higher Education, Open University Press, Milton Keynes.

Usher, R.S. & Edwards, R. (1994) *Post-Modernism and Education. Different Voices Different Worlds*. Routledge & Kegan Paul, London.

Walby, S. (1990) *Theorizing Patriarchy*. Blackwell, Oxford.

Walkerdine, V. (1985) Dreams from ordinary childhood. In *Truth, Dare or Promise: Girls Growing up in the Fifties* (L. Heron, ed.), Virago, London.

Walklate, S. (1989) *Victimology: The Victim and The Criminal Justice System*. Unwin Hyman, London.

Walter, T. (1990) *Funerals and How To Improve Them*. Hodder & Stoughton, London.

Walter, T. (1991) Modern death–taboo or not taboo? *Sociology*, **25**(2), 293–310.

Walter, T. (1994) *The Revival of Death*. Routledge, London.

Walter, T. (1996a) A new model of grief: bereavement and biography. *Mortality*, **1**(1), 7–25.

Walter, T. (1996b) *The Eclipse of Eternity: A Sociology of the Afterlife*. Macmillan, Basingstoke.

Warr, P. (1983) Work, jobs and unemployment. *Bulletin of the British Psychological Society*, **36**, 305–11.

Watkinson, G.E. (1995) A study of the perception and experiences of critical care nurses in caring for potential and actual organ donors: implications for nurse education. *Journal of Advanced Nursing*, **22**, 929–40.

Watson, P. (1980) *War on the Mind: The Military Uses and Abuses of Psychology*. Penguin, Harmondsworth.

Weedon, C. (1987) *Feminist Practice and Post-Structural Theory*. Blackwell, Oxford.

Weiner, N.A. & Wolfgang, M.E. (eds) (1989) *Violent Crime Violent Criminals*. Sage, London.

Weiss, R.S. (1976) Transition states and other stressful situations: their nature, programs and management. In *Support Systems and Mutual Help: Multidisciplinary Explorations* (G. Caplan & M. Killilea, eds), pp. 213–32. Grune & Stratton, New York.

Weston, R. (1997a) *Evaluation of Cancer Prevention Programmes: The Way Forward*. Report to the European Union, Luxembourg.

Weston, R. (1997b) *The Mythmakers in Health Promotion. Is the Randomised Control Trial the Gold Standard?* Unpublished PhD thesis. University of Southampton, Southampton.

Weston, R. & Scott, D. (in press) *Evaluating Health Promotion*. Stanley Thorne Publishers, Cheltenham.

Wetherell, M. (ed.) (1996) *Identities, Groups and Social Issues*. Sage Publications in association with the Open University, London.

Wetton, N. & McWhirter, J. (1997) Image based research and curriculum development in health education. In *Image Based Research: A Source Book for Qualitative Researchers* (J. Prosser, ed.), Falmer Press, Brighton.

Whitehead, M. (Compiler) (1995) *Health Update: 5 Physical Activity*. Health Education Authority, London.

Wilkinson, A. (1996) *The Church of England and The First World War*. SCM Press, London.

Williams, D.T., Wetton, N. & Moon, A. (1989) *A Way In*. Health Education Authority, London.

Williams, M. (1997) *Cry of Pain*. Penguin, London.

Williamson, G.A. (1959) *Josephus, The Jewish War*. Penguin Classics, Middlesex.

Winnicott, D. (1965) *The Maturational Processes and The Facilitating Environment*. Hogarth Press, London.

Winnicott, D.W. (1958) *Through Paediatrics to Psycho-analysis*. Hogarth Press, London.

Winnicott, D.M. (1965) The Maturational Processes and the Facilitating Environment. Hogarth Press, London.

Wisniewski, D. (ed.) (1997) *Monthly Digest of Statistics No. 613*. Office of National Statistics, The Stationery Office, London.

Wolley, N. (1990) Crisis theory: a paradigm of effective intervention with families of critically ill people. *Journal of Advanced Nursing*, 15, 1402–1408.

Worden, J.W. (1982) *Grief Counselling and Grief Therapy. A Handbook for the Mental Health Practitioner*. Springer, New York.

Worden, J.W. (1991) *Grief Counselling and Grief Therapy: A Handbook for the Mental Health Practitioner*, 2nd edn. Tavistock/Routledge, London.

Wortman, C.B. & Silver, R.C. (1987) Coping with irrevocable loss. In *Cataclysms, Crises, and Catastrophes* (G.R. Vandenbos & B.K. Bryant, eds), pp. 189–235. American Psychological Association, Washington, DC.

Wright, N.T. (1997) A post-modern princess. *Church Times*, 12 September, 6–7.

Wright, W.R. (1991) Nurses knowledge, attitudes, and beliefs regarding organ and tissue donation and transplantation. *Public Health Reports (USA)*, 106(2), 155–64.

Young, R.M. (1997) *Princess Diana, The 'Constituency of the Rejected' and Psychotherapeutic Studies*. Unpublished paper available on the World Wide Web at URL: http://www.shef.ac.uk/uni/academic/N-Q/psysc/staff/rmyoung/papers/index.html

Zimbardo, P.G. (1973) On the ethics of intervention in human psychological research with special reference to 'The Stanford Prison Experiment'. In *Dialogues and Debates in Social Psychology* (J. Murphy, M. John & H. Brown, eds), pp. 178–187. The Open University Press.

Zola, I.l (1991) Bringing our bodies and ourselves back in: reflections on a past, present and future 'medical sociology'. *Journal of Health and Social Behaviour*, 32, 1–16.

Glossary

Aberfan: A coal mining village in South Wales; in 1966 the Aberfan disaster occurred, where a coal tip built over a stream collapsed, flowing down and burying the local school, killing 144 people, 141 of them children.

Affective psychosis: Also called manic-depressive psychosis, results in changes in mood. A sufferer may swing between being overactive, talkative, and impulsive (manic) to being morose, withdrawn, and even suicidal (depressive). Judgement is also often affected and the sufferers may say or do things that they would not normally do. A common result is that they seriously overspend, or make unrealistic plans which never get carried out. Some people may become aggressive. Sleep patterns are disturbed and, in the manic phase, sufferers may not sleep for several days at a time. Often the family are more distressed by this than the sufferer, who may feel very happy and energetic and often fails to understand the effect that this behaviour is having on those around them (Microsoft® Encarta® 98 Encyclopedia).

Aggression, aggressive: Threatening behaviour which does not respect the basic human rights of other people. It is usually expressive of archaic anger (see below) which is unacknowledged and of which the individual is unaware.

Annihilation: To have destroyed the sense of self (by others, events or self).

Anomie: From the Greek *anomia*, 'lawlessness', a term for sociology which denotes complete alienation or rootlessness from the mores or values of society; to feel outside mainstream society.

Anticipatory grief: Rehearsal of 'possible events' especially death and associated feelings. Also can be related to the deep feelings of anxiety we have about our own death, commonly called existential anxiety.

Archaic anger: Anger which is 'old' and related to past, often unresolved, issues which can be triggered by current experiences but may to others feel out of place in the current situation. This is often an unconscious process.

Archaic anxiety: This anxiety is the presenting symptom, on the fringe of consciousness, of the repressed distress of the past – the personal hurt, particularly of childhood, that has been denied so that the individual can survive emotionally (Heron, 1989: 33).

Arche-health: Resistance to over-professionalised agendas; the person desires to do something different to that expected of them and therefore challenges held perceptions thus resisting what is expected.

Assertive, assertiveness: Self-expression through which a person stands up for their own basic human rights without violating the basic human rights of other people.

Assumptive world: The world that we know and feel secure in; the one created from our experiences and which we take for granted.

Attachment behaviour: Behaviour expressive of the first emotional ties we make with primary carers and which gives us our basic sense of security.

Bargaining: When a person is faced with overwhelming events which cause them to question 'Why me?', then they may try to bargain with God (even though they have hitherto not been religious) that if their loved one is spared, they promise to be good, not be selfish, take care of others, etc.

Bereavement: The objective situation of an individual who has recently experienced the loss of someome or something significant to them.

Breaking through: The confrontation of 'self' with personal painful experiences (often unresolved in some way) which once faced and resolved allow them then to be able to help and understand others, speak on their behalf and without over inter- pretation.

Cataclysmic events: Those which come suddenly, without warning and involve many unexpected deaths or injuries. These could be flood, famine, accidents, mass violence and so on. They are always devastating, partly because they are unex- pected but also because they are mainly outside of human control. Violent upheaval.

Catharsis, cathartic: The purging of emotions.

Cathexis: A way of bringing repressed ideas or feelings to consciousness.

Congruence, congruent: The quality or state of agreeing, in this case feelings, values, beliefs and behaviour.

Constructivism: Using our learned experiences, skills and knowledge to help us reconstruct our worlds especially when it has been changed in some way and disrupts what we know – our assumptive world.

Dialectic, dialectically: The art or practice of assessing the 'truth' of a theory by dis- cussion and logical disputation.

Difference: Derrida's own term which he suggests explains the space between two polarised positions. If we concentrate on that space he suggests that we can see many 'truths' all of them possible ways to look at an issue.

Discourse, discourse analysis: The formal treatment of a subject in speech or writing, a unit or text. Discourses contain the values, beliefs, reasoning and world view of writers/researchers/authors and how they perceive and conceptualise things.

Disenfranchised grief: That which others ignore, choose to interpret in a way that suits their purposes. This leaves the grieving person disenfranchised, they feel they have no right to grieve or feel the way they do.

Dislocation of self: In Bettelheim's terms, the ego (that which is our centre) fractures, comes apart, feels as though there are parts of you in pieces all around.

Dissonance: An absence of congruence or agreement between feelings, beliefs, values and behaviour; everything jars just as a wrong note in music. This causes tension which needs to be resolved to return to congruence. When someone grieves it is dissonance, their assumptive world has been disturbed, it will never return to what it was but through grief they can reconstruct their world and feel comfortable in it.

Dual process model of grieving: A model of grief in which a bereaved person oscillates between attending to their feelings of loss and attending to their immediate needs of the present and future.

Dunblane: In March 1996 Thomas Hamilton killed 13 primary-school children and a teacher in the village of Dunblane, in Scotland, with two automatic pistols. In response, all handguns were banned in Great Britain in 1997 (Microsoft® Encarta® 98 Encyclopedia).

Emotional competence: Being able to express clearly in your own words how you feel and think and thus managing anxiety to cope with situations.

Ethnocentric: Behaving and believing that the culture in which one lives is the only one and the ways of this society have primacy over all others.

Existential anxiety: Anxiety in the here and now about issues of acceptance, orientation and performance (Heron, 1989: 33); anxiety about the ultimate issues of meaninglessness, death and guilt (Tillich, 1967).

Experiential learning: The practice-theory-practice process; learning through personal and professional experience and integrating the two.

Foucauldian: After the work of Foucault; his thoughts, ideas, views, beliefs, academic knowledge and discourse.

Fragmented: To literally feel 'all over the place', as though you are in many pieces rather than whole.

Grief: The emotional (affective) response to loss; a process not a state (Parkes, 1996a).

Herald of Free Enterprise: The name of a ferry which left the harbour of Zeebrugge on 6 March 1987 and capsized having not had its bow doors closed; 155 lives were lost and of those who survived many were traumatised.

Hermeneutics: The study of the theory and practice of interpretation. It is founded upon a belief in the possibility of achieving a single correct interpretation. However, a more sceptical view of interpretation holds that there are no stable grounds for judgement, and thereby runs the risk of foundering in a quagmire of subjectivism and relativism (the realisation that knowledge is not absolute). The German philosopher Martin Heidegger and his pupil Hans-Georg Gadamer describe this dilemma as a 'hermeneutic circle', referring to the way in which, in understanding and interpretation, part and whole are related in a circular way: in order to understand the whole it is necessary to understand the parts and vice versa. This is the condition of possibility of all human experience and enquiry (Microsoft® Encarta® 98 Encyclopedia).

High modernity: The current phase of development of modern institutions, marked by the radicalising and globalising of basic traits of modernity (Giddens, 1991).

Hillsborough Disaster: The overcrowding of a football stadium in 1989 which led to the deaths of 96 spectators. Many survivors, police, ambulance and medical service were affected and traumatised. There is still anger about how this whole incident was handled by the police force.

Homo taxonomicus: The way men have rationally decided what counts as valid knowledge, what categories of knowledge are acceptable.

Ideology, ideological: The set of beliefs and practices, cultural, behavioural, moral, economic or political, that make up sets of ideas.

Illuminative research techniques: Those which allow people to tell their own stories, or explain how they think, feel and behave; examples are bubble dialogue, auto/biographical writing, drawing, writing and drama.

Immobilisation: Being literally frozen so that one cannot take action. This can be because of fear, anxiety or being emotionally upset. It can, though sometimes be positive in that it slows responses down to give one time to think, clarify and come to terms with things.

Individuation: After Jung, the recognition and integration of all aspects of ourself. The acceptance of the parts of ourselves which we may wish not to acknowledge.

Laddering: A powerful technique within personal construct theory for eliciting a person's core constructs.

Lockerbie: Town in Dumfries and Galloway, Scotland. Recently, however, it has become known throughout the world because of the Lockerbie air tragedy of 1988. On 21 December a terrorist bomb exploded in a Pan-Am aircraft flying from Frankfurt to New York, via London. Everyone on the aeroplane was killed. Parts of the aeroplane crashed into houses in Lockerbie, also killing people on the ground. The final death toll was 270 (Microsoft® Encarta® 98 Encyclopedia).

Manslaughter: The killing of a human being by another without premeditated thought or planning.

Meaning: The personal world view which we use to interpret phenomena; this depends on our views, beliefs, values, perceptions and cognitions.

Metamorphosis: The change which can take place after a person has undergone development and growth; if they are pathologically grieving this may be a negative manifestation of their former self. It is like the transformation of the chrysalis of the butterfly.

Modernity: Gidden's term for the global, economic and political organisation of the world and institutions, following the Enlightenment. He suggests that this has now changed yet again into high modernity.

Murder: Unlawful killing of another person which is premeditated and planned (the difference between this and manslaughter can cause much confusion and indeed grief if people do not understand this, e.g. the driver of a car who is drunk and then kills someone will be tried for manslaughter not murder even though you could argue he/she was breaking the drink driving law).

Myers Briggs: They developed theories about the personality and ways of testing which personality type you are expressed in terms of the Myers Briggs Type Indicator (MBTI).

Neuro-linguistic programming (NLP):   A way of teaching people to visualise their current situation and how they might change it; changing cognition through visualisation which can be guided by the therapist.

Normative needs: Those needs which fit with the society mores in which one lives but also can be the needs of professionals who represent the norms of society.

Ontological security: A sense of continuity and order in events, including those not directly within the perceptual environment of the individual (Giddens, 1991).

Parasuicide: Attempted suicide.

Personal construct theory: After Kelly (1955) and used by Rowe (1993), constructs are the way one sees and understands the world from experience. However, we are always testing these constructs like scientists against new constructs, or other people's, to constantly challenge the way we see the world.

Phenomenology: The study and description/interpretation of phenomena – those things we see, can touch, observe and feel, tangible and intangible.

Post-modern, post-modernism: See modernity and high-modernity.

Post-traumatic stress disorder (PTSD):   The development of particular symptoms following a distressing event outside the range of usual human experience.

Psycho-social transitions: The development and change process throughout the life cycle. Some cultures have rites of passage which are ceremonies, recognised by the community in general to mark such changes.

Qualitative: Research which seeks to interpret and explain behaviour, observations, issues, events and subjective experience.

Quantitative: Empirical research, numbers and statistics, 'objective science'.

Reflexivity: The ability to know that we construct our world, whether that be through research, personal experience or professional practice.

Regression: To return to earlier life stages of thinking and behaving, babyhood, childhood and adolescence.

Rite of passage: See psycho-social transitions.

Samaritans: The organisation who voluntarily listen to those contemplating suicide.

Schizophrenia: Any of a group of disorders, which are psychotic and characterised by progressive deterioration of the personality; withdraw from reality.

Social constructionism: An approach within social psychology which emphasises the constructed nature of the world and the ways in which knowledge is sustained by social processes.

Trauma: A powerful shock which may have long-lasting effects.

Violated: To break, disregard or infringe personal and human rights; entering the 'personal space' or body of another.

Violence: The exercise of an insistence or physical force usually to effect injuries or destruction. A powerful, devastating force. This can be language or great strength of feeling and the violence can be psychological as well as physical.

World view: The way each of us interprets, constructs, explains and uses feelings, experiences and behaviour to negotiate life and living. It is the way we perceive and thus make sense of all aspects of our world. The 'whole picture'. In writing or speech how we seek to represent how we see the world.

Index

Key concepts and headings are given in italics.